PUBLIC POLICY
IN BRITAIN

PUBLIC POLICY
IN BRITAIN

Martin Burch and Bruce Wood

MARTIN ROBERTSON · OXFORD

JN
318
.B87
1983

© Martin Burch and Bruce Wood, 1983

First published in 1983
by Martin Robertson & Company Ltd.,
108 Cowley Road, Oxford OX4 1JF

British Library Cataloguing in Publication Data

Burch, Martin
  Public policy in Britain.
  1. Great Britain—Politics and government
  I. Title   II. Wood, Bruce
  354.41   DA592

  ISBN 0-85520-586-5
  ISBN 0-85520-587-3 Pbk

94757

Typeset by System 4 Associates Limited, Gerrards Cross
Printed and bound in Great Britain by
Billing and Sons Ltd., Worcester

To our parents

Contents

Contents   ix

Preface

Many important political issues are largely ignored in standard texts about British politics. Television, radio and newspaper reports constantly refer to budgets, public spending, taxes, the impact of expenditure cuts and other causes for concern which most textbooks neglect to consider. This book is different in that it does examine these and other neglected issues, as well as many of those that are conventionally handled on courses at school, college and university.

We do not claim to provide neat answers. Rather we view politics as inherently concerned with political argument and values. Our aim is to encourage thought and discussion, and we do this by concentrating on ways of studying public policy in order to present a framework for the analysis of particular policies, events and issues.

Our framework, which we call the 'Policy Approach', has been tried and tested on the second year undergraduate course in British Public Policy at Manchester University initiated and developed by Martin Burch. Seven sets of students have now sampled the Approach, and helped to refine it. To four — Tony Gearing, Susan Salts, Lin Spandley, and Kathryn Teesdale — we are particularly grateful, as the local government case studies in Chapter 6 are largely based on their project work.

Our gratitude also extends to colleagues in the department — Michael Moran, Maurice Wright and Geraint Parry — who read and commented on the draft. Finally we could not have produced this book without the efficient and good-humoured help of departmental and faculty secretaries.

Manchester
October, 1982

Martin Burch
Bruce Wood

PART I

APPROACHES AND VIEWS

1

Introducing the 'Policy Approach'

Our aims in writing this book are two-fold. Our first aim is an intellectual one: to outline and apply a particular approach to the study of politics and government. In the course of so doing, we hope to achieve our second aim, which might be termed empirical: providing an understanding of British politics and government. In this chapter we introduce our approach, indicating its main features, the subjects it isolates for study, and some of the assumptions on which it is based.

The intellectual aim of the book may be queried by some on the grounds that what is required is not a theoretical model or framework but a straightforward factual description of British politics. Like the imperious schoolmaster, Mr Gradgrind, in Dickens' *Hard Times*, the reader might demand 'facts sir, nothing but facts' (Dickens, 1970, p. 47). The belief that one can dispense with viewpoints, and simply look in a wholly impartial way at the real nature of British politics, is certainly widely held and therefore deserves careful consideration, but we affirm to the contrary that because the study of politics is bound to involve political judgments, the way it is studied is of great importance. We begin by indicating why this is so as well as why we think it necessary to use a particular approach.

WHY USE A PARTICULAR APPROACH?

We suggest four main reasons. The first concerns the organization of material. A clearly articulated approach helps make material more ordered, logical and hence easier to comprehend. So a particular approach can help to get the information across and aid understanding. This alone is a good reason for developing one.

More important, a clear approach is essential for analytical and practical reasons. Analytically, it develops and deepens study by concentrating attention and giving focus to inquiry. It guides the observer and ensures the selection of relevant factual material from the vast range that is available. To be told, for instance, that there are 650 Members of Parliament and 660,000 civil servants tells us little unless we relate these observations to a theory about why these numbers are relevant and important. Imagine drawing up a list of political facts without any criteria for selection or emphasis; it would be a very long and very random list. It would not aid understanding, but obscure it.

An explicit approach makes analysis possible and productive, whereas its absence leads to incoherence and muddle. But there is a deeper, more compelling reason for openly adopting a theoretical approach: quite simply, there is no choice. We cannot make sense of the political universe around us without some prior notion of the scope of that universe and the nature of the elements within it. The idea that the real political world only awaits observation is misleading. It is not something which exists wholly independently of the way in which the observer perceives it. We begin to make sense of the political universe by distinguishing the political from the non-political (from the economic, social, technological, and so on). Only then can we proceed to say what, within the political domain, is especially relevant and worthy of study. We cannot do this without some preconception or theory about what is relevant and important. In other words, we cannot avoid using an approach.

We can illustrate these essential analytical and practical reasons with further reference to Mr Gradgrind and his pursuit of facts. Take the case of the unfortunate Sissy Jupe ('girl number twenty') and her inability to define a horse. After being reprimanded for being in possession of 'no facts, in reference to one of the commonest of animals!', Mr Gradgrind turns to Sissy's classmate, Bitzer, for a definition and elicits this response:

'Quadruped. Graminivorous. Forty teeth, namely twenty-four grinders, four eye teeth, and twelve incisive. Sheds coat in the spring; in marshy countries, sheds hoofs, too. Hoofs hard, but requiring to be shod with iron. Age known by marks in mouth.' Thus (and much more) Bitzer.

'Now girl number twenty', said Mr Gradgrind, 'you know what a horse is' (Dickens, 1970, p. 50).

But does she? She has a description which could enable her to identify a horse. Yet she knows nothing about its purpose or usefulness. She has discovered nothing about the qualities that make up a horse, its temperament or its breeding. Much has been left out. All that Sissy has been given are certain observations selected on the basis of what, from amongst the many things pertinent to a horse, the speaker thinks important. Judgments of what is important will differ. The way people perceive an object depends on their backgrounds, their experiences, and their expectations of the object they are viewing. So it is that the farrier sees a horse differently from the horsemeat butcher, the punter from the jockey, and the farmer from the huntsman. No two views will be wholly alike and each will concentrate on different facts when it comes to describing a horse.

In the case of Mr Gradgrind and Bitzer, what we are faced with is a theory. Their theory lacks sophistication, but in essence it holds that what is important is the description of the immediately observable and more obvious physical features of an object. Knowing and understanding the world is, therefore, a matter of collecting this kind of information, preferably in a highly manageable form. What matters is hard information and quantities (he even reduces his pupils to numbers), the physical properties of a thing rather than its qualities, essence, purpose or value. Really Mr Gradgrind is not dealing in the world of facts at all, but the world of perspectives and values.

Figure 1.1 shows just how significant is the choice of an approach or theory in shaping our perception of the supposed 'facts' of politics. In it two ways of understanding British politics are compared: a 'conventional' view and a 'ruling-class' view. These are outlined in greater detail in Chapter 2. For the present, our concern is merely how each focuses on different elements as main objects for political study, raises different issues for consideration, and uses different empirical or factual material to provide supporting evidence. In contrast to the conventional view, for instance, the ruling-class view sees politics as ultimately a product of non-political forces, especially those located in the economy. Instead of concentrating mainly on representative agencies, it provides a wider definition of government and the state to include the military and public services; instead of focusing on political institutions, it pays attention to social movements and classes. Both approaches offer distinct and coherent analyses, and both draw attention to important features of British politics. Both can be illustrated and developed using factual material. To some extent they use different facts, and to some extent they use the same facts differently interpreted and applied, as in

View	Major elements for attention	Some major issues for discussion	Some central empirical concerns
Conventional: representative and responsible government	Political institutions and actors, especially (1) Parliament and MPs (2) departments, Cabinet and ministers and civil servants (3) elections and voters	The relations between the major elements in terms of how representative and responsible they might be considered to be	Parliamentary machinery Legislative role: passage of bills, amending powers. Controlling and scrutinizing role: select committees, ministerial questions, adjournment debates. Executive links: responsibility of ministers to Parliament, role of Prime Minister, collective responsibility, minister–civil service relations. Representatives and people: social origins of MPs, electoral system, links between MPs and constituencies, selection of MPs etc.
Ruling class:	The economy The state (including conventional institutions plus public services and control agencies such as the police, the military and the judiciary) Class structure	(1) Relations between the economy and the state (2) The purpose of the state (3) The connections between economic power and political power (4) Class structure and political change (5) Techniques and tactics for political and economic change	Social and class background of top policy makers. The operations of the control functions of the state. Role of business interests in politics. The means of creating and maintaining political values: the media, socialization etc.

FIGURE 1.1   *Studying two views of British politics*

the use of data on the social background of MPs and ministers to see how representative they are of the population at large or, in the case of the ruling-class view in particular, how closely connected they are to the worlds of business and finance. But neither the conventional nor the ruling-class view can be judged right or wrong by a simple appeal to objectively observable facts.

These illustrations suggest that we can only make sense of political activity by using an approach, or even a range of approaches. Each approach emphasizes different facts and concentrates on different aspects of the political system. The intelligent study of politics is thus bound to be partial, for it focuses on only a part of the potential area of political inquiry. Indeed, because approaches precede facts, it follows that there cannot be any impartial, objective accounts. All approaches will be based on certain assumptions and judgments about what is important and noteworthy. Such judgments will involve the application, knowingly or unknowingly, of political values and opinions. Hence the study of politics involves a high degree of subjectivity, reflecting either the values of the individual observer, or more deeply, those pertaining to the group, economic interest, or culture to which the observer belongs. In this sense, also, the study of politics is bound to be partial, involving an unavoidable element of bias. Some would even suggest that, in consequence, the study of politics is itself a form of political activity (Mackenzie, 1975, p. 90).

As political values are bound to be inherent in any approach, it is essential that the approach being used should be open and clear. The readers will then be able to see what political views are being put forward, so that they can, as is only proper, make a judgment on them. In our view, political questions and opinions are ultimately for the individual to decide. This constitutes a fourth, moral reason for using a particular and clearly articulated approach. Indeed, as there are no unbiased, impartial accounts, the reader should always ask what values are being put over and why.

In sum, approaches are needed to assist clarity, interpretation and meaning. As approaches cannot be avoided, as there is no sense without them, and as there can be no impartial, objective accounts of political reality, we are left with two important questions: which approach should we choose, and by what criteria?

CHOOSING AN APPROACH

If we cannot choose between different viewpoints and approaches solely on factual evidence, what are we left with? Of course, empirical evidence will play its part, for it may help to clarify, shape or correct a particular viewpoint, but it follows the application of theory rather than precedes it. Various considerations that might govern choice are outlined below. This is not a comprehensive list and is intended as a basis for discussion. But consider which of the following criteria you find appropriate:

(1) *Comprehensiveness?* Are approaches that can handle and explain a wide range of phenomena preferable to narrower ones?

(2) *Flexibility?* Are approaches that can take account of changing circumstances and can adapt to new material preferable to those that are static and unchanging?

(3) *Falsification?* Are approaches preferable which allow research-able propositions to be put forward and examined in relation to empirical evidence, and thus allow the validity of the approach to be tested?

(4) *Prediction?* Are approaches which can produce predictions about likely political events in a given set of circumstances preferable?

Many would argue that (3) and (4) offer a degree of rigour and clarity in analysis not otherwise available. They make the study of politics more certain and reliable. While such aims are worthy of pursuit, it is worth considering just how difficult it is to apply such 'scientific' notions to the complex, subjective, political world.

(5) *Aesthetic Appeal?* Are those approaches preferable which are pleasing to contemplate? This is not a criterion often put about in contemporary political study, but the symbolic pro-perty of an approach has been very strongly emphasized in certain cultures, such as Marxist—Leninist perspectives in the USSR, or Hindu perspectives on politics and hierarchy as expressed in traditional Indian political thought. In Britain, the late medieval notion of a 'chain of being', involving distinc-tions of political degree and importance as an approach to

understanding politics, was primarily visual and symbolic (Tillyard, 1963, Ch. 4).

(6) *Sophistication?* The more subtle the approach the better? But what is subtle and what would be sophisticated? Over-subtle approaches may lead to obscurity, cruder approaches may oversimplify.

While the above criteria may help (for instance our emphasis, as teachers, would fall on comprehensiveness and flexibility), the choice of a particular approach will in part be a matter involving the exercise of personal beliefs and values. People will tend to choose ways of looking that they find sympathetic and in keeping with their own underlying sense of how things are and ought to be. There is nothing remarkable about this, and given the partial and theory-based nature of politics, it could not be otherwise. But this means that choosing is partly — and we stress partly — a moral process, a matter for individuals to decide in line with their beliefs and views about what is important.

The matter of choice also depends on the individual's situation in life and purpose in choosing. Though making a choice is difficult, in some situations it may not be necessary or useful to make absolute or narrow choices between approaches. Take, for instance, three basic activities central to politics: the practitioner involved in day-to-day political action; the researcher studying a particular aspect of the political universe; and the teacher and student interested in giving and gaining some general understanding of politics. The practitioner feels a need to choose a particular approach because he has to act in the world of everyday political events, and has to appear consistent and relatively intelligible. The researcher also needs to choose, in order to give clarity, meaning and direction to his research, otherwise his efforts would be indiscriminate and ineffectual. The student and teacher, however, can perhaps be more eclectic. As their aim is understanding, they can best do this by developing a broad framework to give some structure to inquiry, but from there on keeping an open mind and attempting to perceive politics from a variety of perspectives. As each perspective will highlight different issues for discussion and different aspects of the political system for attention, a multi-perspective approach can help understanding.

This perspective on the role of student and teacher suggests that the initial task is to set out an approach within which many views can be accommodated. The task is made easier if we distinguish two kinds of approaches to teaching and understanding: those that are primarily concerned with the initial selection and organization of material for inquiry, and those that are largely concerned with explaining the nature of that material once it has been selected. *Organizational* approaches are broad and over-arching, they concentrate attention by mapping out the area of study and pinpointing the key questions that arise. They open up inquiry by presenting issues for consideration. *Explanatory* approaches concentrate on the detail and attempt to draw conclusions. They close or round off inquiry by offering answers and solutions to the questions and issues identified in the organizational approach. Of course neither category is wholly distinct: organizational approaches, for instance, are likely to limit or exclude certain explanatory approaches; and explanation implies selection and categorization. The distinction is nevertheless useful and we consider our own Policy Approach to be in the organizational rather than explanatory category. It pinpoints areas and issues for inquiry, and can allow a variety of explanatory approaches to be applied to the issues raised.

Answering the question why one should use a particular approach, has led us to cover some abstract and difficult material. We have emphasized the necessity of choosing an approach for organizational, analytical, practical and moral reasons. We have indicated that approaches, while essential, are bound to be based in some degree on political assumptions and beliefs — hence the need to clarify and set out the chosen approach. We have also said that the student and teacher, by contrast perhaps with the activist or researcher, need not be committed to a single explanatory approach. Rather, within the essential organizational approach, different ways of looking at the political universe should be encouraged. In part we have chosen the Policy Approach because it allows us to cover many of these points satisfactorily.

WHAT DOES THE POLICY APPROACH INVOLVE?

We begin with some basic elements by way of introduction and then move on to the main features of the Policy Approach with its emphasis upon government, public policy and public resources.

Some Basic Elements and Definitions

The Policy Approach is centred on government. It recognizes that in Britain, as well as in many other industrialized states, 'big' government is an important fact of social, economic and political life. For instance, in 1981 the expenditures of government in Britain amounted to about 45 per cent of Gross Domestic Product, about 30 per cent of the workforce were employed in the public sector, and more than half the adult population received their main source of income from the government, in wages or in cash benefits such as unemployment pay and old age pensions.

Our emphasis on government enables us to define 'politics' fairly precisely as being government related. We call actions 'political' if they involve government or are concerned with government. Hence, the members of a local Women's Institute are acting politically if they attempt to influence, say, their local council or their MP. When they are not concerned to influence the activities of government, they are not acting politically in our sense of the word.

We define the scope of government primarily in institutional terms to include central government (including Parliament), local authorities and nationalized industries and public corporations. This is the definition used by the Central Statistical Office and, as we use figures based on a great many official statistics in the course of the book, the definition is helpful. But it is important to recognize that defining what is and is not government is fraught with difficulties and is a matter of judgment. There are always agencies and functions which are difficult to classify. Some might argue that our definition is too narrow and ought to be expanded to cover such agencies as British Leyland and the universities which rely on public funds for most of their income (Parry, 1980, p. 2).

Government is central in the Policy Approach, but it is not pictured as an isolated set of institutions. It is seen as part of a wider political system. The political system we define as consisting of two elements: on the one hand government, on the other the citizenry. Nor is the wider political system itself independent: it is part of the wider society, subject to influences from outside its own boundaries, such as those from the economy and other parts of the social system. Thus neither government nor the political system is autonomous; to some extent they are shaped by non-political forces.

These, then, are the basic elements: the centrality and scope of government and the wider context within which it operates. In order to develop the Approach further, we need to say something about how government operates and what public policies are.

Government, Policy and Process

The Policy Approach is concerned with examining what government does (or chooses not to do, or neglects to do), why and with what consequences for the citizen. It is also concerned with what government should do. This concern with prescription can be contrasted with many of the more traditional approaches to the study of government which emphasize what government is, and are concerned to describe the institutions of government and its personnel and their behaviour.

What does government do? One of its most important activities is the making of public policy. In order to make policy, governments engage in a series of operations. By studying these operations, an understanding can be gained of the activities of government, the forces shaping these activities, and their wider effects on society.

Policy we define as the products of government: what. it is that government produces. The policies or products of government can be defined in terms of two sets of indices: either public expenditure programmes (such as the amount of government money allocated to defence, social services or education); or types of policy product, of which we distinguish three main categories.

(1) *Rules and regulations and public pronouncements:* as laid down in a variety of ways ranging from Acts of Parliament to more general statements of intent.

(2) *Public goods and services:* the facilities that governments provide for the population, or a section of it, to use or benefit from, such as roads, health care, police forces and defence facilities.

(3) *Transfer payments:* the transfer of money from one group of citizens through government to another, such as grants to industry, old age pensions, unemployment pay. All involve cash flows from governments to particular groups of claimants.

These three categories overlap; rules and regulations, for instance, will apply to the proper distribution of transfer payments and the efficient management of public services. However, in order to aid analysis, the three categories are treated as relatively discrete.

The public policy-making activities of government are best seen as a process. This word process implies two things: first, an activity taking place over time, and second, an activity that changes and transforms an entity in the course of handling it. Hence, policy making is not seen as static and motionless, but as a continual operation. Nor is government seen as passive and ineffective, for it reshapes national resources by drawing them into the policy process and thereby altering them.

The idea of process can be further developed with reference to a simplified analogy drawn from the economics of production. The processing unit (say a manufacturing firm) gathers in certain raw materials (product components) and draws together other required factors of production such as land on which to site the firm, labour to man the machines, capital to pay for the raw materials and running costs, and expertise to design the product and manage the manufacturing process. The raw materials are manufactured and transformed into products which are then packaged, marketed and sold to consumers. The record of their purchases feeds back into the processing unit as an expression of consumer demand for the product, and as an indication of future production potential. In the light of this new information, the process is then repeated (Figure 1.2). In theory the procedure is continuous unless the market collapses, raw materials dry up, or the factors of production cease to be available. The procedure is also assumed to be adaptable in line with changing consumer demands.

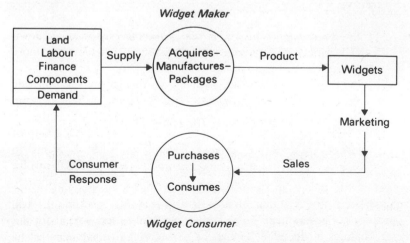

FIGURE 1.2   *The Manufacturing Process*

This economic analogy indicates some of the components of a process model: raw materials, transformation procedures, products, marketing, consumption, and feedback. The latter word refers to the modification of a process by its results or effects. Similar notions can be applied to the public policy process centred on government. Government can be seen as collecting public resources such as political support, and raw materials like finance and capital. These resources are then processed into products or policies (expressed in terms either of types of policy product or proposed expenditure programmes) which are applied to the citizenry and are consumed by them. Citizens also articulate demands for future policy provision and provide support for or opposition to policy proposals. These elements of public support and demand feed back into the policy actions of government (see Figure 1.3).

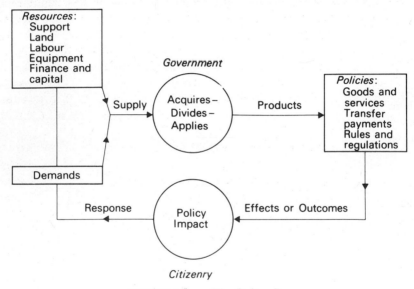

FIGURE 1.3   *The Policy Process*

In a broad sense, this model helps to indicate some of the main features of the Policy Approach: its concern with the activities of government, the emphasis on policy as a means of studying them, and the use of the notion of process as a way of visualizing the key operations of government. To go further we need to say more about the main features of the policy process by considering the precise nature of the operations of government.

The Operations of Government:
Acquisition, Division and Application

We can understand the policy process more precisely by picturing policy making as a cycle which can be divided into certain discrete, though overlapping, phases. At a minimum and most simple level, a distinction is often made between three phases:

(1) *Initiation:* the source, generation and early development of a policy proposal.

(2) *Formulation:* the development of a policy in detail and its outline as a concrete set of proposals.

(3) *Implementation:* the carrying out of the policy once formally agreed to or approved.

The precise demarcation between each stage is difficult, and must to some extent be arbitrary. In the case of an Act of Parliament, the policy initiation phase might be defined as ending when the proposal is discussed for the first time at ministerial level in the sponsoring department or ministry. Formulation would cover the period from there on until the proposal is legislated and has received the royal assent. Implementation would then cover the period thereafter, including the interpretation and application of the Act, its impact upon the public and its consequences for future government reaction.

The important point about the policy cycle approach is that it usefully suggests that the policy process can be broken down into elements. But there are problems with the approach which make it unattractive from our point of view. The emphasis upon phases suggests some kind of chronological sequence which is inevitably involved in policy making. We believe the process to be more fluid than this suggests, and prefer to concentrate on procedures of government which do not involve to the same extent the adoption of a rigid time sequence. Perhaps more important, the policy cycle approach is somewhat neutral in its attitude towards the role of government. It does not necessarily centre on government but rather on particular policies, so it does not fully allow for the positive, shaping role of public agencies, which we see as an important characteristic of 'big' government in the modern age. A more pertinent alternative is to be found in the Policy Approach, based on the resources of government. This implies active government, characterized in terms of three major procedures.

(1) *Acquiring resources:* the extraction and gathering in of public resources from the wider political, economic and social systems. Public resources we define to include public support and the raw materials necessary for the operation of government, namely land, equipment, labour, finance and capital.

(2) *Dividing resources:* the division or allocation of public resources amongst the agencies of government in terms of policy programmes or types of policy products.

(3) *Applying policy:* the carrying out of policy and its consequences, including the distribution of policy benefits and burdens.

This resources approach lays emphasis on the shaping role of government as well as suggesting some of the main operations in which government engages. Acquiring resources and dividing them amongst policy products are essential tasks facing any government. The notion of application allows an important distinction to be made between, on the one hand, the policies produced, and on the other, their effects upon the citizenry — between the products of government and the consequences of government actions. For the products of government are in effect propositions for action, while the consequences relate to the actual results or impact of policy (once applied) upon the citizenry. This again points to an essential consideration facing any government. The impact of policy is bound to shape the relationships between government and citizenry. In particular the reactions of citizens feed back into government and affect the nature and constitution of the resources available for further government action.

The Policy Approach, as we have defined it, is set out in Figure 1.3, and it forms the framework of the book. But why choose this in preference to any other? And what are the assumptions which underlie the Policy Approach?

WHY CHOOSE THE POLICY APPROACH?

The Policy Approach meets the particular needs of students and teachers which we outlined earlier. It is comprehensive, wide ranging and flexible. Like any other approach it is bound to be partial, because it concentrates attention on certain aspects of the political world, and because it looks at those aspects from a particular viewpoint. Despite these inevitable limitations it has the merit of being broad enough to encompass a number of perspectives, as we will see in Chapter 2. Its purposes are best regarded as organizational rather than explanatory: it focuses on certain aspects and issues, but allows them to be examined in a variety of ways.

More substantively, the Policy Approach raises important and pertinent questions about the operations of governments and their relationships with citizens. For instance, how are resources acquired? Which sections of the community bear the burdens of policy making? Which sections benefit? How are policy options chosen and expenditures divided? Why are some policy demands more effective than others? How do governments attempt to carry out their policies and what problems arise? How can observers sensibly judge and evaluate the operations of governments?

SOME UNDERLYING ASSUMPTIONS

We have already stressed that any approach to understanding politics is bound to be partial, involving assumptions which reflect, at least in part, the political opinions and beliefs of those originating or, sometimes, putting forward the particular approach in question. We have emphasized that approaches should be made clear and, as far as possible, assumptions should be revealed. The readers need to know what is being put across in order to make their own judgment on the political content of the argument. The other aspect of partiality is a problem here also, for any approach must involve an element of simplification. Reality 'out there', if it exists at all, is far more complex and wide ranging than the human intellect can handle. Hence, in order to make sense we simplify; we cannot do otherwise. By simplifying, however, we may also ignore or obscure important or interesting features of the political world. By looking at underlying assumptions, the reader can see what is being neglected and why.

Certain basic assumptions inherent in our Policy Approach have already emerged in this chapter. There are three in particular that we would wish to emphasize.

Assumption 1: Government is Central

We assume that government is central to the study of politics: hence our definition of politics and policy making. We also assume that government helps to condition and shape (as well as being shaped by) the wider political, social and economic context within which it operates. We assume further, that government personnel share some interests which are peculiar to themselves as government employees and which, at times, are primary or paramount over other interests they might hold as members of, say, social classes or other groupings.

Many would question our assumptions that government is central, conditioning and self-interested. Most Marxists, for example, would argue that government is primarily conditioned by external, mainly economic forces. They would maintain that, though there may be a close connection between the state and the economy, it is the latter which is central to an understanding of politics; and that in the final analysis the attitudes and aspirations of key government personnel are likely to conform with the interests of key sections in the economy. Other theorists argue that the nature and scale of policy provision is largely a reflection of national material wealth and degrees of economic development and, hence, the nature and operations of government are not substantially important in shaping either social conditions or public provisions. Both of these views are tenable on the basis of their own assumptions. We do not agree with them, though we recognize that both have some valid points to make. These arguments are taken up in later chapters.

Assumption 2: Distinguishing Government and Citizens

We assume that it is possible and valid to distinguish between government and citizens. The distinction does not always apply and it can be misleading. For instance, most government personnel are also, in a different guise and circumstance, citizens: the civil servant and local government officer both pay taxes and may vote in elections. Some government personnel — for instance, the backbench MP or local councillor — are more properly pictured as middlemen between citizen and government. It is also difficult, as we have noted, to distinguish the precise boundaries of government, especially in the case of such difficult-to-place institutions as 'quangos' (quasi autonomous non-governmental organizations), and when government cash grants to industry or individuals are involved.

More fundamentally, the government–citizen distinction tends to imply that a basic difference of interest and endemic conflict necessarily exists between these two elements. (This point also relates to the assumption of the centrality and self-interest of government.) In some instances, this may be the case, in others there may be an element of harmony, a unity of interest between government and citizen. This can occur, for instance, at times of national crisis. Because of this distinction, however, the Policy Approach does tend to veer towards a notion that the relationship between the public and the authorities is often one of conflict.

Assumption 3: Distinguishing Sections and Phases in the Policy Process

Some argue that dividing the policy process into procedures and sections is invalid, because policy making is continual and involves the constantly varying interplay of the actions of many individual policy makers. To break it into sections (such as acquisition and division) oversimplifies, imposes unreal categories on the world, and creates a sense of consecutive action, and cause and effect, where no such things apply.

Such dangers exist. But it is undoubtedly useful to sectionalize the policy-making process. It helps in handling material and it aids comprehension. The notions of acquisition, division and application focus attention on important and neglected areas of government and politics. As indicated earlier, they are not meant to imply a strictly chronological sequence as does, for example, the policy cycle model. However, unless handled flexibly, there is always a danger that any categories may prove too tight and too absolute.

There are certainly many other assumptions underlying our approach, some of which, because of our basic prejudices, we may not find easy to recognize and identify. The reader may wish to look out for underlying assumptions in the book. But remember, when criticizing a particular viewpoint or approach, that you should always strive to have something to put in its place.

In the remainder of the book we develop the Policy Approach. In Chapter 2 we outline a number of ways of looking at the behaviour of policy makers and the structure of policy making in Britain. In Part II we consider the topic of acquisition. An examination of the main resources of government in Chapter 3 is followed, in Chapter 4, with a look at some of the problems of acquiring resources and on which sections of society the burdens and costs of the operation might be said to fall. Part III is concerned with the division of resources. In Chapter 5 certain broad criteria for making policy choices are examined and, in Chapter 6, we focus in detail on the operation of expenditure politics. In both these chapters the notion and concept of power serves as an important and interlinking theme. The topic of policy application is considered in Part IV. Attention is given, in Chapter 7, to the problems facing government when it comes to carrying out policy, and particular emphasis is given to the importance of discretionary powers and the role of minor officials in carrying out policy. Chapter 8 focuses on the impact on society of public policy. It looks at the problems and practices involved in evaluating policy, and considers who might be said to benefit from public policy. In the concluding chapter, we first identify themes which recur in the earlier part of the book and then go on to consider ways of judging the operations of government and the content of public policy, with special emphasis on the moral and political dimensions involved.

REFERENCES

Dickens, Charles (1970) *Hard Times*, Penguin.
Mackenzie, W. J. M. (1975) 'Politics', in P. Barker (ed.) *The Social Sciences Today*, Edward Arnold.
Parry, R. (1980) *United Kingdom Public Employment: Patterns of Change 1951–76*, Centre for the Study of Public Policy.
Tillyard, F. M. W. (1963) *The Elizabethan World Picture*, Penguin.

2

Views of Policy Making

In Chapter 1 we explained that we had chosen the Policy Approach because it raises a number of pertinent questions about policy making in Britain. We see the Approach as a way of studying what government does or does not do, why, and with what consequences for the citizen. In Chapter 1 the focus was primarily on the 'way of studying' politics. The Policy Approach was seen to help the student organize material by raising issues for inquiry and investigation; by defining what is meant by 'policy'; by separating from one another the actions of government as, on the one hand, the acquirer and divider of public resources, and, on the other hand, the distributor of policy products; and by identifying certain assumptions which lie behind the Approach. We emphasized the organizational strength of our Approach, its intelligibility, and its comprehensiveness. In this chapter we turn to its explanatory potential, and we consider various explanations of both why and how particular policies are made.

There is, in fact, some explanatory material contained within the Policy Approach as outlined in Chapter 1. It suggests, for instance, why governments need to acquire resources such as finance, and why citizens seek to influence the activities of public authorities. The assumptions which underlie the Approach will also play a part in shaping the range of explanations provided in this chapter. Thus, our focus on 'government' means that explanations which emphasize the overwhelming primacy of non-governmental factors in shaping policy are liable to be relatively neglected. Hence earlier research on the determinants of local authority spending on education would not be highlighted, for it claimed to show that social factors such as the number of children and the social class composition of the area accounted for most of the variation between authorities, with government unimportant. In the main, however, the Policy Approach is not much concerned with explanation. It sets out a series of categories and issues for investigation, and has little to say explicitly about such matters as how policies are made, how policy makers operate, and how influence is distributed within the policy-making process. Explanations relating to these types of issue have to be introduced into the Approach.

Thus in order to develop the Policy Approach further, we extend its explanatory power by outlining some widely held views about the operation of the policy process and behaviour of policy makers. The breadth of the Policy Approach enables us to consider as many as nine distinct views.

All nine views claim to involve description (explaining how things are), all also involve an element of prescription (explaining how things ought to be). All have some validity, all can be supported with empirical evidence, but no one view is 'right'. Each gives a different way of looking at and talking about policy making. Often the standpoint of the particular observer or commentator (his life experience, his values and beliefs) will influence his views – the politician, the civil servant, the pressure group leader, the academic will each describe and interpret a particular series of events differently. So too, will two politicians or academics, for assessments are affected not only by the angle of vision but also by people's underlying philosophies.

Each view is partial in that each concentrates on certain aspects of the policy process: the conventional model, for example, focuses on the role of institutions at the centre of government, while the administrative dispersion model concentrates on why, due to the organizational complexity of government, it is very hard to make and carry out any new policies. The nine which we have selected we divide into two categories. Two, which we label 'behavioural', are concerned with how policy makers actually go about making policy and the strategies they adopt, as individuals or in groups, when reaching policy decisions. 'Policy makers' are often vaguely and variously defined and can include all who seek to influence the policy-making activities of government. Narrower and more precise definitions arise when discussion is restricted to one of the seven views which we term 'structural'.

We use 'structural' because the second set of perspectives attempts to look at the deeper structure within which policy makers operate. Each view refers to certain fundamental or structural features of the system as a whole. Each attempts to identify forces shaping the process of policy making (what are and what ought to be the major elements and actors, such as Parliament, bureaucracies or social classes); to consider the distribution of influence within the system (including the nature and selection of key policy-makers such as MPs, councillors, civil servants and/or party activists); and to examine what is and what ought to be the role of public authorities.

This distinction between behavioural and structural views is not an absolute one – the two overlap. Some views of policy-makers' behaviour reflect deep structural notions about the role of interests and of specialist information. But we find the distinction useful both in organizing the material on policy making and in offering explanations of how policy is made and carried out.

BEHAVIOURAL VIEWS

How do policy makers set about making policy decisions? Do they consciously adopt what we call 'strategies' for taking policy decisions? Are they likely to pursue a particular approach when confronted with a problem? Do they set out objectives and attempt to achieve them, or do they act more politically, compromising objectives so as to pursue other considerations? Should they behave in a certain manner?

Each of the behavioural views which we consider contains both descriptive and prescriptive elements. Each has something to say about how policy makers perceive, inform themselves about, and tackle policy problems, and about how and to what extent policies are altered and changed.

The Rational View

A rational strategy for tackling policy issues involves proceeding through a sequence of stages which follow on logically from one another. Thus the policy maker, having identified a problem which requires a response, should:

(1) identify, and place in rank order of importance, his objectives;
(2) identify all possible responses to the problem;
(3) go on next to consider all possible consequences resulting from the adoption of each response;
(4) and, finally, select the response which will most nearly achieve the objectives.

The rational model, then, assumes that a given problem will be tackled by following cumulative and logical steps in the search for the best response. But first the policy maker must identify the nature of the problem, and this in itself may be a matter of controversy. The nature of the 'inner-city problem' offers a good illustration of this. Today it is seen as resulting from the interaction of social, economic and physical forces and the policy response is a comprehensive approach to tackling both the economy and the environment of the inner city. This is very different from the analysis of the 1960s, when policy makers believed poor quality housing to be the central issue and responded by bull-dozing large areas and building blocks of flats (Home, 1982, Ch. 1). With hindsight those policy makers failed to identify correctly 'the problem': the 1980s identification is also debatable, for there remains controversy about the cause of the inner-city problem and consensus tends to be limited to its symptoms.

Once the problem has been identified, objectives should be listed and ranked. This is far from easy for there are at least three different types of objectives. Broad political and personal objectives apply to all problems and at all times. They include retaining power, maintaining status, developing a favourable image, and leading a peaceful and pleasant life. Rarely, if ever, do they appear in policy statements. Issue-related objectives are of two sorts. 'Primary' objectives would include, in the case of inner-city housing, equality of opportunity, social stability, public participation, adequate supply, and financial efficiency. 'Detailed' objectives relate to low cost (housing, for example, is extremely expensive to provide), low density of occupation (a response to criticism of modern flats), good standards of design, provision for varying sizes of family and for low-income households, achieving a social mix, and ensuring a fair distribution of dwellings.

This list of objectives, which is certainly not exhaustive, immediately reveals potential contradictions. Are low costs and good standards compatible? Can a social mix and a fair distribution both be achieved? Do low density and adequate supply conflict? In addition, the chances of policy makers agreeing to an order of importance are slim or even non-existent. Each will attach a different weight to political, primary and detailed objectives in general, let alone to the components of the three types.

Identifying all possible solutions and all likely consequences of those solutions is both a technical and an intellectual exercise. Technically, the advent of the computer allows policy makers to process vast quantities of factual information, but not all information about potential policies is factual, or measurable, or available. Measuring accurately the amount of unhappiness among inner-city flat dwellers, or the likely impact of introducing a social mix into a single-class dominated community is particularly tricky because personal satisfaction is less tangible than physical features, though modest indicators of social malaise are being developed. We consider a range of measurement problems in Chapters 4 and 8. Intellectually there are two major difficulties. First, the human mind has a limited capacity. It can cope better with issues with which it can identify than with hypothetical situations, which can mean that potential radical solutions get missed entirely or dismissed immediately because they are inconceivable to the policy maker. Secondly, at this stage in the process anticipation and forecasting are crucial, but the future is uncertain. Assessing accurately the possible consequences of a range of policy options is a mammoth task. Our failure to foresee the economic depression in the late 1970s, and to plan ahead for it is understandable.

The complete rational model is an ideal, a target at which to aim, prescriptive rather than descriptive. It became fashionable to discuss the application of the pure model to public policy making in the 1950s, at first in the USA and later in Britain. Limits on the extent and accuracy of information and on man's intellectual skills and ability to identify problems and rank objectives presented severe practical hurdles and a restricted version of rationality was developed. Of practical value were thought to be the exercises of listing objectives, considering a range of options, and forward planning. Civil servants became trained in this version of rationality, local authorities developed systems known as corporate planning, and White Papers began to state policy objectives. Though we have become aware of the problems of planning, of setting objectives and of analysing options and consequences, the rational view does offer an explanation of some aspects of the behaviour of policy makers.

Incrementalism

An increment is a small step away from an existing position. The term is commonly used in discussions on pay where, for example, a civil servant is on a pay scale under which he receives annual 'increments' for a number of years. Status (executive officer, assistant secretary, etc.) is unchanged but salary takes regular small steps upwards. As an approach to policy making, incremental theories tend to emphasize the extent to which policy makers stick with the known, the accepted, the familiar and the manageable. They avoid the global, fundamental and wide-ranging analysis sought by proponents of the rational view.

Charles Lindblom is usually considered to be the father or inventor of incrementalism. He and his supporters argue that the pure rational model is never sustained or achieved in the real world of politics, and that policy makers are primarily concerned to cope with problems rather than solve them. This alternative strategy of small steps away from the *status quo* is variously labelled 'disjointed incrementalism' or 'successive limited comparisons'. Incrementalism, the common shorthand phrase, has five central characteristics.

Firstly, policy making is restricted in that policy makers do not wander far from the *status quo*. They seek new policies, or responses to problems which differ only marginally (or incrementally) from existing policies. For example, in 1981 the Secretary of State for Health and Social Security produced a consultative document, *Care in Action*, which explored ways in which patients now in large, often geographically remote, long-stay mental hospitals might be provided with accommodation in the community from whence they came. Seven options were listed. One involved a fairly radical restructuring of the public sector, so as to make a single authority responsible for such patients; it received little support in consultations with interested parties. The solution most favoured during these consultations was an extension of joint financing, whereby health authorities contribute funds to local authorities which build suitable hostels and sheltered housing schemes, yet research has indicated that collaboration between the two authorities has been far from successful (Booth, 1981).

Policy makers, then, keep to the familiar. Just as a housewife uses a regular shopping list of requirements, so too, do governmental budget makers tend to begin with a column of expenditure in previous years. That column is the base on to which additions are made under some or all headings due to inflation and new policy developments, or – in recent years – from which small deductions are made in response to government calls for cuts. The base (i.e. what government has been doing) is broadly taken for granted and is not the subject of a full review.

A standard response of politicians to charges of being restrictive has frequently been that 'the time is not ripe' for a wide-ranging review of policy, a reflection of the broad political objectives which we discussed when considering the rational approach. If this response lacks credibility, a second approach may be to set up a body to review the issue, a body without executive powers and with terms of reference which either restrict it or ensure that it takes years to complete its work. Here lies the genesis of many Royal Commissions.

The second characteristic of incrementalism is that it is means-oriented. Means, rather than objectives, determine policy. A clear example lies in the policy of charging NHS patients part of the cost of drugs, pills, glasses and dental treatment. The Labour Party has always favoured free treatment, but successive Labour governments have found it impossible to remove all charges (and have sometimes increased them) because of financial considerations. Policy change becomes more possible when technology changes the means available — the massive flat-building programmes in the inner cities became feasible due to the development of prefabrication and industrialized building; tall blocks resulted from improvements in steel structures.

Thirdly, incremental strategies are remedial. They deal with issues or problems as they arise. Policy makers do not normally go out in search of work, and have no idealized future state by which to test whether or not action is needed, and towards which they are working. The *status quo* is satisfactory until it cannot be maintained any longer due to the extent of dissatisfaction with it. There is often a reluctance even to recognize the existence of a problem. In 1976 Peter Shore, Secretary of State for the Environment, made an important speech in which he officially recognized the inner-city problem and promised new policies. The speech came only after years of pressure, research activity and limited policy experiments. A further flurry of activity came in 1981, but largely as a reaction to urban riots in Bristol, Brixton and Toxteth. Rural deprivation remains almost unrecognized by governments, despite considerable statistical evidence of its existence and the efforts of an articulate lobby to place it on the agenda for action.

Fourthly, incrementalism is reconstructive and serial. Policy makers recognize that problems change over time, that a problem is quite likely to alter in the course of being dealt with, and that solutions will in turn raise new problems. Policy making becomes a never-ending activity. Post-war housing policy provides a good example. In the early years poor physical standards were thought to be the key problem, and the policy response was demolition on a vast scale. Later the problem was reconstructed to one centred on social and environmental issues. This, in turn, changed and financial considerations became the focus. The policy response has been a switch of emphasis towards the refurbishing of older houses, but many poor owners and numerous private tenants have not benefitted because of a shortage of money or lack of financial incentive. The decline in house building may also lead to a chronic shortage in the mid-1980s, and a further reconstruction of the problem would then be necessary (Donnison and Ungerson, 1982, Chs 9 and 10).

Finally, incrementalism is fragmentary. Policy is made across both space and time. By 'across space' we mean that different actors and institutions are involved in the same policy area. Housing policy for England is made in the Department of Environment, in the Treasury (the financial allocation), in Parliament, and in 366 local authorities (365 city, borough and district councils and the Greater London Council). Wales, Scotland and Northern Ireland have separate arrangements. But this list excludes numerous other actors who seek to influence housing policy: housing associations, building societies, the local authority associations, builders and developers, trade unions with building worker members, professional organizations like the Royal Institute of British Architects, pressure groups such as Shelter, and so on. Finally, actual and potential house purchasers and occupiers must be considered, even though they are not organized. By 'across time' we mean that the involvement of each group of actors varies and is not static. This is the case both from year to year and in relation to particular policy decisions about housing. Housing associations, for example, have developed rapidly in the last 20 years and today are responsible for 10 per cent of new building. In places they have outstripped the district council as the major developer.

According to Lindblom, all these policy makers are coordinated through 'partisan mutual adjustment'. This apparently clumsy expression means that policy makers will be prepared to negotiate and bargain with one another, and to make concessions in the interests of achieving some agreement and making some advances. Negotiations are, in effect, continuous and policy decisions emerge continually. Concessions eat into radical proposals as each actor realizes that he can only achieve so much (usually very little) without the active or passive support of other actors. Hence aspirations are checked and small steps result. On the other hand there can be frequent small steps, and collectively they may add up to considerable policy change over a fairly short period of time.

Lindblom argues that there are good reasons for policy makers adopting an incremental strategy. Policy making is made manageable when only limited comparisons with the *status quo* are made. Disagreements over objectives can be avoided because objectives are seldom considered. The information and intellectual skills needed are likely to be available. For most actors, focusing on the familiar is more comfortable than assessing the unknown.

Although superficially the incremental view appears to offer a useful description, it does suffer from a number of weaknesses. It fails to make a clear distinction between incremental and non-incremental change; it offers no adequate guide to help us answer questions such as 'are the creation of the National Health Service and the decision to join the Common Market examples of incremental policy making?'. After all, both can be viewed as major shifts in policy. Secondly, it does not appear to have universal applicability and is relevant only in stable, industrialized states with continuity, deep-seated values of consensus, and support for the regime. Britain can be so characterized, though, as we shall see in Chapter 3, there are some signs of change. Thirdly, even in Britain partisan mutual adjustment can be inefficient and ineffective. There has been considerable criticism of coordination between public authorities, well illustrated by the government's 'think tank'. This discovered that Whitehall departments were pursuing different and sometimes incompatible policies towards local authorities. Treasury calls for spending cuts coincided with other departments requesting higher levels of expenditure on nursery education, on health and safety at work, and on the physically and mentally disabled, for example (CPRS, 1977). A process of partisan mutual adjustment had not resulted in consistency.

A fourth weakness of incrementalism is that, by starting with the *status quo*, it seems to ignore the problem of how fair and equal is today's distribution of resources in society. The assumption is that society is sufficiently fair and just to satisfy all of its citizens, and that fundamental questions do not need to be examined. Some challenge this as being too complacent. It may be that the system of policy making prevents certain viewpoints from being heard properly, and recent events in several of our inner cities give credence to this criticism. The 1980 and 1981 riots in Bristol, Brixton, Liverpool and Manchester can be interpreted as resulting from the failure of government to tackle urban deprivation (Scarman, 1982, pp. 35–6, 158–60).

Like rationality, the incremental view offers a useful explanation of some aspects of the behaviour of policy makers. The notion of partisan mutual adjustment accounts for features such as the emphasis on coordination and on consultation and negotiation. At the heart of continuous debates about the organizational structure of central and local government and of the health service has been a concern with coordination. Consultation is now so fashionable as to be, in effect, an established convention of politics. Failure to consult is heavily criticized, and rights to be consulted are increasingly given recognition in Acts of Parliament. By law, ministers must consult with local authorities before decisions on the distribution of the Rate Support Grant are made, town planners drawing up a Structure Plan must consult with the public, and so on.

This search for common ground in turn helps to explain the lengthy timescale of policy making. A delay of months, or even years, between a problem being identified and a policy being carried out is commonplace. The process of local government reform took from 1966 to 1974, for example, but the alleged benefits of the new system which came into being in 1974 were unlikely to be felt until it had had a few years to settle down. The search for common ground also offers a possible explanation of the contents of the policy finally chosen. The 1974 reforms were closer to the *status quo* than were the 1969 proposals of the (Redcliffe-Maud) Royal Commission on Local Government in England. The Redcliffe-Maud Report came under heavy attack from existing vested interests bent on pointing to the potential difficulties which radical reform might create (Wood, 1976, Ch. 3). It does sometimes seem that major changes of policy are impossible or, at the very least, unlikely when policy makers face a range of established interests.

A number of commentators have been critical of both the rational and the incremental views of policy making. A common criticism is that one overemphasizes significant changes in policy, while the other suggests that any change is difficult to achieve. Compromises between the two include Etzioni's 'mixed scanning' and Vickers' 'appreciative judgements'. Etzioni emphasizes the need for both general objectives and immediate, incremental policy decisions (Etzioni, 1967). Equal benefits for all was a general objective of the welfare state towards which detailed policies were aimed in the immediate post-war period. By the 1960s, however, new sets of values and principles had emerged. Widespread poverty was 'rediscovered', and detailed policies to combat it moved towards selectivity.

Vickers' contribution centres around his notion of 'appreciation'. He believes the way in which policy makers view the world affects their policy choices and that the major limitations on policy makers are institutional and cultural (Vickers, 1965; Vickers, 1980). Normally 'appreciative settings' change only slowly, and in these circumstances Vickers is close to the incremental view. But he also sees the possibility of larger and quicker changes in appreciative settings, with consequences for the nature of policy changes. The worldwide economic recession in the 1970s, for example, rapidly caused Keynesian economics to be reassessed as the basis for economic policy discussions.

Etzioni, Vickers and others offer compromises between the rational and incremental views on which we have concentrated. They indicate the folly of selecting either and concluding that the one not preferred is wrong. Rational and incremental approaches are valuable alternatives, but are not opposites: there is evidence to support both, and each helps us to explain the nature of public policy.

STRUCTURAL VIEWS

So far we have identified a number of ways of talking about how policy makers go about making policy. Because these focus on the behaviour of policy makers, they have little to say directly about the nature of the system itself and about who is involved in the making of policy. We turn now to consider these matters through the perspective of seven views of the operation of the policy process.

To help elucidation and understanding, each view is considered in terms of what it has to say about:

(1) the nature of the policy-making system, especially the key elements that make it up, such as institutions and broader social grouping and interests;

(2) the distribution of power, influence and leadership within the policy-making system, with particular reference to the definition of policy makers and the means of their selection;

(3) the role of government and/or the state: what does it do and what should it do?

Each view is put forward by a different set of practitioners and commentators, and each can be supported by empirical evidence. As already indicated, there are connections between some structural and some behavioural perspectives, and these are brought out where appropriate. Like their behavioural counterparts, all seven views involve prescriptive and descriptive elements.

The Conventional View

Here the policy-making system is characterized as being responsible to, and representative of, public opinion. The key elements are those elected institutions that exist at the centre of the web of (representative and responsible) relations which bind government to popular opinion. The central focus is on a representative assembly, Parliament or the local council, and a system of election which ensures popular control. This was illustrated in Figure 1.1, on page 6.

Power is ultimately in the hands of the citizen but is mediated through the members of the representative assembly, who have the dual role of being accountable to the public and of controlling the executive through mechanisms such as the local council committee system, parliamentary scrutiny of the work of government agencies, and the responsibility of individual ministers to Parliament for the work of their departments. Hence leadership is in the hands of the people's representatives, some of whom (e.g. ministers and local government committee chairmen) play a more prominent role than others (backbenchers).

These issues of power and leadership indicate that those who constitute the policy makers are relatively few in number. An important role is fulfilled by ministers and the elected leaders of local authorities, who are advised by impartial civil servants and officers, all of whom are accountable to the people's representatives in Parliament and council. Backbench MPs and councillors also have a policy-making role to play in the passage of legislation and the making of decisions in council committees. These policy makers are selected through elections in parliamentary constituencies and local government wards, though leaders (ministers etc.) are selected usually by election or appointment within Parliament or the council. There is a strong element of popular control in this model. Though the people don't actually make policy, they do, through their representative, have some kind of broad influence on policy decisions.

Clearly then it is the role of government, according to the conventional view, to carry out the demands of the citizenry as interpreted by their representatives, the MPs and councillors. Conformity with citizens' demands is ensured through periodic elections and through contact and consultation with citizens in their local community.

The conventional view is very much the accepted way of talking about the British system of government, hence our label for it. Many academic textbooks emphasize elections, the sovereignty of Parliament, and the idea of accountable ministers (advised by expert civil servants) as key policy makers. Practitioners such as politicians, civil servants and local government officers often put forward this view, at least in public. It is frequently used as a language for justifying their activities.

The conventional view can be supported with reference to a variety of evidence. There are times when Parliament, for instance, is clearly authoritative in the making of policy. There are issues of conscience (hanging, abortion law, homosexual rights) which are traditionally left to Parliament to resolve (Richards, 1970). In recent years, the role of Parliament appears to have expanded. Since 1974, three major Finance Bills have been amended in Parliament; in 1976 the Scotland and Wales Bills were defeated; 14 new select committees, established in 1979 to scrutinize the actions of particular departments, have made ministers and civil servants more answerable to Parliament; and in the 1974—9 Parliament there were more cross-party votes recorded (MPs voting against the party line) than at any time since the 1867 session (Norton, 1980). Although the 1974—9 Labour government was for some time a minority government, there are clear indications that the reassertion of Parliament is a continuing phenomenon and that the 1980s could be a decade in which Parliament's influence is at its highest for many years.

The Party Government View

Derived from the conventional view, here the key institutions in the system are political parties rather than elected assemblies. It is political parties that mediate the public's opinion, which they then fuse into broad policy proposals; it is political parties that control the operations of the assembly. Parties thus predominate in the formulation of policy, and control the policy process.

In Britain this view has usually emphasized the existence of a two-party system, with Labour and Conservative competing with each other for office. Thus power is interchanged between these two major parties. But the view is not wholly invalidated by the existence of other parties such as the Liberals or Nationalist parties and, more recently, the Social Democrats. The City of Liverpool, for example, has had a three-party system since 1974, with political control dependent on agreement between any two of the three. Such agreements have not extended to election time, and the three fight one another in the quest for sole power.

From the party-government view, party activists form the main body of policy makers and party leaders are the key personnel. These leaders are selected through party machinery from amongst party activists at both national and local levels. The exact system of selection varies from party to party. For example, the Labour Party Leader and Deputy Leader are elected by the various wings of the party in the proportion 40 per cent trade unions, and 30 per cent each for the parliamentary party and the constituencies; the Conservative Party Leader is elected by Conservative MPs; and the Social Democratic Party gave every paid-up member a vote in its 1982 leadership contest. Other key personnel, such as MPs and councillors, are selected to stand as party candidates by their party's local constituency and ward committees in line with regional and national guidelines.

The role of government is to act in conformity with the policies and demands of the party, when it is in power. These policies are formulated within the party in line with the wishes of party activists and in keeping with that party's ideology and values. This partisan control of government is assured by the existence of a manifesto (or policy programme) which has been endorsed by the electorate, and by the concept of a mandate: the winner of an election has a mandate to govern in accordance with its programme and objectives. These notions of manifesto and mandate are at the centre of the party government view.

The party-government view has been articulated by political activists, particularly party members, and especially in the Labour Party. In recent years the Labour Party has become embroiled in a series of debates about the proper application of the party-government model to its own operations. This has involved deep argument about the relationship between the Party Conference and its National Executive Committee on the one hand and the parliamentary leadership on the other, and an attempt has been made to assert party control over the activities of Labour governments. In Chapter 6 (page 148) an example of a dispute between the local party and the Council Labour Group in Manchester in relation to cuts in council spending illustrates this. However, it is not only in the Labour Party that the party-government model is put forward. Recently the Conservatives have placed greater emphasis on manifesto commitments and the idea of having a mandate to carry them out. Interestingly, this goes against the traditional, more flexible Conservative approach to policy formulation and application. Both Mr Heath and Mrs Thatcher presided over the production of detailed policies in opposition, and both, when their party was elected to office, claimed a mandate from the electorate as justification for attempting to carry out their programmes (M. Burch in Layton-Henry, 1981).

Evidence for the party government view can be considered on two levels. In part it is overtly prescriptive, involving the belief on the part of many activists that parties should be the main and predominant policy-making bodies. Such people often express the model in reformist terms, arguing that changes are required to ensure a greater accountability of leaders to members and parties to citizens than is at present normal. In other words, it is what some party activists would like to see happen. But the view does also have a descriptive quality. Many policies are initiated within a party, presented to the electorate, and carried out in government. The Conservative's 1971 Industrial Relations Act was a direct product of party thinking, so also was Labour's policy in the mid-1970s to renegotiate the British terms of membership of the EEC and to subject these to referendum. The Conservative's 1979 election manifesto contained detailed commitments to the reduction of government borrowing, trade union reform, assisting small businesses, improving the pay and conditions of the police, the further limitation of immigration, the encouragement of council house sales, and increased expenditure on defence – all of which the Thatcher government has since attempted to carry out.

The Bureaucratic Power View

This focuses on government institutions, especially ministries and local government departments (rather than assemblies and parties), as the key elements in the policy-making system. These institutions are at the centre of the policy process; most if not all policies have to pass through them, and some policies are actually generated within them. Thus, the argument goes, these bodies either create policy or significantly shape it.

The presence of the civil service and of local authority departments is, of course, recognized by those who articulate the conventional and the party-government views of policy making. With more than three million staff this is inevitable! The key difference between this and the two previous views is in the alleged location of power: this third view is based on the premise that, in reality, it is the paid officials – particularly top civil servants and council chief officers – who are the main policy makers. It is they who are central, not ministers, chairmen, MPs or councillors. Their substantial role in policy making is a result of their position at the heart of government, and their supremacy is exercised through sheer weight of numbers, superior knowledge, control of information, continuity (politicians come and go), and the ability to work away from the glare of publicity that inevitably surrounds politicians. This last point is less true in local government for, while civil servants are anonymous, council officers are not.

Top officials are initially selected through civil service and local government recruitment procedures, usually on the basis of qualifications, tests and interviews. Career advancement thereafter depends more on personal qualities. In the civil service, promotion is decided by colleagues with, at the most, marginal ministerial involvement, usually only when it comes to the filling of top departmental positions (permanent and deputy secretary posts). In local government, councillors are involved in the appointment of deputy chief officers and upwards, but rarely in the promotion of younger officials. Whenever they are involved in selection, politicians are, of course, advised by senior officials. Career advancement, then, is usually markedly influenced by the opinions of more senior 'official' colleagues about the merits of subordinate staff, and is not subject to the effective control of elected politicians.

The role of government is seen as central to policy making; its personnel, especially officials, manage the policy process. They regulate policy demands by interpreting those demands and preparing responses for ministers to articulate. They also supervise, and to some extent control, the flow and application of policy ideas and decisions. A key role is best described as 'filtering' – regulating the flow and content of information. (We develop this idea in Chapter 5.) For example, a headmaster may seek additional teaching staff for his school in order to cope with a rise in the number of pupils with learning problems. When this request reaches the council's education committee, it will be accompanied by a paper from the chief education officer which points out that agreement to extra staff might result in similar requests from other schools, that peripatetic teachers from a 'learning centre' visit the school more often than previously, and that schools with a high level of social deprivation are nationally recognized (known as

Social Priority Area schools) and automatically obtain extra resources anyway. The 'problem' has thus been reinterpreted and given a council-wide focus which makes a political initiative less likely.

Some argue that, as this example indicates, officials are particularly adept at, in effect, defending the *status quo* by pointing to difficulties in moving away from it. Thus, the bureaucratic power view can be seen as a conservative view, which accords with many of the features of incrementalism. Others go further and suggest that it is the proper role of the government to ensure a degree of continuity in policy making, regardless of alterations in the political complexion of particular governments. Hence, officials may claim to represent some notion of the public or national interest, a middle way between the extreme oscillations of party politics. Viewed in this light, the role of official-dominated government is to bring politics closer to what are seen as the realities of governing.

Many who articulate the bureaucratic power view do so in a critical manner. It is at odds with the apparently 'democratic' conventional view. Former Ministers (Crossman, Shore, Benn, Barbara Castle) have, in recent years, been scathing about the power of the civil service. Equally critical are academic analyses of bureaucracies, which suggest that public agencies tend to become self-serving rather than serving the public. The recent television series 'Yes Minister' conveyed this view of the civil service to a wide audience — personal reputation and the interests of the department were central to the thinking of the Permanent Secretary. The frantic activity of Dame Evelyn Sharp (Permanent Secretary) when seeking to retain responsibility for planning within 'her' Ministry were, according to Crossman (her Minister), based mainly on departmental self-interest (Crossman, 1975, p. 25). His doubts about the wisdom of retaining this responsibility within the Ministry of Housing and Local Government had to remain private: there was simply no way in which he could be seen, as a new minister, to 'sell the department down the river'.

As indicated above, much evidence is available to support the bureaucratic power view. In government, the burden of work is such that politicians have no alternative but to delegate extensively to officials. When Crossman insisted on seeing every policy output from the Ministry of Housing (which is now only part of the larger Department of the Environment), he very quickly found this to be impractical. In that sense, the civil service and local government departments are indispensable. Indeed, the idea that officials play a significant role in policy making seems self-evident (it is strange that it should ever be denied) and many case studies of policy decisions have highlighted the influence of officials. For example, the concept of Community Development Projects to combat urban deprivation was developed in 1969 by a senior official in the Home Office (McKay and Cox, 1979, p. 233, 238–9).

The Technocratic View

Just as the party government view was derived from the conventional, so too is the technocratic view a derivative of bureaucratic power. However, it differs in its emphasis upon the skills and expertise of officials and the purpose and particular nature of the system of policy making.

The key elements within the system are well organized agencies or departments which deal with the specialized functions of government such as land-use planning, health, education and transport. These agencies (often, though not always, coterminous with ministries and local government departments) are staffed by personnel qualified in their specialism and backed up by teams of research workers and information gatherers. The primary feature is the purpose of the system, which is to ensure that the resources of government are organized and managed 'effectively' and 'efficiently' on behalf of the population. Such a task is not seen as being mainly a political one, but rather as a matter of technical administration.

Power lies in the hands of those who possess technical skills and know-how: the specialist or professionals. It is these that constitute the main policy makers. It is they who are 'most competent' and thus 'most able' to make judgments about policy matters, such as nuclear power, which are allegedly too complex for non-specialists such as politicians or even 'generalist' civil servants to handle. Leaders are those who have risen to the top of their profession within the agency and they are, like all technocratic personnel, selected on the basis of their training and qualifications. Thus, the system claims to be meritocratic. It lays emphasis on expertise rather than accountability or personal connections.

According to this view, it is the role of government to formulate and carry out the 'best' policies at reasonable cost, and to ensure the successful distribution of public goods and services among the population. The latter may be consulted about the level of goods and services required through the use of surveys and other 'impartial' ways of discovering what the public wants. Additionally, or alternatively, the nature and distribution of public services may be determined in line with 'objective' definitions made by specialists of what it is that people need. Doctors, for example, may decide on the extent and type of need for health care: more hospital beds in this or that medical speciality, or more local clinics. We develop the idea of 'need' further in Chapter 5.

This view of how policy is, and ought to be, made has been articulated in recent years by some management specialists who seek efficiency in the public service. It accords with the underlying ethos of, for example, the Fulton Report (1968) on the civil service and the Seebohm Report (also 1968) on the personal social services. It builds upon the rational view of policy making in that it contains the suggestion that there are objective, correct policies to be found by expert analysis. Critics challenge this along the lines of our earlier comments on rationality, and fear the emergence of a technocratic elite with professional dominance over politicians. The belief that government should be run like a private company derives from the technocratic view, as does the demand for 'politics to be taken out of local government'. Both imply that policies should be 'non-partisan', that there is a group of best-qualified men who can take the best measures.

As a description of the policy process, the technocratic view has some supporters. Benington claims that 'management reforms' in town halls have led to the transfer of power from politicians to specialist officials (Benington, 1976). The power of doctors over the utilization of National Health Service resources has been emphasized (Elcock, 1982, pp. 275–6). School curriculum is traditionally formulated by teachers. However, some point out that there are parameters within which specialists must operate – the amount of money allocated to health or education. Politicians also cannot be excluded from discussions on highly technical issues such as the choice of type of nuclear reactor, and their input (perhaps stressing objectives like cost, public safety, the desirability of 'buying British') may be critical. On the other hand, as the tasks of government have become more specialist, so the role of technocrats and professionals has expanded.

The Pluralist View

Pluralists emphasize interests rather than formal institutions as the key element within the policy-making system. Society is seen as being made up of interests such as agriculture, business or consumers. Some are highly organized, others are more amorphous (for example, 'the City'). These interests interact with one another and policy emerges after a process involving bargaining and conciliation. Some see policy as conforming to the demands of particular interests. Others, however, see policy as a consensus of all the interests competing in the political marketplace.

The pluralist view is less tangible than the previous four in that it is concerned with ideas, desires and demands rather than with institutions like Parliament or government departments. It encompasses at least two approaches to the location of power, influence and leadership. Some argue that power is diffused. There are many different interests of roughly equal influence and, therefore, there are many power centres and the system is balanced fairly between them. Moreover, the influence of individual interests varies across different policy areas and particular issues, while even the personalities involved may add a further degree of variation. Taken to its extreme, power and policy-making personnel are not only dispersed but also vary across time and place and, in the case of power, personality. Others challenge this 'free market' approach and point to a concentration of power in the hands of certain key, usually highly organized, interests which are 'incorporated' in the policy process. We call this 'elite pluralism'. The suggestion is that some interests — those of consumers, of NHS patients, of parents of schoolchildren — are effectively excluded from policy making.

Both approaches accept that leadership is in the hands of spokesmen for particular interests and of those who arbitrate in the case of any disputes and adjudicate between competing interests. These are the key policy makers. Some are selected by organized interests, perhaps by election amongst members (as in the case of the President of the National Union of Mineworkers) or by appointment on the basis of qualifications (as in the case of the Director General of the Confederation of British Industry). Some emerge almost naturally to speak for a particular, usually amorphous, interest, such as Mrs Mary Whitehouse speaking for television viewers. Those who arbitrate and adjudicate are often appointed by ministers, but ministers and their civil servants may also fulfil these tasks.

There are at least three views of the role of government in a pluralist society. First, some say that government's task is to establish the rules under which competition between the various interests takes place, and to ensure that there is fair play. In sporting terms, government is like the Football Association, which determines the laws of the game. Second, government can be seen as an adjudicator. It balances competing claims and settles disputes rather like the referee in a football match. But a third view is that government actually plays in the game, because government is itself an interest (or a collection of interests) and may also be expected to ensure a balance of interests (which means that it may need to represent minorities such as patients in mental hospitals). All three views are compatible with the pluralist view, for each recognizes the existence of, and importance of, groups or interests.

Some academic political scientists see pluralism as a more realistic version of British policy making than the conventional view allows. They usually stress the important role played by organized groups (Richardson and Jordan, 1979). The emphasis on policy making as a complex activity involving several interests accords also with much of our earlier discussion on incrementalism and especially the notion of partisan mutual adjustment. But it does seem to undervalue the important and shaping role of institutions and the active and initiating role sometimes played by British governments and parties in direct opposition to powerful interests.

Critical concerns relevant to a pluralist view are often put forward by journalists and commentators who fear the development of elite pluralism and what has been termed a 'corporate state'. By this they mean a system of policy making in which a few powerful and highly organized interest groups become, in effect, incorporated into the process of policy making. They negotiate and liaise continually with the departments and agencies of government, and policy emerges from this private, unrepresentative and unaccountable relationship.

The Administrative Dispersion and Diffusion View

This view concentrates on the scale and, particularly, institutional complexity of the state. Contemporary British government is seen, not as a logically ordered and clear-cut set of institutions, but as an amorphous mass of interlocking organizations attempting to provide for the many public service demands of a modern industrial society. Often the relationships between these bodies is confused and even contradictory, and as a result, policy making is inherently difficult, frustrating and only partly effective. Indeed, some maintain that in general the system is beyond effective direction and control.

The link with our earlier discussion of incrementalism is immediately apparent. Our final feature of the incremental model, for example, was its fragmentary nature and we listed a number of public and private bodies involved in housing policy. Consider, alternatively, responsibility for care of the elderly. Depending on their particular needs, senior citizens may be receiving attention from hospital and community staff employed by health authorities (doctors, nurses, health visitors, chiropodists), from social services departments of local authorities (home helps, day centres, old people's homes, meals on wheels), from housing departments (sheltered housing schemes, rent rebates), and from the local offices of the Department of Health and Social Security (pensions and supplementary benefits). In addition, transport, library and education authorities frequently make special arrangements for them. Because there is no clear-cut division of responsibility, demarcation disputes frequently arise: should someone be in hospital or in a home for the elderly, for example. Moreover, there is bound to be difficulty in coordinating the activities of this mixture of agencies, each with its own objectives, time-scales and interests to pursue.

Thus power and influence, under this model, are diffused widely and often ineffectively. The system is so complicated that there are no real centres of power. To take one small example, the consultant geriatrician, as controller of admissions to geriatric hospital beds, may seem to be all powerful, but in practice he can be placed under tremendous pressure to admit someone by his medical colleague in general practice or by other community health and social services staff; alternatively, he can be bypassed when a patient is admitted to hospital through the Casualty Department (under the control of a different consultant). Nominally, leadership is in the hands of politicians, civil servants and other policy makers identified in our discussion of the 'conventional' model, but it is argued that their hands are, in practice, tied. It is hard for policy makers to make any substantial impact on the system: communications do not get through or are not interpreted as hoped; other actors oppose; demands change from day to day; the problem continually alters and can never be fully comprehended; people forget, lose information, or are overburdened with work. The inertia inherent in any large-scale structure takes over.

What, then, is the role of government under this profoundly pessimistic view of policy making in Britain? One approach is merely to survive without too much upset. 'In political activity men sail a boundless and bottomless sea; there is neither harbour for shelter nor floor for anchorage, neither starting place nor appointed destination. The enterprise is to keep afloat on an even keel' (Oakeshott, 1962, p. 127). Others argue, more positively, that odd forays should be made into the morass of complexity and contradiction in an attempt to create some order out of chaos. Such forays should be restricted to narrow and clearly identified topics, and governments should realize that any improvements made will be temporary and illusory as new problems will quickly arise. 'Good' topics relate to structures rather than attitudes: it is easier to reform the structure of the NHS than it is to change the relationships between doctors, nurses and social workers. This may be why governments, anxious to appear 'active', spend a large amount of time on institutional reorganization — local government reform, NHS reorganization (two in eight years, in 1974 and 1982), reshaping the civil service and government departments, the creation and abolition of quangos (*ad hoc* appointed bodies to handle a particular problem or service).

This view of British policy making has been articulated both by organization theorists who emphasize complexity and limitations, and by some former politicians and civil servants. It has become fashionable in recent years as justification for governmental failure or inaction. It is a subtle but rather negative view which owes much to the rediscovery of the concept and problem of 'implementation' (see Chapter 7 below) in the early 1970s.

The Ruling Elite and Ruling-Class View

According to this view, the nature of the policy-making system is not what it immediately appears to be. The institutions of government, and the associated ideas of accountability to, and control by, the public are no more than a facade. Behind that facade is a structure which effectively maintains control in the interests of the few, against the real interests of the majority of the population. The key concern is with the state (including its policing and military functions). Its policy production serves to maintain and extend the inequitable distribution of real resources between those who hold power and those subject to it.

Central to this view is the concept of power. Political power is seen to have a wider social and economic base. The *ruling-class* view is that the key state personnel (politicians and officials) exercise political power in accord with the interests of the owners and controllers of capital (i.e. the means of production, distribution and exchange). The basis and purpose of political power is thus largely determined outside the political system in line with the nature of the economy. Political leaders (key state personnel) share the values of the dominant economic class. They may personally have no direct involvement in the ownership and management of capital, but they identify with those values through socialization and work experience, and through education and training.

The *ruling-elite* view also stresses that political power rests with the few, and that access to positions of leadership is closed to most people. However, it differs from the ruling-class view in not necessarily subscribing to any theory about the economic and social basis of political power. A ruling elite — the few governing the many — is seen as inevitable in any large-scale society. There are bound to be those who rule and those who are ruled. Also inevitable is the likelihood that those at the top will seek to maintain their position by promoting to high subordinate positions those who are close to them and share their point of view. So it is that key state personnel tend to form a closely integrated, self-perpetuating group which is held together by a common desire to maintain their privileged position, and by shared ideals, social contact, and similarity in terms of origins and backgrounds.

The role of the state (rather than government) under both views, is to operate in the interests of the ruling class or elite, either to perpetuate their political power, or to maintain the economic and social systems on which their power is based (or both). The state is thus an instrument of control over the powerless majority. That control is exercised either through the provision and manipulation of public goods, services and benefits or, more overtly, through the use of force or coercion (police and military aspects of the operation of the state are a key concern). Dissent is limited because citizens are made dependent on the state and because they are manipulated to ensure a lack of awareness of the real nature of the system.

The ruling-class view is articulated by Marxist theorists and some politicians on the left of the political spectrum. The exact nature of the view is a matter of some contention. Theorists argue about such matters as the nature and purpose of the state, the relations between the political and economic spheres, and the relevant means of political change. The ruling-elite view, developed by sociologists and, later, political scientists, on the other hand, has an appeal to some activists on the political right, partly because it provides an explanation of, and justification for, the unequal exercise of political power.

Clearly, access to positions of leadership is greatly helped through the possession of a certain social and economic background and connections with those already holding important positions. For example, there are not very many leading politicians and top officials with a genuine working-class background in Britain, and there is no doubt that other sections of society (women, young people, ethnic groups) are dramatically under-represented in Parliament, local councils and government in general.

CHOOSING BETWEEN VIEWS

As we said earlier, all nine views are different ways of looking at the operation of the policy process and the making of particular policies. They are neither 'right' nor 'wrong'. Each focuses on different elements and questions, and ignores others; in that sense each is narrow, and each is biased. Some views might be considered more partial than others. But be warned, the definition of partial will be highly subjective and will depend on who is making the judgment and why.

The Policy Approach, because it is broad and flexible, allows a number of explanations to be considered. In fact, all nine perspectives outlined in this chapter can be accommodated, with one possible exception. The ruling-class view conflicts with the assumption of the Policy Approach that politics are central to policy decisions by suggesting that government is substantially a creature of economic and social forces. We have included it because it is important and is widely discussed, and because it offers a critical assessment of our Approach. We ourselves question the notion that government can best be regarded as ultimately having no purpose of its own, and as secondary to some external set of influences. We believe it is feasible to argue that the public sector does have predominant purposes and interests which are peculiar to that sector.

Given that there are so many ways of looking (our nine do not exhaust the possibilities), how then do we choose between them? If we do choose, our choice will be influenced by empirical evidence, but will also be guided by our own moral views and our values. But in Chapter 1 we made the point that, as scholars attempting to understand British politics, we do not actually need to choose. Indeed, choice would be highly undesirable if it led to certain views being excluded from further consideration. Far more desirable is the maintenance of many different ways of viewing policy making in order to gain a wider understanding than would be provided by adopting only one perspective. The material in this chapter helps us to examine a particular event, issue or set of circumstances from at least nine different vantage points. Not all are applicable in every instance, but in later chapters we maintain this multi-perspective approach and we refer back to these explanations as we investigate the acquisition, division and distribution of public resources.

TOPICS FOR DISCUSSION

1. Should attempts be made to achieve pure rationality in policy making?
2. Can policy making simultaneously be both incremental and rational?
3. How representative and responsible is the British system of policy making?
4. Should a party elected to office carry out its mandate regardless of circumstances?
5. What empirical evidence would you need to support the technocratic view of policy making? (Repeat for other views.)
6. Can government be run like a private company?
7. Is there a ruling class in Britain?

KEY READING

Our aim here is to cite one source for each of the nine views. There are, of course, many others.

On the rational and incremental views, see R. G. S. Brown and D. R. Steel (1979) *The Administrative Process in Britain*, Methuen, Ch. 7. The conventional view is outlined in A. H. Birch (1980) *The British System of Government*, Allen & Unwin, 4th edn, Ch. 2. On party government, see R. Rose (1976) *The Problems of Party Government*, Penguin, Introduction and Chs 15 and 16. Bureaucratic power is outlined in H. Young, and A. Sloman (1982) *No Minister*, BBC; the technocratic view in J. Meynaud (1968) *Technocracy*, Faber, Chs 1 and 2. Pluralism, elitism and the ruling-class view are all covered in F. G. Castles, D. J. Murray and D. C. Potter (eds) (1971) *Decisions, Organisations and Society*, Penguin, Part Three. This book also covers several other views in Part One. On administrative dispersion and diffusion see A. King (ed.) (1976) *Why is Britain Becoming Harder to Govern?*, BBC, pp. 8—30.

REFERENCES

Benington, J. (1976) *Local Government Becomes Big Business*, CDP Information and Intelligence Unit.

Booth, T. A. (1981) 'Collaboration between the health and social services', *Policy and Politics*, Vol. 9, Nos 1 and 2.

Central Policy Review Staff (CPRS) (1977) *Relations Between Central Government and Local Authorities*, HMSO.

Crossman, R. H. S. (1975) *The Diaries of a Cabinet Minister*, Vol. I, Hamish Hamilton and Jonathan Cape.

Donnison, D. V. and Ungerson, C. (1982) *Housing Policy*, Penguin.

Elcock, H. (1982) *Local Government*, Methuen.

Etzioni, A. (1967) 'Mixed scanning: a "third" approach to decision-making', *Public Administration Review*, Vol. 27, No. 5.

Home, R. K. (1982) *Inner City Regeneration*, Spon.

Layton-Henry, Z. (ed.) (1981) *Conservative Politics*, Macmillan.

McKay, D. H. and Cox, A. W. (1979) *The Politics of Urban Change*, Croom Helm.

Norton, P. (1980) *Dissension in the House of Commons, 1974—9*, Oxford University Press.

Oakeshott, M. J. (1962) *Rationalism in Politics and Other Essays*, Methuen.

Richards, P. G. (1970) *Parliament and Conscience*, Allen & Unwin.

Richardson, J. J. and Jordan, A. G. (1979) *Governing Under Pressure*, Martin Robertson.

Scarman, Lord (1982) *The Scarman Report: The Brixton Disorders, 10—12 April 1981*, Penguin.

Vickers, G. (1965) *The Art of Judgement*, Chapman and Hall.

Vickers, G. (1980) 'The assumptions of policy analysis', *Policy Studies Journal*, No. 2, 1980—1.

Wood, B. (1976) *The Process of Local Government Reform, 1966—74*, Allen & Unwin.

PART II

ACQUIRING RESOURCES

3

Acquiring Resources:
the Policy Ingredients

In Chapter 1 we drew an analogy between the manufacturing of goods and the making of public policy. We pointed out that manufacturing requires raw materials which are later transformed into products and marketed to consumers. These raw materials are the basic elements on which manufacturing depends. Without them the process could not work. Similarly, public authorities require basic, essential resources in order to operate and produce policies. We distinguish five of these and loosely term them the ingredients of policy making. Four — land, equipment, labour, and finance and capital — are relatively tangible and easily identifiable; but the fifth — support — is altogether more difficult and less easy to describe. All are essential and necessary if governments are to operate and policies are to be made. The ingredients of policy making, especially in terms of their form and quantity, like the raw materials in manufacturing, have important effects upon the whole process. In particular, they help to determine the nature, products and consequences of policy making.

Of course, governments, like manufacturers, have to get hold of resources. The means used to draw in these resources will affect the make-up of the resources that are gathered in. For instance, the machinery for acquiring particular resources may break down or may operate inefficiently. Moreover, the costs of gathering in and the burdens of contributing may fall more substantially on some sections of the community than on others. It is this broad set of issues that the topic of acquisition seeks to cover: not only what is gathered in but also how, and to what effect.

In this and the next chapter acquisition is explored. Our immediate task is to set out and examine the basic resources of government and the main means of their acquisition. This takes up the remainder of Chapter 3. The chapter falls into two main parts, beginning with support and proceeding thereafter to look at more tangible resources. For reason of clarity we deal with each resource separately, which is slightly misleading as in reality they are interlinked and interdependent. This is a point to which we return in our conclusions. A good deal of detailed information is put forward, especially in the second part of the chapter. The reader should not be daunted by this. It is material which is not available in easily located sources. It is essential background information, especially when it comes to discussing, in Chapter 4, some of the problems of acquisition.

SUPPORT: THE INTANGIBLE RESOURCE

Support is arguably the key raw material, for governments cannot easily acquire land, labour or finance, or achieve policy objectives, or survive in the long term, without a degree of support from both the public and, importantly, from amongst their own personnel. Yet it is an elusive notion. It is difficult to define, locate or measure. We cannot usually be precise about the amount of support required for, say, the survival of a government or the success of a particular policy. We can be precise in situations where there are formal and observed rules about required degrees of support, such as when a majority ruling applies, as in a vote in Parliament or a local authority council chamber. We might also be able to be precise after the event, when a policy has failed or a government collapsed. In many cases, however, there is no precise formula to tell us the nature and exact degree of support needed for institutional survival and policy success.

These difficulties stem from the fact that the notion of 'support' has a number of complex components. In effect, what we are considering when we talk about support is something much more complicated than any simple notion of, say, majority or unanimous public support. We are considering, rather, the support of 'key' and 'influential' sections of the politically 'important' population. Here lies a difficulty, for the definition of 'key', 'influential' and 'important' depends on judgments about power and influence, and, as we noted in Chapter 2, there are many ways of tackling these matters. For instance, when looking at support from a pluralist view we would expect it to vary across political structures, policy areas and issues, and time. So support would need to be gauged in relation to particular issues and could not be easily generalized across a multitude of issues or policy-making systems. The ruling-class view would suggest the contrary, that, in equivalent types of societies and economies, the key and influential sections, though varying in detail, in substance would be the same. In a capitalist system, for instance, the critical elements would be those controlling industry, commerce and finance. Pronouncements about support are, therefore, secondary to prior judgments about power and influence. Hence problems of measurement and assessment are intensified, for even the basic parts of the equation are not agreed.

The difficulty of assessing support is further complicated by the extent to which it varies according to the intensity of commitment involved. In effect there are different qualities or degrees of support, and these will have consequences for the effectiveness of government, though the relationship is in no sense easy to unravel. We can, at the most simple level, distinguish between support (a) which is given voluntarily and involves a high level of positive commitment; (b) which is unconcerned and disinterested, and is acquiescent and apathetic; and (c) which is compelled and given grudgingly under duress, involving a low level of positive commitment. A policy-making system which rests on high positive support may have a much greater capacity for survival and policy success than one that depends on acquiescence or compulsion, though even this is arguable. One thing is clear: most systems, including Britain, involve a large measure of public acquiescence and disinterest.

Finally, the difficulty of predicting what level of support is likely to be required by government is also complicated by the fact that all governments actively try to generate and maintain support. Their success varies and is greatly enhanced by modern techniques such as mass propaganda, physical controls and other inducements. Governments may thus be able to enhance or preserve support to an unexpected and unpredictable extent.

We have now seen just how difficult and slippery the notion of support is. In the following pages we narrow our focus to consider the expression and nature of broad public support in Britain, though, of course, questions remain as matters for debate and argument: which or whose support matters? And which level of support is most effective?

Nature of Public Support in Britain

It is important to distinguish between two main types of political support. First, there is support for the overall structure of policy making, which we call *regime support*. A consideration of this aspect of support is concerned with the extent to which the overall structure of government is seen as legitimate or acceptable. Regime support needs to be considered as distinct from support for particular administrations, their personnel and the measures they pursue. This dimension we term *governmental support*.

There are two main sets of arguments about the nature of *regime support* in Britain. The traditional view is that, in comparison to most other states, Britain enjoys a high degree of regime support which is positive and committed. This has given the British policy-making system a high level of popular acceptance and stability. In part this acceptance of the regime is a legacy of a long continuity of relatively peaceful political development. Arguably the British system has evolved and adapted peacefully to changing circumstances for over 200 years without major disruption from external or internal sources (the last major internal threat to the regime being the ill-fated Jacobite rebellion of 1745).

This traditional view can be supported with reference to contemporary evidence such as the apparent absence of any substantial popular desire for fundamental changes in the system. The major British political parties for example – Conservative, Labour, Liberal and Social Democratic – generally tend to be regime-supporting. They are concerned to preserve and, perhaps, develop the existing structure, but not to transform it. Likewise survey evidence amassed during the late 1950s and early 1960s suggests strong popular support for the regime. The classic, cross-national study by Almond and Verba concluded that the British public reveal great trust in the 'fairness of the system', show emotional attachment to the 'democratic process' and believe in 'consensus' (Almond and Verba, 1963, pp. 455–69). Equally, it is maintained, the British, to an unusual extent, generally operate through the accepted channels of political discourse and action and show a high degree of deference to authority. Compared with other national populations, the British are not much given to indulging in protests, demonstrations or violent and disruptive behaviour (Birch, 1973, p. 25).

In recent years this traditional view has been questioned. The counter-view contains two related, yet distinct lines of argument. Some query the evolutionary theory of British political development and the consequent notions of a gradualist and consensus-seeking approach to politics with its emphasis on the accepted channels and the avoidance of extra-constitutional or violent means of political expression. While it is not denied that the British system has a relatively good survival record, this does not provide evidence for strong and positive regime support, but is rather the consequence of astute political manipulation and adaptability, and an absence of external disruption.

Indeed, so this first counter-argument holds, the history of political conflict and counter-regime activity in Britain is a long and varied one. Over the last 200 years the frequency of conflict and extra-constitutional action has been, and has remained, high. Direct action, including rioting, can be traced back through unemployment marches, Mosley's blackshirts, strikes, suffragettes and the Irish question, to nineteenth century events like Peterloo and Luddite disorders to the earlier, late eighteenth century, London mob (Kiernan, 1972). The 1950s saw popular demonstrations over Suez in 1956 and the non-violent activities of the Campaign for Nuclear Disarmament. These were the start of a trend of extra-constitutional activities which can be traced through into more recent and violent forms such as terrorism and inner-city rioting. According to one international analysis, during the relatively tranquil period from 1948–67, Britain recorded 132 major political demonstrations 'perceived as significant at the national level', the tenth highest score of the 136 countries surveyed. Britain's 82 'riots' placed her 36th in the overall ranking (Taylor and Hudson, 1972). And this was before the IRA became active in the late 1960s.

This alternative analysis of endemic conflict and underlying political instability suggests a political tradition based, not so much on gradualism and constitutional means, but on concerned and at times virulent opposition to the regime. According to this analysis, the persistent survival of the regime is not in itself adequate evidence of positive regime support. More truthfully, political support in Britain is usually acquiescent, yet strongly vigilant at times of crisis, and in essence highly cautious of authority.

The second counter-argument accepts that regime support in Britain is well established, but maintains that this support has never been as consensus-based nor as positive as the traditional view has it. Moreover, while the immediate post-war period might be seen as a high point for regime support, since the mid-1960s there has been a marked decline and, as a consequence, an increasing degree of instability has been introduced into the system. Over the last two decades the British have become less trustworthy of government and more willing to condone and even indulge in extra-constitutional activities such as protests, demonstrations and strikes. This recent disenchantment with the regime appears especially evident amongst the younger members of the population, and in certain regions — notably Wales and especially Scotland — where significant nationalist movements have developed.

Some evidence relating to a shift in citizens' values was revealed in a cross-national study of public attitudes towards regimes and legitimate tactics of political action, undertaken in 1974. The traditional notions of positive support and British political passivity are substantially undermined. Sixty-three per cent of those questioned felt they had no say in what government does and 60 per cent indicated a limited trust in government. A clear majority of respondents believed that Britain is governed by self-interested men on behalf of a few big interests. The study concludes that 'political trust in Britain is at a very low ebb' (Marsh, 1977, p. 117). At the same time, unconventional, direct action types of political influence have found their way into the potential repertory of a wider segment of the population, especially amongst the younger age group; according to the survey 35 per cent of the population would engage in lawful demonstrations and 22 per cent in illegal ones, and less than half the population are wholly opposed to unconventional tactics (Marsh, 1977, p. 51).

In assessing these different views of regime support, much of the difficulty lies in the problem of comparison. It seems that, when set against some other European nations, the British population does show a marginally higher degree of regime acceptance. But this tells us little about the nature and possible implications of regime support in Britain as such. One point is clear, however — regime support is not static, it is continually changing. A major weakness of the traditional view is that it does not adequately handle this dimension. It is based mainly on evidence drawn from, and assumptions which were fashionable in, the late 1950s and early 1960s, a period which, when placed within the context of the overall span of British political development, appears remarkably tranquil and exceptionally peaceful. We might even call it a golden age of regime support. More recent surveys and events do suggest that the British population has either become, or perhaps always was, far less accepting of and deferential to authority than was previously assumed. The trend appears to be in the direction of heightened conflict, a commensurate decline in consensus, and at least a marginal weakening of the stability of the political framework.

Government support for particular governments of different party political persuasions, is both more tangible and more fluctuating than regime support. In Britain, at the national level, governmental support

— as revealed at successive general elections since 1945 — has tended to move between the two major parties, Labour and Conservative. Superficially, therefore, governmental support patterns give some credence to the two-party government view of policy making. However, as in the case of regime support, what initially appears simple turns out to be rather more complicated.

The common characterization of Britain as a two-party system is misleading. Insofar as it is accurate, it applies mainly to parliamentary politics, especially in England. It has not generally been applicable to local government or, more recently, to national electoral politics in Scotland and Wales. Even in parliamentary terms, the notion of a two-party system is historically inaccurate. From 1885 to 1915 British national electoral and parliamentary politics were multi-party involving Conservatives, Liberals and Irish Nationalists. From 1915 to 1945, with the decline of the Liberals and the emergence of Labour, coalition governments ruled for 24 of the 30 years. It was only after 1945 that a two-party system emerged.

Neither has the pattern of two-party support been monolithic or unchanging. In order to characterize accurately the nature of the system, it is useful to distinguish between support amongst the electorate and support in the parliamentary-government arenas. Seen in these terms, we can distinguish two main phases in the development of two-party governmental support. From 1951 (perhaps earlier) to 1964, the two-party model was dominant in electoral terms with between 93 per cent and 97 per cent of voters supporting Labour and Conservative candidates. Each party seemed to enjoy a bedrock of support amongst certain sections of the electorate. Labour appeared strong amongst working-class voters and trade unionists, while the Conservatives gained votes from amongst the middle as well as a proportion of the working class (Blondel, 1974, p. 65). During this period major party electoral support was stable, party allegiance was high and voters remained loyal to party across elections. It was on this firm foundation that the two-party electoral system rested.

In parliamentary-government terms, however, the period from 1951 to 1964 was dominated not by two parties alternating in office, but by one party: the Conservatives. For these 13 consecutive years Conservative majorities dominated Parliament and Conservative leaders were in power. This provided an element of policy continuity and stability and ensured that the keen party conflict reflected in the electoral arena was not generally transferred into government. In essence, therefore, the period from 1951 to 1964 was one of two-party electoral politics and one party dominated parliamentary politics.

Since the early 1960s the situation has changed and the two-party base of electoral support appears to have weakened. The percentage of voters casting their votes for Labour or Conservative fell below 90 per cent in the 1966 and 1970 General Elections, then declined to only 75 per cent and 77 per cent in the February and October 1974 polls, and rose slightly to a relatively low 81 per cent in 1979. As support for the two major parties declined, so votes for other parties (especially the Liberals and, in Scotland, the Nationalists) increased. There appears to have been a persistent, if erratic, erosion in the social foundation of two-party support. The electorate has become less partisan, voting behaviour has become more volatile, and more electors appear to be choosing instrumentally on the basis of a broad, often crude, considera- tion of the issues and their likely impact upon their own well-being. As this happened, the influence of social and family background as the source of strong party identity appears to have weakened. The pattern of increasing instability and declining party allegiance is reflec- ted in parliamentary by-election voting, local government voting and opinion poll results (Butler and Stokes, 1974, p. 207). Moreover, various electoral surveys have revealed a weakening in the strength of electors' identification with both the Labour and the Conservative Parties and, according to one comparison of the October 1974 and 1979 General Elections, less than half the electorate voted for the same major party at both elections (*The Economist*, 1981).

At the parliamentary-government level, the period since 1964 has seen alternating two-party government in superficially close con- formity with the party-government view. Power has switched between the two parties, Labour from 1964 to 1970, Conservative from 1970 to 1974, Labour again until 1979 and Conservative thereafter. Although there have been periods of very small major party majorities (1964 to 1966 and part of 1974 to 1979), both parties have been in full control of government for a relatively short period, followed by a broadly equivalent period in opposition. This alternating two-party pattern has had consequences for policy production, continuity and presentation. Both parties have tended to produce policies in the more partisan and distant context of opposition, which they have then placed before the electorate and attempted to carry out in government. Because of the emphasis on partisan policy making and the highly competitive nature of this arrangement, the two parties have tended to present programmes which emphasize the differences between them rather than the similarities. The public impression revealed in opinion polls is one of a lack of continuity in policy making and a shifting of policy objectives from one party extreme to the other.

In sum, the 1951–64 pattern stands in contrast to what emerged after 1964. The two-party character of electoral politics has been weakened, and public support may well be developing in the direction of a form of multi-party politics. At the parliamentary level, however, a clear competitive two-party system has operated. Of course, the nature of parliamentary politics is likely, in time, to reflect changes in the electoral arena. Despite the distorting effect of the British 'first past the post' electoral system, *if* the decline in two-party voting continues, it seems likely that there will be increasing instability at the parliamentary and government level, possibly in the form of coalitions, alliances or small majority governments.

Interestingly, perhaps disturbingly, we find that the apparent erosion of positive regime support is parallelled by an increasing instability in governmental support.

Acquiring Support

How is public support maintained and generated by government? There exist a number of possible means, ranging from the use of force to persuasion as in a political speech or a campaign. In Britain overt coercion is seldom used. Occasionally it is applied in order to suppress opposition of a violent or potentially disruptive nature which is judged to pose a threat to the structure of government, as in the case of the IRA. Avoiding overt coercion means that support has to be acquired by means which are less obtrusive and more subtle and acceptable. In making sense of this subject, it will help if we distinguish between a machinery of acquisition, some techniques employed, and more primary conditioning influences.

The machinery of acquisition consists of the whole range of political institutions and the personnel who operate within them, such as elections, political parties, Parliament and local councils, government departments, and the media. From a conventional, representative and responsible viewpoint most political institutions operate primarily as channels for the expression of public demands. However, they also inevitably operate in the opposite direction: as means through which public support is created and maintained. Elections, for instance, allow voters broadly to express their demands, but they also provide support for particular groups of office-seeking personnel. In a less obvious way elections, by giving citizens an opportunity to participate and feel part of the system, serve to reassert democratic and participatory values and thus strengthen regime support. Likewise political parties, in addition to their representative role, accumulate support for or against particular governments and, by operating through established and conventional channels, affirm the values and support the structure of the regime. The same is equally true of established interest groups which, while pursuing the interests of their members or clientele, are often called upon to support and even help to carry out particular policies, as has been the case with both the CBI and trade unions in the operation of successive prices and incomes policies. All political institutions to some extent fulfil this dual representative and supportive role.

Techniques for acquiring support include a number of manipulative and control devices ranging from physical restrictions, through inducements involving the use of information, advice and finance, to exhortation and persuasion. (Some of these are more fully developed in Chapter 7, where they are considered in relation to the carrying out of policy.) In essence policy makers gain, maintain or lose support by creating and altering policy products. By satisfying the demands and expectations of key sections of the population, policy makers can strengthen both regime and governmental support.

National economic success and the general standard of people's material wellbeing appear to have important, though uncertain, consequences for the stability of regime support. A developing economy and rising real incomes are generally associated with a high degree of political satisfaction on the part of the population. Assuming this to be the case, it is interesting to note that over the 23-year period from 1951 to 1974, real personal disposable income per head almost doubled. Since 1974, however, the pattern has been more patchy with real personal disposable income declining slightly to 1977, rising to 1980 and falling by 2 per cent in 1980 — the biggest yearly fall since 1945 (CSO, 1982). The relative decline in the standard of living may offer some explanation of the apparent weakening of regime support already noted in this chapter.

Policy products can also create and maintain support for governments. They can be regarded as ways of bidding for support, of preserving and extending voting coalitions. This is particularly the case with reforms in tax levels, alterations in levels of social security benefit, and changes which especially assist identifiable sections such as, in recent years, small businessmen, mortgage payers, old age pensioners and single parent families. Moreover, the size and scope of the public sector, and the techniques of economic management now available, provide governments with an unparallelled opportunity to influence citizen behaviour. Some have argued that, since at least 1955, successive governments have attempted to create economic 'booms' prior to general elections. Indeed in Britain, as elsewhere, the growth rate in real incomes has tended to be higher in election years (Alt, 1980). But if policy manipulation was intended and not just fortuitous, success was by no means certain. For, despite election year booms, incumbent governments lost the 1964, 1970, 1974 and 1979 elections!

Support is also shaped by conditioning influences, such as the family and home environment, the school, the workplace, and the community. These primary institutions, it is often argued, help to mould citizens' attitudes, a process sometimes referred to as socialization. Few systematic studies of the effects of socialization on regime support have been undertaken. In relation to governmental support, it is clear that home and family background have some connection with voting behaviour. For instance, there is a relatively close relationship between the party allegiance of parents and their children, though recent research reveals that the degree of intra-family allegiance is declining and suggests that, in any case, its extent may have been exaggerated in earlier studies (Butler and Stokes, 1974, Ch. 3; Dowse and Hughes, 1971). Labour voting has tended to be strongest amongst workforces in large, unionized enterprises, especially in urban areas. Conservatives and Liberals have done better where enterprises are smaller and union ties are less established, often in rural areas. The workplace and community may complement and reinforce the influence of the home environment and create a particular, localized subculture with strong traditional patterns of voting for either Conservative, Labour, or even Liberal candidates. Increased educational opportunities, job mobility and the national influence of the media, especially television, may have served to weaken these subcultures and these developments offer some explanation of the decline in class voting patterns and party allegiance, observed earlier.

We have noted significant movements in the stability of popular regime support and the weakening of two-party governmental support. We have indicated that the extension of state provision and the techniques of manipulation which are now available have provided new opportunities for building and maintaining support, while, conversely, changing social and economic patterns have made such operations both more difficult and less certain in their outcome.

The effective acquisition of other resources greatly depends on the degree and quality of support. Without a certain level of support, for instance, taxes are difficult to raise, loans hard to come by and voluntary labour difficult to recruit. It is in this sense that support can be seen as the key to the process of acquisition and it is for this reason that we have devoted a substantial part of the chapter to its consideration. We now turn to examine in detail the more tangible resources of government — land, equipment, labour, and finance and capital. As with support, we look at the nature of each resource and at the means by which it is acquired.

TANGIBLE RESOURCES

Land and Equipment

Government land is used to build on, to train on (by armed forces), to conserve, to rent out and to put to immediate productive use. It contributes some revenue to the public purse and much is available, in the form of parks and open spaces, for the use and enjoyment of the public. Public land can be seen, therefore, as both a resource and a product of policy making. Closely connected with land is the equipment used by government in order to carry out its operations. The National Health Service, for instance, requires hospitals, health centres and surgeries, nurses require uniforms and doctors require medical equipment and pills. Likewise, the education service requires school buildings, books and paper, desks and chairs, blackboards and chalk.

Public Land in Britain. Public authorities have acquired land through a variety of means. Some, such as common lands, involve historical rights which have passed from the hold of the lord of the manor to the local authority. Others, such as Crown lands and some conservation lands, have passed to the public domain in exchange for undertakings about income being given to the previous owners. In the case of the Crown, for instance, a large part of the monarch's personal land-holding — known as the Crown Estate — was transferred to the public purse in 1760 in return for an annual 'Civil List' payment. Public agencies also receive land in lieu of payment of taxes, especially those relating to capital and estate duties.

Land may also be gifted to the public sector by private benefactors, as is the case with many local parks and open spaces. In the past some lands have been acquired through seizure, as were some of the monastic lands during the reign of Henry VIII. Nowadays such overt methods are not used, although land may be compulsorily purchased by public agencies in order to carry out schemes such as the clearance of slums, building of roads and the provision of public housing. In such cases the government is legally obliged to pay compensation. Most public land is now acquired on the open market, usually by the Property Services Agency acting for central government and by local authorities. Public authorities also acquire some land through tenancy agreements and the payments of rents.

There is a paucity of information about the extent of public land in Britain. The last comprehensive survey of land ownership was undertaken in 1873, and the one prior to that was in 1086, commonly known as the Doomsday Book! Recent surveys (undertaken in the 1970s) lack total accuracy, but on the basis of these we calculate a total public land-holding of nearly 3.85 million hectares, or just under 17 per cent of the land surface in Britain. These calculations include common land and land held by conservation bodies such as the National Trust. If we add rented land the figure is probably nearer 20 per cent.

Table 3.1 shows the distribution of public land between categories of public authority. The Crown Estate is administered by the Crown Estate Commissioners and accounts for about 3 per cent of all public land. A further 30 per cent of all public land is held by the Ministry of Agriculture and the Scottish and Welsh Offices and is mainly forest land administered by the Forestry Commission. The Ministry of Defence also has a substantial share, nearly 7 per cent of all publicly-owned land.

About 80 per cent of the holdings of nationalized industries and public corporations are in the hands of the National Coal Board, British Railways Board and the electricity authorities. Two-thirds of the 30 per cent of public land owned by local authorities is taken up with houses and flats, smallholdings and roads.

In the post-war period the amount of land owned by public authorities has grown, although, given the limited nature of the information available, it is impossible to say by precisely how much. According to one estimate, in 1936 the total public land-holding in Britain amounted to about 5.5 per cent of the British land surface, while another estimate for the year 1941 suggested a higher proportion of about 8.5 per cent (Harrison *et al*, 1977, p. 52). As our calculations indicate a public land-holding of between 17 and 20 per cent, we might conclude that, relative to 1941, by the mid-1970s the size of the public land holding in Britain had more or less doubled.

TABLE 3.1   *Public Ownership of Land in Britain*
(calculated from figures for 1972 and 1977)

	Area in Hectares	A	B
The Crown Estate and central government	1,617,583	7.0	42.0
Nationalized industries and public corporations	246,867	1.1	6.4
Local authorities	1,138,826	5.0	29.6
Common land and conservation bodies	845,012	3.7	22.0
Total public land	3,848,288	16.8	100.0
Total land surface of Britain	22,999,000	100.0	

Source: Dowrick, 1974; Harrison *et al*, 1977.
Key: Column A shows public lands as percentage of overall British land surface. Column B shows each holding as percentage of total public land. Percentages rounded to the nearest decimal point.

Though land provides a limited amount of revenue to the public purse, its importance lies in its usage. Some, such as that owned by the Forestry Commission and National Coal Board, is largely put to productive use. Other lands are let to private agencies such as tenant farmers, property developers, and mineral extractors. A further segment of public lands has an immediate use by public authorities for the location of public sector utilities such as offices, hospitals, schools and factories. It is here that our discussion of land tends to merge into matters which are more pertinent to the topic of government equipment.

Government Equipment. Just as governments require land on which to locate their activities, so they also need equipment with which to carry them out. The range of government equipment is potentially vast and includes items as various as battleships, computers, deks, filing cabinets, power stations, motor vehicles, offices, printing presses, typewriters and tea-urns. Government equipment has never been fully catalogued nor extensively studied and, in the limited space available, we can only provide some very rough indications of what is involved.

The most recent figures available on the value of tangible public sector assets are those for 1975 which reveal a market value of £189 billion. These include plant and machinery (£29 billion); vehicles, ships and aircraft (£3.9 billion); and dwellings (£73.5 billion). About 49 per cent of these tangible public sector assets were held by local authorities (mainly council houses), 14 per cent by central government, and the remaining 37 per cent by nationalized industries and public corporations (Treasury 1982c). Additional figures are available on the unit number and sizes of many public goods and services. In the United Kingdom in 1978, for example, there were 2,592 hospitals (nearly half in the 250–499 bed range), about 36,000 schools and more than 336,000 kilometres of public roads.

There are also statistics relating to central government's Civil Estate, which in 1979 comprised a total of 10,616 holdings of land and buildings throughout the UK. The largest single element of the Civil Estate is the office estate; in 1979 this included 6,163 properties ranging from major office blocks in central London to small suites in provincial towns. Over 60 per cent of the office estate is outside London. A further major component of the Civil Estate is the defence estate, which consists of 821 separate defence establishments (such as barracks, airfields, dockyards, research establishments, housing estates, hospitals, stores, factories, warehouses, workshops and wireless stations). Some of these are relatively small, while others cover large tracts of countryside such as Salisbury Plain.

The major part of the Civil Estate is administered by the Property Services Agency. In 1977–8 the PSA spent some £320 million on office accommodation and equipment, including about £125 million on fuel and maintenance and £30 million on furniture (Department of the Environment, 1979, Appendix). Such statistics, though selective and impressionistic, give a rough idea of the very widescale and substantial nature of the equipment used by public authorities.

Labour

In addition to land on which to locate their activities and the equipment with which to carry them out, governments require personnel to man their offices and installations. Public employment has undergone considerable growth in most major industrial societies. As abroad, the trend in Britain has been towards the recruitment of more specialist, qualified personnel. In terms of recruitment the system has become more meritocratic, less based on command, but also, because of the growth in numbers, less accountable to the public and politicians.

Means of Acquisition. Conscription and forced labour were once relatively common. Indeed, before and during the feudal system people were obliged to undertake public works as part of their labour dues. More recently conscription was used in both the First and Second World Wars to recruit armed forces and it continued until 1961. Because conscripted or involuntary labour is difficult to organize and motivate, its use has tended to decline. There are still some examples of tasks that involve an element of compulsory public employment such as the imposition on offenders of community service orders, or the use of labour in prisons and places of detention. In general, however, little public employment is based on forced labour recruitment.

Another traditional way of recruiting labour was through inheritance; the acquisition of public office through birth and kin connection. This again has declined in importance but significant elements remain in institutions such as the monarchy and the 820 hereditary peers who are members of the House of Lords. Connected with inheritance and still very prevalent is the use of command and favour as a means of recruitment. This applies to some of the most prestigious jobs and becomes increasingly important higher up the hierarchy of government. Prime Ministers and their advisers, for example, dispense Cabinet and ministerial positions partly on the basis of favour and command. The same applies when it comes to the creation of life peers, of which there are now more than 330. The Prime Minister and other ministers can appoint people to the various commissions, committees, and other quasi-governmental or non-governmental organizations (quagos or quangos) that come within their responsibility. More than 5,600 paid public appointments are dispensed in this way, and some (like the Chairman of British Steel, who was paid £31,390 in 1978, and British Rail, £25,895) are very well remunerated (Civil Service Department, 1978). Leaders of majority parties in local governments often have considerable scope in the appointment of committee chairmen and occasionally senior officers, and councillors appoint people to public bodies such as district health authorities and community health councils, school and university governors, and gas and electricity consultative councils. As in all political systems it is not only a question of what skills you have or of what you know, but also who you know and how well you are accepted.

While command and favour remain essential elements in high level political recruitment, the other traditional means of acquiring labour (conscription and inheritance) have tended to be replaced by techniques of election and especially selection on the basis of specialist qualification and skills. Election accords with the conventional representative and responsible view of policy making. From this viewpoint, recruitment through election by periodic, popular ballots is the central means whereby public agencies are rendered accountable to the citizens. In England and Wales there are more than 22,000 elected MPs, district and county councillors, with a further 70,000 elected to parish councils. These are not usually included in public sector employment figures and indeed most councillors and some MPs are part-time and have other occupations.

Although much attention is given to the responsible and democratic nature of the British system, very few public sector personnel are subject to election. The bulk of recruitment to the modern public sector is based on selection using prescribed criteria such as age, skills and qualifications. One main avenue of entry into the higher grades of the civil service is through the administrative trainee scheme which usually recruits a number of graduates each year on the basis of their academic achievement and tests. Likewise local government officers, if they are to be candidates for promotion, generally require to be fully qualified in their particular speciality, be it social services, town and country planning or legal services.

Increasingly, therefore, as government has become more complex and substantial, the acquisition of labour has become more firmly based on the merits, skills and qualifications of those recruited. Once labour is recruited, command and favour play a more substantial part, and at the very top of the system these techniques remain significant in both the placement and even initial recruitment of personnel. The elective element is much promoted in public discussion but in reality has a more contained and limited role. Indeed recruitment patterns suggest a system of policy making closer to the technocratic, bureaucratic power, administrative diffusion and elite views of policy making rather than the conventional, representative and responsible government view. It is a contemporary problem for theories of democratic account-ability that, as the size of public employment has expanded, and as its recruitment has increasingly relied on meritocratic criteria, the idea of a small number of elected, non-specialists supervising and controlling a vast contingent of highly specialized manpower becomes increasingly difficult to sustain both in theory and in practice.

The numbers and trend in public employment. In 1978, the latest date for which full figures are available, 29.7 per cent (7,383,000) of employees in the UK were employed in the public sector: 9.2 per cent (2,309,000) in central government, 12.1 per cent (3,013,000) in local government and 8.3 per cent (2,061,000) in public corporations and nationalized industries (Semple, 1979).

Of that central government total, 13.8 per cent (318,000) were employed in the armed services, 50.9 per cent in the National Health Service, 3.4 per cent (80,000) in publicly constituted bodies such as the UK Atomic Energy Authority and the Forestry Commission, and 31.9 per cent (736,000) in the civil service. Among the civil servants, just over 567,000 were non-industrial, policy-making and administra-tion personnel who man the various ministries.

At the local government level 52 per cent (1,566,000) of local authority personnel were in the education services and a further 11 per cent (334,000) were employed in the public health and social services. Amongst the public corporations the major employers were British Rail (217,800), the Post Office (401,300), the electricity industry (158,700), and British Steel (197,000).

The trend in public sector employment over the last 130 years has been one of intermittent but persistent expansion, followed by con-traction in the late 1970s. From 1851 to 1961 public employment as a percentage of the labour force rose from 2.4 per cent to 23.8 per cent. The main growth in numbers (nearly 4 million) took place be-tween 1938 and 1951; in the 1950s there was a decline in public sector employment (Parry, 1980). Expansion, however, was renewed in the 1960s but not at the same pace as previously. Between 1961 and 1978 public sector employment increased by 1.5 million. This is accounted for almost wholly by developments in central government's NHS (which doubled from 575,000 to 1,175,000) and by local autho-rity education, health and social services (which also doubled). The other categories of the public sector have remained relatively the same or have marginally declined.

Since 1978, however, there has been an overall decline in the size of public sector employment. By mid-1982 civil service numbers had fallen to 666,400 (a drop of about 69,600 since 1978), while local authority employment declined by 1.6 per cent between 1979 and 1980 and by a further 2.5 per cent in 1980–1.

Who is influential? Not all of the 7 million plus public employees are equally influential. The question of who are the key policy makers is a difficult one. As noted in Chapter 2, what is defined as 'key' depends upon the chosen view of policy making and the nature of power and leadership contained therein. The question of 'key' also depends on which section or part of the policy process is being observed: the personnel involved in acquiring resources are generally different from those involved in their division or distribution. However, there is an obvious distinction to be made between:

(a) those engaged in the day-to-day operation of a service or public undertaking who have little discretion or original decisions to make about their task, such as lower ranks in the armed services, general public service maintenance and cleaning staff, miners, railwaymen and workers in ordnance factories and the Royal Mint;

(b) those who are engaged in the day-to-day operation of a service and have some discretion to determine the way they operate and how they carry out their tasks (such as teachers, social workers, policemen, tax collectors, social security officers, doctors, judges, factory inspectors);

(c) those who in some part determine the broad framework within which day-to-day operations and tasks are carried out (such as senior local government officers, chief constables, senior civil servants, managers of public corporations and nationalized industries, councillors, members of parliament and ministers).

Of course these categories overlap — judges, for example, could fit into either (b) or (c), — but we can say that category (a) has at most a very marginal influence on policy making: they can protest, go on strike or go slow, for instance. Those in category (b) are likely to be more influential. It is these types of personnel that are often closest to and most in contact with the public. It is they who carry out policy and, as Chapters 7 and 8 illustrate, they can have an important effect on the nature of the programmes actually applied and on the impact of policy upon particular citizens.

Those in category (c) who set the broad framework are generally important, particularly when it comes to dividing resources (as we shall see in Chapter 6). In the conventional view these, especially elected representatives and senior officials, are the key policy makers. This, we believe, is a narrow focus which ignores the complexity and wide range of government and its operations. However, as in the case of each view of policy making, it has credence. In terms of their scope for making, though not necessarily seeing through or controlling the application of major policy choices, individual senior civil servants are clearly more important than individual government inspectors or policemen; individual Cabinet ministers are more important than individual doctors or social security officers.

At the national level the conventional view suggests that there are probably fewer than 2,500 key policy makers. These are the 110 or so members of the government (Cabinet and junior ministers), the 2,200 civil servants in the four most senior grades (permanent, deputy, under and assistant secretaries), and the 100–200 heads and immediate advisers of the main public corporations and nationalized industries. Possibly we might add the 550 backbench MPs and 6,000 principal grade or higher executive officer civil servants for they may also have an intermittent role in influencing policy. At the local authority level, the conventional view focuses on top departmental officers – directors and deputy directors of housing, education, planning and so forth – the councillors and, especially from among the latter, leaders of the ruling group and chairmen of committees. On this reckoning, the key policy makers in Manchester City Council, for example, number about 150 out of an overall workforce of 38,000.

Such generalizations can be helpful but they can be misleading. The structure of policy making is not always as neat, nor as simple as they suggest. In fact it is a useful exercise for the reader to apply each of the views of policy making discussed in Chapter 2 to the question; who are the key personnel? According to the pluralist viewpoint, for instance, more attention would need to be given to the personnel in different policy arenas or areas such as health or industrial policy and to the leaders of interest groups. The idea of a single, overall policy system would be questionable. From a ruling-class perspective, personnel dealing with social control and socialization would take on some importance, as would connections between state personnel and key personnel in the economy. We suggest you refer back to Chapter 2 and do this exercise for each of the views of policy making described in it.

Finance and Capital

All governments require finance and capital in order to pay for building, land, equipment and personnel. The main means of acquiring public finance include levying taxes, charging for the use of public services, contributions from public enterprise and investment, grants from superior authorities, the sale of public sector assets, and borrowing to make up any shortfall between the amount raised and the amount spent.

Taxation. In Britain about 80 per cent of public revenues are derived from taxation, amounting to about £101.5 billion in 1981–2. Because of its importance as the major means of acquiring finance and capital, and because of the complexity, the tax system deserves careful examination.

The bulk of taxation revenue is raised by the central government through four main types of taxes (see Figure 3.1). Those levied on (1) *income*, (2) *capital*, (3) *spending*, and (4) *national insurance and health contributions*, which are strictly speaking not a tax but an insurance payment, though we include them in taxation as they represent a major source of revenue and operate as a kind of crude payroll tax. At the local authority level revenue is raised through rates, which are a form of property tax based on the value of property in conjunction with a rate level set by each local authority.

Figure 3.1 contains details of the major taxes and their yields in 1981–2. This shows that an important feature of the British tax system is the key role played by income tax (about 28 per cent of tax revenue) and taxes on spending (37.4 per cent of tax revenue). Very little, only about 1.5 per cent of tax take, is raised from capital taxes and only a small amount, about 5 per cent, from company or corporation tax. The reliance on income and spending taxes as the main source of tax revenue has been constant since the Second World War, but there have been important changes in the balance of contributions made by these taxes. The main trend until 1979 was an increasing shift to taxes on personal income, but since the June Budget of that year, there has been an important move back to taxes on spending, following cuts in basic income tax rates and an almost doubling of VAT from a basic rate of 8 per cent to 15 per cent. Since the 1970s, also, new sources of tax have been developed in the case of North Sea oil

A. NATIONAL TAXES

The central government raises about 89 per cent of tax revenue — about £90.5 billion — through four main types of taxes.

1. *Taxes on Income* : yield about £37.4 billion — 36.7 per cent of tax take
   (i) *Income Tax:* yield about £28.5 billion.
       In theory a progressive tax which varies according to income level and family circumstances.
   (ii) *Corporation Tax:* yield about £4.8 billion.
        A tax on company profits levied at the rate of 52 per cent on large companies, 40 per cent on small and 40 per cent on building societies. Qualifying limit £90,000.
   (iii) *Petroleum Revenue Tax:* yield £2.4 billion.
         A tax levied on the market revenue, at the rate of 75 per cent, on all North Sea oilfields with a production exceeding 500,000 tonnes a year after allowances. Between April 1981 and December 1982 a supplementary petroleum duty was levied at 20 per cent of gross revenues.

2. *Taxes on capital:* yield about £1.6 billion — 1.6 per cent of tax take. Some examples:
   Capital Gains Tax: yield £540 million.
   A tax levied on capital gains over £5,000 at the rate of 30 per cent — various exemptions allowed for personal property.
   Capital Transfer Tax: yield about £470 million.
   A tax on transfers from one individual to another of personal wealth above £55,000, at rates rising from 15 per cent to 50 per cent.

3. *Taxes on spending:* yield about £38 billion — 37.4 per cent of tax take — including national insurance surcharge yielding £3.6 billion. Some examples:
   Value Added Tax: yield £12.3 billion.
   A tax collected at each stage in the production and distribution process; excludes basic necessities — rate 15 per cent.
   Revenue Duties: from tobacco £3.3 billion; oil £4.5 billion; alcohol £3 billion; gaming £500 million, etc.

4. *National Insurance Contributions:* yield about £13.5 billion — 13.3 per cent of tax take.
   Paid by all employers and employees.

B. LOCAL TAXES

Rates: taxes on property: yield about £11 billion — 11 per cent of tax take.
[Estimated overall tax yield = £101.5 billion]

Source: Treasury (1982b)

FIGURE 3.1. *An Outline of Taxation in Britain*
(All figures are estimates for the year 1981—2.
Percentages have been rounded)

extraction. Petroleum Revenue Tax was introduced in 1975 and in the 1981 Budget a supplementary petroleum duty was levied until December 1982.

Compared with other industrialized states the level of taxation in Britain is neither exceptionally high nor exceptionally low. Amongst 12 OECD (Organization of Economic Development) countries Britain ranked fourth in 1971 and seventh in 1978, and in the 1971−8 period the percentage of Gross National Product taken by taxes and social security contributions actually fell by 2 per cent. Hence, contrary to much popular belief, Britons were not more heavily taxed than their competitors, nor was the tax burden rising. This false impression probably arises from variations in tax systems: France (43 per cent and West Germany (35 per cent) depend far more on social security contributions than does Britain (18 per cent) for example. We, on the other hand, have high expenditure taxes (we rank second) and household income taxes (fifth) and the public is very conscious of these (Newman, 1980).

Traditionally tax levels are reviewed annually. Local authorities set their rate level in February or March, and the Chancellor of the Exchequer presents his budget in March or April. Often the Chancellor's proposed changes in taxation are implemented immediately (petrol may go up the same day if the tax is increased), but it is not until the House of Commons has passed a Finance Act later in the summer that certain tax changes become legally binding. In recent years there has been a tendency to introduce 'mini budgets' in mid-year in order to keep economic policy on course, and some tax levels can be altered without recourse to legislation in a Finance Act but by means of delegated legislation.

In central government relatively few people are closely involved in determining tax measures. They include, apart from the Chancellor and his junior ministers, officials from the fiscal policy division of the Treasury and the tax collection departments. Traditionally, with the exception of the Prime Minister, the Cabinet only hears of the Budget proposals the day before the Chancellor's speech and so has little opportunity to influence the details, though they will, of course, have had opportunities to debate overall economic policy. The secrecy surrounding the Budget has been much criticized and under the recent chancellorships of Messrs Healey and Howe there has been some relaxation − prepublication of background data and leaks to the press.

The collection and administration of national taxes is mainly the

concern of the two major tax collection departments: Inland Revenue
and Customs and Excise. The former, with a staff of 85,000, is concerned with capital and income taxes, while the latter, with 35,000
personnel, deals with expenditure taxes and duties. In addition the
Department of Transport administers the motor vehicle duties and the
Department of Health and Social Security the national insurance fund.
Locally, district councils administer the rating system. They collect on
behalf of county and parish councils, as well as for their own coffers.

User Charges and Public Enterprise and Investment. About 5 per cent
of public sector revenue is raised from user charges and this is largely
derived from local authority housing rents. However, public authorities
also charge in full or part for the use of a wide range of public goods
and service, including medical prescriptions, airport charges, parking
fees, bridge tolls and dental treatment. About 10 per cent of local
authority revenue is derived from user charges, while only about 2 per
cent of central government's revenue comes from this source. In recent
years user charges as a proportion of revenue have been marginally
increasing.

Public enterprise and investment accounts for about 7 per cent of
general government revenues. The bulk of this (estimated to be about
£7.3 billion in 1981–2) is contributed by nationalized industries and
public corporations. The rest is derived from other forms of government investment such as shares in private companies. The yield from
public enterprise is unpredictable as much depends on the trading
capacities and opportunities of the organizations involved. In a reces-
sionary economic climate, revenue from this source will tend to decline,
hence pushing the burden of revenue extraction upon other means of
acquisition. High unemployment, for example, means fewer people
travelling to work and a reduced income from bus and train fares.

Grants from Superior Authorities. Public sector institutions may gain
some income from superior authorities, either supra-national in the
case of EEC grants, or national in the case of central government
contributions to local authorities, nationalized industries and public
corporations. The gross receipts from the EEC are fairly minor and
variable: in 1980–1 they amounted to £971 million, well below 1 per
cent of general government receipts (Treasury, 1982a, vol. II, p. 8).

In 1981–2 local authorities collectively obtained 59 per cent of
their income from central government grants, though the proportion

varies from council to council. The major allocation is in the form of a Rate Support (Block) Grant which is determined on the basis of each local authority's resources and needs in line with a national definition of reasonable expenditure patterns. In 1981 local authorities received grants worth just under £16 billion from central government.

Public corporations and nationalized industries also receive subsidies from central government. In 1981 these bodies received about £3 billion from this source, the bulk of which went to the National Coal Board (£251 million) and British Rail (£673 million).

The Disposal of Capital Assets. Revenue can be raised through the sale of public sector holdings, such as shares in companies, land, buildings and/or mineral resources. This is not a constant, nor consistent source of income. It is a one-off transaction for obviously, once the asset is sold, it cannot be re-sold. Moreover any regular income (such as rent) that the asset contributed to public revenues is lost. A further difficulty arises in that assets can only be sold when they are available and market-able and this will vary according to the state of the asset and the state of the market. In addition some administrations are less willing to sell off assets than others. The 1970–4 and post–1979 Conservative governments accepted 'denationalization' or 'privatization' as an important policy aim and the 1979 government, for example, gave 5 million council house tenants a legal right to purchase their homes. Between 1979 and 1982 more than 370,000 houses were sold. Labour governments have been more reluctant, though in the autum of 1976 a Labour administration did dispose of 10 per cent of the public shareholding in British Petroleum in order to deal with an immediate economic crisis.

For the above reasons the contribution made to national revenues through the sale of assets is liable to vary from year to year. Though the recent trend has been towards a greater use of this means of acquisi-tion, this development is unlikely to continue as it involves an erosion of the resource-base of the public sector on which the process of dis-posal ultimately depends. Put simply, if there is nothing left to sell that is saleable, no money can be raised in this way. Despite the importance attached to the sale of assets by the 1979 Conservative government, receipts remain small in relation to the overall total of government revenue. Excluding oil receipts (for example, premiums levied on licenses to explore in the North Sea) the 1979–80 and 1980–1 totals were only £370 million and £210 million respectively, the former figure being bolstered by further sales of £276 million worth of BP shares (Treasury 1982a, II, p. 97).

Borrowing to Make Up the Shortfall Between Receipts and Expenditure.
In recent years, borrowing by the public sector from other sectors of the economy and from overseas has played an increasingly important part in revenue acquisition. In the national accounts total borrowing is denoted under the heading Public Sector Borrowing Requirement (PSBR). In 1981—2 this was estimated at £10.5 billion, more than 8 per cent of overall public sector receipts. The percentage of public revenues made up by borrowing was less than 5 per cent in 1963, rose to over 5 per cent in 1968, then fell to nil in 1970. Thereafter PSBR rose to around 15 per cent by the middle 1970s, was cut back to 8.5 per cent in 1977 then increased to take up about 11—12 per cent of revenue before falling back in 1981—2.

The PSBR is financed mainly through the sale of government securities called 'gilts', and to a lesser extent National Savings. These two items alone have, over the last few years, accounted for about 70 per cent of the financing of the PSBR, and the money has increasingly come from the non-bank private sector, including institutions such as insurance companies and pension funds, industrial and commercial companies, and individual investors (Treasury, 1981).

Central government is the largest borrower but also sanctions loans raised by local authorities and public corporations. Both the latter sets of institutions have steadily but marginally increased their borrowing since 1963, while overall general government totals have fluctuated quite markedly from year to year (from nil in 1970 to nearly £6 billion in 1978—9, for example). Indeed the PSBR has generally varied in step with large changes in the central government share. Local authorities and public corporations can, and do, raise loans on their own behalf, but, in addition, they borrow from central government itself — in 1979—80 public corporations and nationalized industries borrowed £3.15 billion that way, and local authorities £817 million (Treasury, 1980).

CONCLUSION

The various resources of government are interdependent. While each can be studied separately it is important to realize the connections between them. If there are, for instance, contractions in a particular source of finance and capital, the shortfall will require to be made up either by drawing in more from other sources or to be eliminated by cutting actual expenditure. A cut in the activities of government, especially those benefiting special and influential sections, may lead to an erosion of governmental support and possibly, in time, regime support. Equally an extension of government borrowing may increase the cost of credit and contribute to inflation and rising costs in general, thus affecting the general state of the economy which in turn may reflect back in terms of a weakening of support. An increase in user charges will have immediate consequences for certain sections of the population and could actually lead to a decline in revenue if the charges become excessive and citizens cease to use certain services. In general any extension or contraction in resources will create problems. Extension in taxes depends ultimately on taxpayers' willingness to accept the burden of taxes: too heavy a burden will lead to less acquiescence and cooperation. A contraction in public employment will have immediate consequences for those made redundant, long-term consequences for the labour market, will reduce tax and national insurance revenue, and will raise spending by increasing the amount devoted to unemployment pay and social security benefits.

As we have mentioned already, a key place in the interwoven web of resources is held by support. Without the support of substantial and important sections of the public, government cannot easily and effectively acquire land, equipment, labour, or finance and capital. Yet if support *is* the central resource, it is closely dependent upon the operation and application of its more tangible counterparts. For, as we have noted, support shapes, but is also shaped by, the nature of other resources and how they are acquired.

As far as these more tangible resources are concerned, we have seen that the post-war period has been one of growth. Government land, employment, and finance and capital have been greatly extended. Towards the middle of the 1970s, however, the expansion of resources slowed considerably and by the end of that decade there were clear indications of a marginal reversal in the volume of government resources.

The chapter also reveals the important and influential position of central government in Britain *vis-à-vis* the other component parts of the public sector. Central government controls the bulk of revenue, and local authorities and public corporations are greatly dependent on grants and loans from, or sanctioned by, the centre. The dominance of central government, however, is not so substantial when it comes to the consideration of land and labour.

Over time there have been major changes in the methods of resource acquisition. The traditional reliance on coercive and command techniques as well as clearly defined obligations and responsibilities has been replaced by more modern techniques involving exchanges and inducements such as cash payments, and more open means of acquiring resources such as skilled labour recruitment and taxation. In general the methods have become more complex, more wide ranging, and have involved a wider section of the population than had previously been the case. Naturally there are both strengths and weaknesses in this. The commitments to, involvements in, and benefits from government fall more widely, as in the case of public sector employment and welfare benefits, and this dependence may strengthen government. Equally, however, the burdens are distributed amongst wider sections, so that more feel the extractive and demanding side of public authorities, and this may have the reverse effect.

Because the resources of government are so interlinked, and because so much depends upon the pattern of political support, the acquisition of resources is not only complex but fraught with difficulties. Also, because acquisition involves the extraction of resources from the population it is bound to involve costs and the imposition of burdens. We consider these issues of the effectiveness of acquisition and its consequences in the next chapter.

TOPICS FOR DISCUSSION.

1. Is it realistic to talk about a distinctive British approach to political change?
2. Do recent changes in government support threaten regime support?
3. Should all land be public land?
4. Why did public sector employment increase during the period from 1959 to 1979? Examine the arguments justifying this increase.
5. Which public services, if any, should be substantially financed through user charges? Why? Suggest some of the likely consequences of your proposals.
6. Examine the case in favour of selling public sector assets.

KEY READING

On support, Marsh (1977), Ch. 2 deserves careful reading, while Butler and Stokes (1974) produce material on the development of voting in the 1960s and Harrop (1982) provides a useful summary of recent research. There are some points on land in Dowrick (1974) and Ch. 2 of Norton-Taylor (1982). Kay and King (1980) offer a comprehensive outline of the British tax system. Semple (1979) provides much information on public employment, as does Parry (1980). Other material on tangible resources has to be gleaned from primary documents such as the most recently published Budget Report (Treasury 1982b).

REFERENCES

Almond, G. and Verba, S. (1963) *The Civic Culture*, Princeton University Press.

Alt, J. (1980) in P. Whiteley, (ed.) *Models of Political Economy*, Sage.

Birch, A. H. (1973) *The British System of Government*, Allen & Unwin, 3rd edn.

Blondel, J. (1974) *Voters, Parties and Leaders*, Penguin, revised edn.

Butler, D. E. and Stokes, D. (1974) *Political Change in Britain*, Macmillan, 2nd edn.

Civil Service Department (1978) *A Directory of Paid Public Appointments Made by Ministers*, HMSO.

CSO (Central Statistical Office) (1982), *Social Trends*, Vol. 12, HMSO.

Department of the Environment (1979) 'Property Services Agency', *Annual Report 1978–1979*, HMSO.

Dowrick, F. E. (1974) 'Public ownership of land — taking stock, 1972–73, *Public Law*, Spring.

Dowse, B. and Hughes H. (1971) 'The family, the school and political socialisation', *Sociology*, Vol. 5, No. 1.

The Economist (1981), *The Economist*, 8 August 1981.

Harrison A., Tranter R. B. and Gibbs R. S. (1977) *Landownership by Public and Semi-public Institutions in the UK*, Centre for Agricultural Strategy, University of Reading.

Harrop, M. (1982), 'The Changing British Electorate', *Political Quarterly*, Vol. 53, pp. 385–402.

Kay, J. A. and King, M. A. (1980) *The British Tax System*, Oxford University Press, 2nd edn.

Kiernan, V. G. (1972) in R. Benewick and T. Smith (eds) *Direct Action and Democratic Politics*, Allen & Unwin.

Marsh, A. (1977) *Protest and Political Consciousness*, Sage.

Newman, K. J. (1980) 'International comparison of taxes and social security contributions 1971–1978', *Economic Trends*, December.

Norton-Taylor, R. (1982), *Whose Land is it Anyway?*, Turnstone Press.

Parry, R. (1980) *United Kingdom Public Employment: Patterns of Change 1951–76*, Centre for Public Policy, University of Strathclyde.

Semple, W. (1979) 'Employment in the public and private sectors 1961–1978', *Economic Trends*, November.

Taylor, C. L. and Hudson, M. C. (1972) *World Handbook of Political and Social Indicators*, Yale University Press, 2nd edn.

Treasury (1980), 'Measuring the public sector borrowing requirement', *Economic Progress Report*, No. 126, HMSO.

Treasury (1981) 'Financing the public sector borrowing requirement', *Economic Progress Report*, No. 136, HMSO.

Treasury (1982a) *The Government's Expenditure Plans 1982–83 to 1984–85*, Cmnd. 8494, Vol. II, HMSO.

Treasury (1982b) *Financial Statement and Budget Report 1982–1983*, House of Commons Paper 237 (1981–2 Session), HMSO.

Treasury (1982c), 'The national debt and the public sector debt', *Economic Progress Report*, No. 147, HMSO.

4

Problems of Acquiring Resources – What, How and from Whom?

In manufacturing industry the nature of the raw materials used will affect the product. The proportions and quality of hops, yeast and water will, for example, determine the taste and strength of beer, and this will vary from brewer to brewer. In the public sector too, the raw materials (or resources) drawn in by government will help shape the policy produced. The acquisition of resources affects the process of policy making, the actual policy products, and the social consequences of those products. Local authority budgeting, for example, is affected by central government policies on the extent and allocation of grants to councils. These policies are sometimes announced late in the local budget process, and a rapid reassessment of proposed council policies can result, as we shall see in Chapter 6. A cut in the level of grant aid, the experience of recent years, has policy consequences such as a postponement of plans to extend the home help service or meals on wheels. This in turn has social consequences including a reduced quality of life for some elderly people living at home, and possibly an early enforced move into a hostel or hospital.

It may seem obvious that the acquisition of resources affects policy products. However, there are theorists who challenge this view. Dye, for example, produces a considerable body of evidence in support of the view that the prime determinant of the standard of public goods and services is the level of material resources of the community (whether it be a city, state or nation). A materially wealthy unit of government will have a high level of public service provision for '*on the whole* economic resources (are) more influential in shaping state policies than any…political variables' (Dye, 1976, p. 29 – his italics). The theory suggests that the ways in which governments acquire, divide and distribute resources are not the main concern when it comes to explaining public policy, and is supported by empirical evidence that technologically developed industrialized nations tend to have superior public service provision to Third World states (Wilensky, 1975).

We accept that the extent of potential material resources is a relevant factor in helping determine the nature of policy products. After all, non-existent resources simply cannot be acquired! But we argue that the anti-political stance is overstated in the theory, in three ways. First, even if material resources do provide some limit on what policy products can be selected, they at the most only rule out certain 'expensive' options. They may provide a ceiling on the size of the public sector, but we are concerned with its shape as well as its size.

Second, the theory tends to assume that the amount of raw materials available to government is given and fixed. But this is not so. Government can positively go out and acquire and extract resources, and government chooses which to extract and which to leave untouched. Whether or not to impose a wealth tax is one example. Another is the policy of some Labour-controlled councils, known as 'municipalization', whereby houses which come on the market are purchased, thereby increasing government holdings of land and equipment. This contrasts with the conscious sale of assets, a policy of the 1979 Conservative government.

Third, the theory ignores the way in which the political choice of what resources to acquire from the community has consequences for the nature and distribution of material resources in society, that is on the actual raw material base. Policy decisions about the type of income tax (progressive, proportional, or regressive), about a wealth tax, death duties and capital transfer tax affect both the distribution of wealth today and, in turn, the nature and quality of resources available for future acquisition.

For these three reasons we believe politics to be important rather than neutral or uninfluential. We contend that different governments do determine what resources are available to them and, further, that a government's approach to the acquisition of resources will greatly influence the scope of public policy which, in turn, will have wide social and economic consequences for society.

In this chapter we are concerned only with the acquisition of resources; their division and distribution are considered later. Acquisition alone raises two major sets of issues on which we intend to concentrate.

The first set of issues relates to problems which governments face when they come to acquiring resources. Some are technical — how best to organize the collection of a wealth tax, for example. Others raise philosophical and moral questions such as how far it is acceptable to extend governmental support by using acquisition policies which favour certain sections of the population. Governments are frequently criticized by other parties on this ground when changes in the incidence of taxation are announced, as was the Conservative government when it reduced the highest rate of income tax paid on earned income from 83 per cent to 60 per cent in its June 1979 Budget. Then there are judgmental problems: how to assess the likely effects of potential new acquisition policies such as a wealth tax, the nationalization of land, or the re-introduction of conscription through national service. Like manufacturing industry, government will be intent on acquiring its resources effectively, an objective not easy to achieve.

The second set of issues relates to the consequences on the community of the acquisition of resources. We shall see in Chapter 8 that the distribution of those resources returned to society, when coupled with their original extraction, affects household income. Our concern in this chapter is solely with the extraction of resources and with an analysis of their source. Which sections of society provide the government with resources? Who bears the burden or costs of acquisition? In particular we go on to focus, as a case study, on perhaps the most tangible and best known (but not well understood) of resources: money. We analyse and question some of the claims commonly made about the British tax system, including the idea that those with high incomes suffer high levels of taxation.

PROBLEMS OF ACQUISITION

Policy makers are faced with a series of problems when it comes to acquiring resources. First, they need to take a view about what is potentially available. Having established the size of the kitty, they need also to judge what proportion of that kitty should be acquired, and to consider how effectively this can be done. These three sets of issues are interconnected, and a theme common to them is the constraint of public attitudes. Taxes on basic foods like bread, milk and potatoes might be judged by politicians as unacceptable to voters, for example. So, too, might invasions into personal privacy or the removal of 'traditional' rights of land ownership.

What is available?

It is extremely difficult to define the scope and extent of the nation's resources with any precision. Yet in the absence of such a definition, fully informed policy decisions about acquisition are not possible. Ideally we need to have some notion of what is in the kitty before deciding what to take from it. But an analysis of what is potentially available to government is faced with problems of definition, of information, and of location.

Proposals for a wealth tax, announced in principle by the 1974—9 Labour government in March 1976 as part of a 'determined attack on the maldistribution of wealth in Britain' (Sandford *et al*, 1980, p. 4), but never introduced, illustrate the problem of definition. The meaning of 'wealth' is unclear and no fewer than five definitions were identified by the Royal Commission on the Distribution of Income and Wealth. Money and assets are involved. Money is relatively easy to assess, though trusts are a complication and may account for 9 per cent of wealth (Atkinson, 1975, pp. 121—5). Assets are often less tangible, and not all are easily valued, particularly those like security and economic and social opportunity which usually go alongside tangible wealth. The question of which tangible assets to include in a wealth tax is also controversial. Most people now own cars, houses and a number of consumer durables. Finally, some argue that a distinction should be made between wealth resulting from hard work and inherited wealth, and/or between wealth invested productively in industry, and wealth wasted on gambling or a high life (C. T. Sandford in Field, 1979).

'Wealth', then, is an elusive concept. But it is not the only example, and similar problems of definition apply to 'income', 'profits', 'skilled labour' or 'public opinion'.

To the problem of definition is added the problem of information, which embraces both availability and reliability. Some data, ideally needed in order to assess what is available to government, may not be collected. In Chapter 3, for example, we saw that estimates of land ownership vary widely, with no comprehensive survey having been made for more than a century. The reliability of some statistics is questionable, often due to errors made during their collection. The 1981 Census, for example, asked householders how many rooms there were in the house, but gave inadequate guidance about counting attics and cellars. Neighbours in a terrace of identical houses gave different replies, but the published results give an appearance of accuracy and precision. In this case there was no obvious motive for concealment, but sometimes there is. Landlords, for example, may leave some tenants off the electoral roll for fear of being found by the taxman to have a greater income from rents than they habitually declare.

Locating what is available is the third problem. Ideally taxation policy, for example, should be based on an accurate definition of the nature and extent of the economy. In practice the formal economy (activities and income flows recorded in official statistics) can be distinguished from the informal economy (which is unrecorded and largely hidden from official surveillance). The formal economy includes fewer than two-thirds of working age citizens, and says nothing about any economic activity of the remaining third, or of the two-thirds outside normal working hours (Shankland, 1980). Household and voluntary work involve no cash transactions, but 'moonlighting' (earning money without it being recorded) does, and is often termed 'the black economy'.

Because it is hidden, its size cannot be precisely determined. Estimates have ranged between 5 per cent and 15 per cent of Gross Domestic Product (O'Higgins, 1980). In 1979 the Commissioner for Inland Revenue opted for 7½ per cent and this meant £3—3.5 billion of lost tax revenue. If collected, this amount would have paid for a cut in income tax of 5—10 per cent (*The Economist*, 1979). The black economy is not new: it was referred to in the very first report of the Board of Inland Revenue. But it has officially become 'one of the most difficult (problems) facing the Department' (Board of Inland Revenue, 1981).

These problems of definition, information and location make it impossible to know precisely what is available. They are common to all the resources identified in Chapter 3, where we spent some time considering the difficulties of locating, isolating and measuring support. This lack of precision means that policy makers must make a judgment about the resources potentially available. They are likely, for purely practical, administrative reasons, to acquire those that are easiest to extract, rather than those which possibly might (for political, moral or philosophical reasons) be drawn in. Hence effective taxes on wealth or on prosperous multinational corporations, for example, are unlikely to be introduced, and government gets by without properly attempting to identify the true extent of resources potentially available to it.

What proportion should be acquired?

Though there are obvious practical consequences, this is essentially a moral question to which there is no single answer. There is a range of views about what it is desirable or proper for government to acquire and, to illustrate these, we take two of the resources identified in Chapter 3 — labour and finance.

On the acquisition of labour, views can be contained under three broad headings. First, there are those who favour a strictly limited amount of public sector employment on the grounds that it is unproductive and a burden on the private, productive sector (Bacon and Eltis, 1976, pp. 16–19). This burden, in the form of taxes or charges for services, should be minimized by limiting the public sector to basic services. Exactly what constitutes basic services is, of course, a matter for debate and those who subscribe to this broad philosophy do not necessarily agree on what government activities are essential.

A contrasting argument favours substantial public employment (again the precise amount is a matter for separate debate) as an aid to the private sector and the economy. Though not all public services are directly productive in the way that nationalized industries are, they support the manufacturer by saving him from making individual arrangements (which could be costly, ineffective, or both) for the provision of roads, water supply, schools for the children of employees, for protection, and so on. Private sector industry can concentrate on what it is best at, manufacturing and promoting services (Galbraith, 1974, Ch. 16).

The third view is concerned with the direction of activities rather than with employment. Government should exercise control over the nature of most employment on behalf of the community at large, an objective which can be achieved either by large-scale public employment or by positive land-use, financial and industrial planning to constrain the freedom of the private sector, or by a combination of the two approaches. The 1974–9 Labour government, for example, introduced the concept of 'planning agreements' with major manufacturers though only one (with Chrysler UK Ltd) was fully negotiated and agreed, and it did not get carried out as intended (Wilks, 1981). Another approach is 'hidden' public employment whereby a firm is so heavily dependent on government subsidies that its managerial autonomy is limited, as in the case of British Leyland. Public corporations, too, come under the influence of government, though their employees may be listed as part of the public sector anyway. In all these cases, government is in a position to use either sticks or carrots to direct major parts of the economy in the public interest.

Within finance and capital, when it comes to deciding how much taxation should be levied, at least four differing viewpoints can be identified. Once again each reflects moral and philosophical values about the proper role of the state.

At one extreme is the view that taxing people is wrong in principle. The argument is that money is earned by individuals, and what they earn is their money, to be spent as they please. Taxation reduces choices about personal expenditure and so limits individual freedom. As Finer has argued, it should be kept to the minimum, and pay only for basic communal services (Finer, 1977). A second view, less extreme than the former, also seeks low levels of taxation. In this case the emphasis is on paying for services received and benefits provided. Charges for services such as health and schooling would be set at a sufficiently high level to meet either all or a large proportion of the costs of provision on the grounds that it is the collective provision of such services that makes an individual's standard of living possible.

The third and fourth views both see taxation as a positive vehicle for achieving certain social goals rather than as the inevitable consequences of the necessity of providing some public services. The third view is that tax systems should promote social stability both through raising money for communal services like policing, fire prevention and the provision of leisure facilities, and through equalizing to some extent, individuals' resources. A progressive system of taxation and policies designed to redistribute resources are the essential components, how progressive and how much redistribution being matters of debate (and matters of practical concern which we investigate later in this chapter and in Chapter 8). Finally, at the other extreme from Finer, there is the view that all personal income is really communal income because income can only be generated when there is a community to provide the essential framework of stability and security. Thus communal interests should always predominate over individuals' interests because community is primary. Hence substantial taxation is proper, and private income is not fundamentally private.

These ideas about the acquisition of resources illustrate clearly the total lack of agreement on the amount of resources which government should extract. Detailed arguments about exact quantities — the rate of income tax or size of the public sector — are secondary to, and can obscure, basic moral and philosophical questions about the role of the state. It is hard to find common ground between extreme views like some of those outlined above, and the examples have illustrated that there is no one, correct answer to the question of what proportion of national resources should be acquired by the government.

How effective is the process of acquisition?

At first sight this seems a more tangible issue than those discussed above about the potential size of the kitty and the proportion of it to acquire for the public sector. We know, for example, that local authorities spend less than 2 per cent of the proceeds of rates on the cost of collecting them. Income tax costs a similar amount to collect, duties on alcohol less than half, but capital transfer tax almost double, 3.5 per cent (*The Economist*, 1980). But effectiveness cannot be limited to the financial costs of acquisition in this way.

A broader and more useful definition of the effectiveness of acquisition might start from 'achieving the objectives of acquisition at the lowest cost'. This is derived from the rational and the technocratic views of policy making discussed in Chapter 2, with their emphasis on goals and efficiency. As indicated above, the administrative costs of acquisition can be measured with some precision, though there may be technical difficulties about the allocation of certain expenditure — income tax collection, for example, is heavily dependent on employers keeping records, but their costs are not included in the 2 per cent cited in the previous paragraph. More problematic are both the 'objectives of acquisition' and the existence of non-financial costs such as public hostility towards local government, caused by complaints that the rating system is unfair and inequitable.

Two examples of acquisition, that of regime support (see Chapter 3) and of labour, illustrate these general points about the difficulties of defining and measuring effectiveness.

In the case of the acquisition of regime support the evidence about effectiveness can be viewed in two totally different ways. Citizens may take an active, maybe occasionally disruptive, interest in politics and public affairs, or they may quietly take no part in it. Does the former illustrate committed involvement, or does it suggest dissatisfaction? Is 'apathy' an indication of satisfaction, acquiescence, or oppression? Furthermore, how do we assess the effectiveness of regime support? The literature on governability and ungovernability, and on the survival of particular regimes has nothing precise to offer. It implicitly assumes that if a regime exists at all there is effective support for it, regardless of the way in which it exists (including the degree of oppression). We spent a lengthy part of Chapter 3 discussing support as a resource, because we viewed it both as the key resource and as particularly difficult to handle. Attempting to measure the effectiveness of the process of acquiring regime support raises difficult problems.

The effective acquisition of labour is equally tricky to judge. The obvious answer is that effectiveness means the public employment of the right number with the right skills, with proper organization and training. To measure this we need to know about the objectives of public sector employment. In the previous section we identified three conflicting views about this and from that discussion it seems that we first need to decide whether or not a responsibility is a proper responsibility of the state before assessing how efficiently it is being undertaken. Defence and policing are commonly accepted as state responsibilities; public sector provision of leisure centres, hospitals and houses can be a matter for debate.

If we accept that there is a common consensus on the need to employ policemen, the next step is to measure the effectiveness of their performance. The police are there to protect the public from one another and to enhance social stability. The traditional use of financial costs tells us little or nothing about how well this is done. The success rate in solving crimes offers some indication of performance, but relates to only part of their work and is in any case dependent on people (including policemen) reporting that a crime has been committed. Recruitment systems, training procedures and policing methods (foot patrols, cars, communication systems) are at least as important – indeed the Scarman Report into the 1981 Brixton riots placed great emphasis on these factors (Scarman, 1982, Part V). The report was highly critical of many facets of police work, but Scarman would be the first to acknowledge that his analysis was based largely on his judgment rather than on precise statistical evidence. His recommendations are not necessarily the single, correct answer to the problems of policing the inner city.

The notion of effectiveness, then, can only be applied when there exist objectives which provide criteria as a basis for measurement. We saw in Chapter 2, when discussing the rational view, that objectives are frequently unstated, unclear or even incompatible, are matters of debate, and may be avoided by policy makers. This makes assessing the effectiveness of acquisition a difficult task.

To sum up, we have so far identified three broad problems about the acquisition of resources. These relate to the size of the kitty, the proportion to be acquired, and the effectiveness of the process of acquisition. Discussion on each has revealed a mixture of general moral and philosophical questions and of practical issues about measurement and the quality of statistics. Brief examples have been given from a range of resources, but inevitably there has been insufficient space to present them in great detail. To take the argument further we propose to focus on the tax system as a case study of acquisition. We do so because, superficially, taxation appears to be quite tangible and to involve a good deal of hard statistical evidence.

Taxation: a case study of acquisition

It is common to hear taxpayers criticizing the high level of taxation in Britain. For instance, 'it isn't worth working overtime, it all goes in tax'. This belief may be an exaggeration, but it is certainly true that there are high nominal rates of tax. In 1982 income tax started at 30 per cent and rose to 60 per cent (with an additional 15 per cent surcharge in the case of unearned income). Capital transfer tax could be as high as 75 per cent on death and 50 per cent during the tax-payer's lifetime, while corporation tax reached 52 per cent (Treasury, 1982a). But these high nominal rates are a poor guide to actual tax yields, which are far lower. One estimate of the average tax rate on all income is only 13 per cent (Kay and King, 1980, Table 15.2, p. 235), because less than half of personal income is subject to tax. Capital taxes contain loopholes and never apply at the statutory rates with the result that capital transfer tax yields only 0.4 per cent of total government income from taxation. This combination of high tax rates and low tax yields suggests that the system may be ineffective and that we should investigate the reasons for these low yields. There seem to be four main ones.

First, the tax system is not solely concerned with revenue raising. There appear to be at least four other, not always compatible, objectives: the management of the economy; protection of industry; redistribution of personal wealth; and the influencing of citizens' behaviour. Taxation, in other words, is also an instrument of economic and social policy (C. Sandford in Sandford *et al*, 1980, pp. 4—5). At this point the additional economic and redistributive objectives can be taken as needing no further explanation, but the attempt to influence behaviour does. There are occasions when taxes are levied or reduced in order to give incentives to citizens to undertake certain courses of action. Import duties may be constructed to encourage people to 'buy British', tax allowances to stimulate house repairs. Two points about the four additional objectives stem from these examples. One is that such objectives can be incompatible with the revenue-gathering function and there has to be a balance struck between the two. The other is that concessions to some potential taxpayers in order to encourage changes in their behaviour help create a complicated system which is difficult, and maybe also expensive, to operate.

This leads directly to the second reason for low yields. These five varied objectives of the tax system have led to a whole host of special allowances and exemptions under which a tax is excused or offset. Whether or not such allowances work as intended, they are usually guarded or defended by a particular interest and this means that the objectives of taxation compete with the need of government to acquire and maintain support.

Major instances of tax allowances include the ability of industry to offset almost all of its expenditure on plant and machinery and the value of its stock against its liability for corporation tax, a concession designed to both protect industry and encourage investment in new technology. This is certainly incompatible with the revenue collection objective, for the nominal rate of 52 per cent is effectively halved at a cost, in terms of lost revenue, of an estimated £9,800 million in 1981−2 (Treasury, 1982a, Table 4.9).

In the 1982 Budget alone, a further nine allowances for industrial and commercial taxpayers were introduced. One example is a 100 per cent first year allowance against tax liability for expenditure on rented televisions which incorporate a 'teletext' facility (Treasury, 1982b). The Confederation of British Industry and other groups constantly pressurize government to retain and add to such concessions. In all there were 108 different kinds of tax relief in 1981−2, ranging from personal income tax allowances for all taxpayers (the married man's allowance alone meant a loss in revenue of £8,540 million) to an annuity paid to the few holders of the Victoria Cross (Treasury, 1982a, Table 4.9).

The predisposition of Chancellors to alter marginally this host of tax allowances was clearly illustrated by the March 1983 Budget.

Just a year after making the nine changes outlined above, the same Chancellor announced a further 19 modifications to tax allowances and exemptions. Some were straightforward increases in the monetary value of existing allowances. Two, however, were entirely new exemptions designed to encourage further exploration for North Sea oil. Other significant developments were aimed at assisting the construction industry, small businesses, and employee profit sharing. These involved changes in the incidence of corporation tax, in levels of stock relief, and in the arrangements for share option schemes.

The cumulative effect of these allowances and concessions on the tax system is enormous. It has been estimated that in the early 1970s only about 45 per cent of declared personal income was taxed, and that income tax revenue would have been 41 per cent higher had all the main reliefs been abolished (Willis and Hardwick, 1979, pp. 89, 103). It may be easier to grasp this point if we consider a simple example of a married man earning £100 per week, or £5,200 per annum. In 1981–2 he was able to claim a personal allowance of £2,145, thus reducing his taxable income to £3,055. If he was paying a mortgage of £100 monthly, he would obtain additional relief against the interest payments made to the building society, and this would further reduce his taxable income to about £2,000. He might have other, much smaller, allowances too: plumbers and joiners can claim for tools, university lecturers for books necessary for teaching, and so on. The lowest nominal rate of income tax in 1981–2 was 30 per cent, but our man paid at most 12 per cent (30 per cent levied on the net taxable income of £2,000).

The complex structure of allowances, concessions and tax exemptions ensures that yields fall well below tax rates. The third reason for low yields takes this point a little further. Taxpayers can actively use the complexities of taxation to reduce their liability for tax beyond the levels originally intended by policy makers. Exploiting the system is perfectly legal and commonly termed 'tax avoidance'. It is deliberately or artificially ordering one's affairs in such a way as to minimize taxation. Loopholes in tax legislation are exploited with taxpayers acting against the spirit, if not the letter, of the law (A. Christopher in Field (ed.) 1979, p. 80). Death duties (replaced in 1975 by capital transfer tax) were a classic example: for every £1 raised, an estimated £3 was avoided. Optimism about higher yields from the new capital transfer tax also seems to be misplaced (Field *et al*, 1977, pp. 157–60). Companies are adept at introducing clever and artificial means of reducing their liability for corporation tax. Multinationals can transfer profits from one country to another by selling goods from one part of the group to another at non-market prices, for example. Individual North Sea divers were wrongly taxed as self-employed, thus benefitting from a more liberal approach to the level of expenses which could be offset against income tax. When Inland Revenue wished to re-classify them as employees, they formed an action committee to defend their status, won, and saved themselves perhaps £3,000 to £5,000 each (A. Christopher in Field (ed.) 1979, p. 88).

'Tax evasion', on the other hand, is illegal. Because it is hidden, its full extent is hard to estimate. Inland Revenue wrote off £28 million of tax debts as irrecoverable in 1978. In 1979 an estimated £75 million of income from vehicle licences was unpaid, and in 1981–2 (despite detector vans) 1.4 million people avoided paying £55 million in TV licence fees. Under-reporting of income by the self-employed is well known. In 1976–7 almost 40 per cent of traders and professional men and women disclosed profits of under £60 per week, at a time when the average manual wage was £70 (A. R. Ilersic, in Seldon *et al*, 1979). We saw earlier that the black economy was estimated to cost £3–£3.5 billion of lost taxation.

Following on from the discussion of tax avoidance and tax evasion comes the fourth reason for low yields: policing the system and collecting the taxes is difficult. The scale of the problem is enormous, with Inland Revenue alone having to keep records and inspect returns covering nearly 26 million individual taxpayers whose employers act as tax collectors under the PAYE (Pay As You Earn) schemes, a further 1,860,000 self-employed taxpayers, and firms and individuals liable for corporation and capital taxes – there are 2 million unincorporated companies alone. The 85,175 staff of Inland Revenue (1979) spend the bulk of their time on the self-employed, where avoidance and evasion are easier than under PAYE, with 67 per cent of inspectors and 43 per cent of collectors assigned to this work. Even so only about one return in eight was examined and a mere 3 per cent were given a thorough, detailed investigation (Board of Inland Revenue, 1979b, para. 60). These few checks led to the collection of an additional £37 million in the 1976–7 tax year, and £47 million in 1977–8.

Customs and Excise face similar logistical problems. Some 1.3 million VAT outlets are supervised by only 11,000 officials, who are able, on average, to inspect each outlet once every five years. An estimated 38 per cent of VAT payers sent in the wrong amount (based on their own figures and not taking into account any tax avoidance or evasion). Customs and Excise estimate an annual shortfall in revenue from VAT of only 1.5 per cent (or £20 million), almost certainly an underestimate. In other Common Market countries a shortfall as high as 30 per cent (France) or 50 per cent (Italy) has been thought possible.

Policing is made additionally difficult by the fluid and indeterminate nature of some taxable assets. The value of a dead person's estate, for example, is partly based on the estimated value of possessions like property and jewellery which may be hard to assess accurately. What is likely is that low valuations will be made by executors, and accepted by tax officials, if only because excessive policing after death will be felt to be distasteful. Public attitudes to policing relate to all types of taxation, and are a further factor which can affect yields. Certain sorts of tax avoidance seem to be widely condoned by the general public, whereas the abuse of social security is not (Field *et al*, 1977, p. 163). Hence Inland Revenue and Customs and Excise tend to avoid criminal proceedings whenever possible. Inland Revenue prosecuted only 154 people in 1977–8 and 184 in 1978–9. Customs and Excise took out 14,000 prosecutions in 1973–4 but almost 13,000 of these were for currency control and smuggling offences. A recent report from Inland Revenue on the black economy typifies its broad approach to relations with the public. The need for stricter policing is made clear but steps taken 'should not impair the good relationships which have always existed between the Department on the one hand and the taxpaying public (and their professional advisers) on the other' (Board of Inland Revenue, 1981, para. 135). Suspected abuse of social security is investigated in a very different manner, with five control procedures which make those aimed at preventing tax abuse 'look pretty weak' despite evidence that 'the amount lost in tax abuse is massive compared with the loss from social security fraud' (Field *et al*, 1977, Ch. 8). According to the Inland Revenue Staffs Association, tax losses in 1982 were probably around £4,000 million but social security abuse was only £50 million.

Conclusion to the Case Study

Our case study of the tax system has revealed that severe constraints operate on government. When seeking to acquire finance and capital, it is limited by public behaviour and attitudes, by the complexities and contradictions of the tax system, and by problems of policing and collecting taxes due to be paid. Continual legislation is needed to close new and ingenious loopholes found by specialist lawyers and accountants, and at times the whole process of extracting resources seems rather like a game, with government experts matched against private experts. To this is added deliberate tax evasion and pressure for additional exemptions and allowances. The result is low tax yields compared with nominal rates of taxation. This seems inevitable, given the several and varied objectives of the tax system, which is an instrument of social policy as well as of revenue acquisition.

Finally, the case study does seem to suggest that the theory that the amount of resources available determines the nature of policy products (outlined in the introduction to this chapter) can be overstated. The way in which governments go about acquiring resources greatly affects the amount collected. Rules can be enforced tightly or largely ignored. Attitudes towards policing can vary from one part of government to another. The system can be changed to increase yields (one intention of capital transfer tax, for example). Furthermore, the approach of government to the acquisition of resources not only affects the quantity extracted, it also determines the distribution of the burden between different groups in society. It is to this issue that we now turn our attention.

WHO PAYS HOW MUCH OF THE COSTS
OF RESOURCE ACQUISITION?

The acquisition of resources is at the expense of the citizen, who provides government with money, land, labour and support. Not all give the same amount — some sections of society contribute more to the kitty than others. Acquisition thus has an effect on the distribution of resources in society, and policies on acquisition will either preserve or alter that distribution. Taxation, for example, can be used to equalize incomes; public sector employment can distribute job opportunities; land policies can alter the ownership and value of land.

At this stage the important point is that the acquisition of resources is *not* a neutral process but one which places a greater burden on some than others. Hence our description of taxation as an instrument of social policy, a simple example of this being the unfulfilled intention to introduce a wealth tax (Sandford *et al*, 1980, p. 4). It is surprising, therefore, to find that political scientists generally have avoided the

question of who pays the costs or bears the burden of the political
system, even though an important way of judging the performance
of government is to consider the social consequences of policy products. One possible reason for this avoidance of a key issue has been
the methodological problems involved in measuring costs. We consider
these first, before returning to our case study of the tax system in an
attempt to find out who bears how much of the burden. Later, in
Chapter 8, we spend more time looking at the consequences of public
policy and discussing ways of measuring these.

Problems of Method

An academic investigation into the effects on society of the process of
resource acquisition must be systematic or it is worthless. But isolating
and measuring the costs of acquisition is not easy. In particular three
major problems of method confront the researcher.

First there is the problem, common to all research and to many parts
of this book, of definition and measurement. What exactly do we mean
by the 'cost' of acquisition? The direct costs of collecting and policing
the tax system — the salaries of 120,000 Inland Revenue and Customs
and Excise staff, and so on — can be identified and measured but
are only a small part of our concern here with costs. More pertinent
is the economists' concept of 'opportunity cost' whereby acquisition
results in the loss to the citizen of money, land or personal freedom,
or in an opportunity foregone. For example, the 'cost' of compulsory
National Service for those aged 18—20 was their inability to join the
civilian workforce for two years, or to go to University and graduate
at 21. The cost of taxation might be a net income (after tax) which
makes a car and modern house too expensive, both being feasible if the
gross income had been received. These examples illustrate the great
difficulty in applying this concept of cost, as knowledge of the opportunities foregone is required, and these will vary from person to person
depending on both personal taste and the range of opportunities
available.

Measurement, too, is far from simple. Financial costs are usually
reasonably straightforward as money is tangible. Income tax, rates,
fees for the use of council swimming baths are all items in the
household budget which get recorded either by government or by
respondents to the Family Expenditure Survey or both. But many
costs are intangible. This is especially true in the case of the acquisition

of support, where factors such as the costs of participation in policy making are perhaps best termed psychological. Psychologists have as great a problem with quantification as do political scientists.

In practice tangible and intangible costs are simultaneously present. The compulsory purchase of property, for example, involves land, money (the enforced sale being paid for by government as compensation) and support (the loss of the property might lead to antipathy towards government, or satisfaction if it was unwanted). Governments spend much time assessing the likely consequences on support of new policies about acquisition and, in effect, such assessments are measurements. If the so-called 'political costs' are deemed too high, government is judging that they are larger than the benefits to be gained by government from the policy proposal.

Definition and measurement, then, raise problems for the student of the costs and consequences of resource acquisition. Some are insuperable in that quantification is not possible. In such instances judgment must be relied upon, and it may be feasible to use estimates covering a range of valuations. An alternative approach, which we follow later, is to limit a study to direct costs and tangible items. In a sense this ignores some of the problems of definition and measurement by avoiding them. Such an approach is acceptable only if it is made clear just what has been ignored, and some of the consequences of the limited methodology must be spelled out in its conclusions, which must discuss assumptions about the possible impact on them had intangibles and indirect costs been included.

The second problem relates to the units of society on which the measurement of costs is to be made. There is no single method of division, and much will depend on the study being undertaken. The costs borne by different social classes would interest those concerned to test the ruling-class and ruling-elite view of policy making discussed in Chapter 2, for example. The administrative dispersion and diffusion view might suggest analysis on a geographical basis, using regions, counties or towns. Other units might include sections of industry and commerce, or demographic factors. But each (except sex) contains ambiguities — a region, for example, can be a so-called standard region (a concept introduced in the late 1940s in an abortive attempt to standardize units of public administration), a NHS region, gas region, electricity region, and so on. Social class was once thought of as being relatively uncomplicated and unambiguous: the head of the household's occupation was used to categorize the family, the Census having listed every occupation and allocated it to a particular class. Today's researcher faces problems when categorizing families for many claim to have joint heads of the household, who may fall into different social classes. This makes it vital in every study that the method of dividing society into groups is explained in some detail.

Thirdly, there is the problem of how to handle benefits in a study of acquisition costs. Arguably a study restricted only to costs is too limited to be of value, for an individual's personal 'balance sheet' covers both costs and benefits. Indeed it is often impractical to separate the two: the example above of compulsory purchase can be viewed as both a cost (the loss of property) and a benefit (the level of compensation). Paid National Service offers the benefit of a guaranteed income, but at the cost of an inability to earn money in the way a person wishes.

We go on to consider studies of the distribution of policy products, including both costs and benefits, in Chapter 8. That is the more appropriate place to present such a study as, between now and then, we will have reviewed the way in which government divides up its resources into policy products and applies those products. In Chapter 8 we also make the point that there is a place both for specialized studies of costs, or of benefits, or of distribution within particular policy areas (as these offer a detailed snapshot of an aspect of public policy), as well as for wider, more generalized studies which attempt to reach conclusions about the overall performance of government. The one needs the other.

Our concern here is to consider whether, and to what extent, the costs of the acquisition of resources fall more on some sections of society than on others. The methodological problems discussed above suggest that a precise assessment is not possible. The range of resources described in Chapter 3 further suggest that an analysis of the whole area of government resources within a few pages is also impractical. What is feasible is to limit our study to taxation in order to examine more closely the distribution of tangible, monetary costs between various income groups. Our choice of income groups as a way of dividing society into units for analysis reflects the hypothesis about the tax system which we wish to test. That is that taxation in Britain is progressive, which means that higher income groups pay a larger proportion of their income in taxes than do lower income groups.

Who Bears the Burden of the Tax System?

In absolute terms (i.e. how many £s) it is clear that high income groups pay more tax than the lowly paid — indeed a senior manager in industry may pay more tax in a year than the gross wages of the worst paid employee. Thus the answer to our question seems straightforward: higher income groups.

The burden of taxation, however, should be measured not only in absolute amounts (implying that £10 has the same value for a man on £80 per week as it does for the £400 executive) but also in relative terms. The British tax system aims to take relative burdens into account by being progressive. It relates to the taxpayer's level of resources and seeks to redistribute these from the richer to the poorer. Hence high income groups are supposed to pay a larger proportion of their income in taxes than are the lower paid. In 1982–3, for example, the basic rate of income tax is 30 per cent, but this rises progressively to 40 per cent, 45 per cent, 50 per cent, 55 per cent and 60 per cent as income increases. The highest rate of 60 per cent is reached when taxable income has increased to £31,500 per annum (Treasury, 1982a).

In theory then Britain operates a progressive tax system. Indeed nominal rates of tax ranging from 30 per cent to 60 per cent suggests that it operates a very progressive tax system. But, as is often the case when analysing public policy, a second look is necessary. Four factors affect the nominal rates of tax, and the orthodox claims for the system can be examined only after they have been outlined.

The myriad tax allowances, the first factor, were detailed in the case study of taxation, where we illustrated that the nominal rate of tax paid by a person on a salary of £5,200 was more than halved. Field has no doubt that, overall, these allowances 'are regressive in their effects, being of greater benefit to the high-income groups' (Field *et al*, 1977, pp. 60–9). Such groups are particularly likely to undertake expenditure which is eligible for tax reliefs, which in 1981–2 were worth £2,030 million in the case of mortgage interest allowance, and £1,530 million in the case of life assurance policies and company pension schemes. All three are beyond the reach of many low-income households. In contrast, house rents and national insurance contributions feature prominently in their budgets, but neither expenditure qualifies for tax relief.

These tax allowances not only favour the better off, but increasingly do so as they improve their income and inflation continues or interest rates rise. One reason is that some tend to be expressed as a percentage rather than in absolute terms. If the rate of interest of a mortgage rises, for example, so does the tax allowance. Another reason is that an allowance against tax of £1 is worth 60 pence to the tax payer on the highest tax band, but only 30 pence to those paying at the basic rate. The substantial exemptions from capital transfer tax and the ease of avoidance and evasion from it must be added to the argument.

The second factor concerns the greater opportunities available to the self-employed to limit their liability for tax than is the case with employees. A tax payer earning £5,400 in 1974–5 paid 26.7 per cent of his income in tax under PAYE, but only 24.5 per cent under Schedule D (for the self-employed), a difference of £120. The self-employed can offset more expenses against income, particularly in the case of transport and travel costs, office premises, and equipment. They are also, in effect, self-assessed, for the Inland Revenue are unable to police more than a fraction of the returns. Tax avoidance and evasion is thus easier. In 1976–7 13 per cent of solicitors, 37 per cent of architects, 49 per cent of barristers, and 81 per cent of accountants claimed to be receiving a taxable income of less than the average manual wage, though many may also have received their share of the profits of a partnership (Board of Inland Revenue, 1979a, Tables 2.18, 2.24).

So far we have concentrated almost entirely on income tax. A third factor affecting the progressive nature of the tax system is that income tax is only one way in which taxation is levied, and that some of the other main taxes are not progressive. National insurance contributions are one instance as they reach a ceiling at about average income and so contribute a lower proportion of income as incomes rise. The rating system is another example, for the amount paid is based on the rental value of property and not on ability to pay. This is regressive in two respects. First, the rateable values of large, detached houses are higher than those of small terraced property, but not in proportion to the difference in average incomes of occupiers of each type of house. Secondly, within a group of similar houses there will be a range of incomes, but the same amount of rates will be paid by each household regardless of its income. The combination of these two factors meant that, in 1974, the poorest households spent 11 per cent of their disposable income on rates, the richest only 2.3 per cent (Field *et al*, 1977, p. 131).

A number of indirect taxes are also regressive. Excise duty on alcohol and tobacco applies per bottle or packet of cigarettes, regardless of the wealth of the purchaser. VAT is a fixed percentage, though in this case because it does not apply to food and certain other essentials, it has little impact on the distribution of income. Overall, indirect taxes (including rates) in 1980 accounted for 21.9 per cent of the disposable income of the wealthiest households, but 28.0 per cent in the case of households above the poorest level but with below average incomes (Central Statistical Office, 1982, Table F, p. 99). Clearly income tax has to be markedly progressive if it is to offset this variation which, if anything, is likely to grow because successive governments since 1977 have pledged themselves to shift the burden towards indirect taxes.

The final factor affecting tax burdens has been inflation. Each year pay rises cause people on fairly low incomes to come within the income tax net. Each year the Chancellor of the Exchequer announces an increase in personal tax allowances, and claims that this will result in many thousands of taxpayers no longer being liable for income tax. But over time, if not every year, the number entering the net has exceeded the number removed from it. In 1938—9 only 3.8 million people paid income tax. This total rose to 13.5 million in 1945—6, 23 million in 1973—4 and 25 million in 1976—7. Economists have termed this process 'inflationary fiscal drag'. It boosts government revenue without any change having to be made in the rate of tax, but at the same time it has profound effects on the distribution of tax burdens. To some extent 'inflationary fiscal boost' counteracts it. This occurs when prices of taxable goods rise but the tax payable does not because it is a fixed amount per unit. In this case the government's revenue is reduced in real terms. 'Drag' affects progressive taxes, 'boost' the regressive indirect taxes on commodities like beer and cigarettes (which is why Chancellors often feel it necessary to increase them on Budget Day). Inflation thus tends to make the system less progressive.

The steady extension of the income tax net since 1945 has been partly deliberate and partly caused by inflationary fiscal drag. A key consequence of drawing lower income citizens into the income tax system has been a phenomenon known as the 'poverty trap'. Lower income families fall into this trap when they not only start paying income tax (at a rate of 30 per cent of each £ of additional income) but at the same time become ineligible (on income grounds) for certain benefits such as rate and rent rebates, Family Income Supplement and free school meals. In 1979 an estimated 59,000 families receiving Family Income Supplement were simultaneously eligible for income tax: they stood to lose at least 65 pence of every extra pound received, and in some cases (where several benefits were lost) they could lose *more than* a pound (D. Piachaud in Sandford *et al*, 1980, p. 72). Another analysis calculates that this loss is not 65 pence but 90.75 pence, and estimates that there are 'millions of low-paid workers' for whom very substantial pay rises are almost worthless or lead to an actual loss in income (Field *et al*, 1977, p. 56).

These four factors about the tax system, when combined, seriously undermine the concepts of progressiveness and redistribution. In 1974 Professor J. L. Nicholson concluded, after a detailed statistical analysis of 1970 data that 'total payments in all taxes combined have formed a remarkably constant proportion of original income among families of any given type at different levels of income'. The Royal Commission on the Distribution of Income and Wealth confirmed in 1975 that 'the tax system had little effect on the overall shape of the distribution of income' (both quotes in Field *et al*, 1977, pp. 172–82). Our hypothesis that the British tax system is progressive is, therefore, not proven. In very broad terms the system seems to be proportional. In detail it is progressive at very high income levels, but regressive at the level of the poverty trap and between groups each side of average income.

Two points must be made about these conclusions. First we are not saying that either a progressive or a proportional tax system is a good thing. That is a moral judgement, to be taken by each of us. We are merely pointing out that a common claim for the tax system that it is progressive, is open to challenge. The intention of the tax system to redistribute income does not appear to be met by its performance. Secondly, except for a brief reference in the discussion of the poverty trap, we have not dealt with the question of benefits in this chapter. Our concern has been solely with the process of acquisition of resources, and with the consequences of that process. Benefits are policy products which also have an impact on the distribution of income, and we go on to look at those after analysing the way in which government divides and applies the resources it has acquired.

CONCLUSION

Our study of the acquisition of resources has revealed seven main points about the making and consequences of public policy. Some of these relate to other parts of the book and are also discussed in Chapter 9, while others are specific to the problems of acquisition.

First, the evidence which we have presented indicates that government policy decisions on acquisition are significant. We challenge Dye's view, outlined on pages 81—2, and conclude that government is important. Its policies on acquisition affect the extent of public goods and services which it can supply, and the distribution of resources within society. What is gathered in, how much of it, and how effectively it is acquired are all issues from which flow social and economic consequences for society as a whole, for groups of citizens, and for individuals. Indeed we find it disturbing that most books on British politics pay very little attention to policies about acquisition and thus imply that these are of little political consequence. Sometimes the key resource of support is considered, but finance, land and labour commonly receive scant coverage.

Second, acquisition raises both technical and moral questions, and policy decisions contain judgments about these. Technical issues include the accuracy and availability of data, and the problem of locating the full extent of the kitty potentially available to government. These were illustrated in the discussions of the black economy and of a wealth tax. Moral issues include the distribution of the burden of acquisition between different groups in society, and the nature and amount of resources which should be acquired.

Third, the process of acquisition is not always effective. Some resources are difficult to obtain or to police — the income from capital transfer tax, for example, was sparse, and the self-employed were largely self-assessed for income tax. Effectiveness, however, was not easily measurable because the objectives of policies on acquisition are not always clear. Raising money, land or labour was only one of the several aims, and could be contradicted by others which involve the creation of allowances and exemptions. In the background was the overall objective of maintaining and extending support for both government and regime.

Fourth, although we have concentrated in this chapter on taxation, our conclusions are equally relevant to the acquisition of other resources. Obtaining labour, land, equipment and support also involves moral judgments and technical issues. The process can be ineffective, as has been the case with the land policies of successive post-war Labour governments. Policies about equipment — computers, defence weapons, industrialized building — have all been criticized by informed observers. Our concentration on support (in Chapter 3) and on taxation was because they raise key questions about policy making, and because they have been rather better researched than have the other resources. Land ownership, for example, has not been properly surveyed for more than a century.

Our fifth point is about the burden of taxation. We came to a preliminary conclusion that taxation was broadly proportional rather than progressive, except in the case of those with very high incomes (where it was progressive) and those falling within the poverty trap (where it was regressive). We call this a preliminary conclusion because we made the point that the burden of taxation is offset, in part, by the receipt of cash benefits and public services. It is the combination of taxes and benefits which determines the extent to which public policy redistributes resources within society. In Chapter 8 we bring together the evidence on taxation and material on the impact of cash benefits and public services in an overall attempt to assess distribution. Some readers may prefer to turn straight to that chapter rather than to proceed, as we do, by looking first at the ways in which resources are divided and policies carried out.

Sixth, our review of acquisition revealed that attempts to introduce a wealth tax and to reduce the profits made by owners of land had been particularly ineffective. Both examples contain the combination of technical problems and a strong party philosophical base. They suggest that controversial policies on acquisition are particularly difficult to introduce successfully, and explain why most acquisition is through long established methods which are now generally accepted by citizens (even if not liked!). Administrative arguments seem to outweigh partisan standpoints, except at the margins when occasional forays into new areas may be made.

Finally this last point suggests that the party government view of policy making is not often applicable to acquisition policies, while earlier conclusions about the importance of judgment and values question the applicability of the technocratic view, with its emphasis on experts knowing the most appropriate policy decisions. The scale of acquisition, involving all citizens and many thousand public servants, suggests that a good deal of discretionary power resides within bureaucracies. The steady growth of tax concessions to cope with problems which arise from time to time indicates that incremental strategies dominate acquisition policy, and elite pluralism also accounts for the development of pressures on government to recognize those problems. On the other hand those who favour the ruling-class view will point to the evidence that taxation is not progressive, and that many poor people are kept in the poverty trap. Once again the advantage of keeping several views of policy making in mind is that it gives us a rounded understanding of, in this case, how resources are acquired and with what consequences.

TOPICS FOR DISCUSSION

1. Is public sector employment necessarily 'unproductive'?
2. What are the intended purposes of taxation and how effectively are these purposes fulfilled?
3. If compulsory taxation is acceptable, why is conscription not?
4. Argue the case for and against tax avoidance.
5. Which is the greater problem with taxation — the equity of the system, or the efficiency of its operation?

KEY READING

Bacon and Eltis (1976), Finer (1977) and Galbraith (1974) offer contrasting arguments about the nature and amount of resources which government should acquire. Material relevant to the effectiveness of acquisition is to be found in C. C. Hood, (1976) *The Limits of Administration*, John Wiley; in Seldon *et al*, (1979); and in Field (ed.) (1979) — the chapter by A. Christopher. The burdens of the tax system are discussed in Field *et al.* (1977) and in *Reports 4 and 5* of Royal Commission on the Distribution of Income and Wealth (1976) Cmnd. 6626.

REFERENCES

Atkinson, A. B. (1975) *The Economics of Inequality*, Oxford University Press.
Bacon, R. W. and Eltis, W. A. (1976) *Britain's Economic Problem*, Macmillan.
Board of Inland Revenue (1979a) *Inland Revenue Statistics*, HMSO.

Board of Inland Revenue (1979b) *121st Annual Report, 1978, Cmnd. 7473*, HMSO.

Board of Inland Revenue (1981) *123rd Annual Report, 1980, Cmnd. 8160*, HMSO.

Central Statistical Office (1982), 'The effects of taxes and benefits on household income, 1980', *Economic Trends*, No. 339.

Dye, T. R. (1976) *Policy Analysis*, University of Alabama Press.

Economist (1979), 'Make the best of the black economy', *The Economist*, 30 June.

Economist (1980), 'Making sense of capital taxes', *The Economist*, 31 May.

Field, F. *et al.* (1977) *To Him Who Hath*, Penguin.

Field, F. (ed.) (1979) *The Wealth Report*, Routledge & Kegan Paul.

Finer, S. E. (1977) 'Taxing people is wrong', *The Listener*, 3 November.

Galbraith, J. K. (1974) *Economics and the Public Purpose*, Deutsch.

Kay, J. A. and King, M. A. (1980) *The British Tax System*, Oxford University Press, (2nd edn).

O'Higgins, M. (1980) *Measuring the Hidden Economy*, London: Outer Circle Policy Unit.

Sandford, C. T. *et al.* (1980) *Taxation and Social Policy*, Heinemann.

Scarman, Lord (1982) *The Scarman Report*, Penguin.

Seldon, A. *et al.* (1979) *Tax Avoision*, London: Institute of Economic Affairs.

Shankland, G. (1980) *Our Secret Economy*, London: Anglo-German Foundation for the Study of Industrial Society.

Treasury (1982a) *The Government's Expenditure Plans 1982–3 to 1984–5, Cmnd. 8494, Part II*, HMSO.

Treasury (1982b) *Financial Statement and Budget Report, 1982–3*, HMSO.

Wilensky, H. L. (1975) *The Welfare State and Equality*, University of California Press.

Wilks, S. (1981) 'Planning agreements: the making of a paper tiger', *Public Administration*, Vol. 59, pp. 399–419.

Willis, J. R. M. and Hardwick, P. J. W. (1978) *Tax Expenditures in the United Kingdom*, Heinemann.

PART III

DIVIDING RESOURCES

5

Dividing Resources:
the Criteria for Choice

Getting and spending are mutually dependent. As already indicated governments are constrained by the resources available to them and by the effectiveness with which these can be acquired. So it is that what is drawn in to government helps to shape what is subsequently handed out and, in the end, who will benefit. But before the spoils are distributed, decisions have to be reached about how they are to be divided amongst the various types of policy product — rules and regulations, public goods and services, transfer payments.

The issue of deciding how to divide resources is at the very heart of the activities of government, and it traditionally focuses attention upon familiar institutions such as departments, committees, cabinets, councils, parliaments, parties and pressure groups. We look at this issue in this and the next chapter, though we take a different line from more traditional approaches. We ask questions about how choices are made and on what basis; and, in Chapter 6, we examine public expenditure politics and budget making at the national and local government levels in Britain. These topics draw the investigator into questions about the nature of influence and power, questions which form an important secondary linking theme throughout this part of the book. We return to the matter of power intermittently as Chapters 5 and 6 unfold. Initially, however, we present some information on the products of government as revealed in the pattern and distribution of public expenditure, both between levels and types of government and across policy programmes.

HOW MUCH IS SPENT? ON WHAT? BY WHOM?

In 1981—2 public expenditure amounted to about £120 billion (including interest payments), which was about 45 per cent of the overall economy (defined in terms of Gross Domestic Product — GDP — at market prices) (Treasury, 1982, p. 7). The long-term picture has been one of more or less consistent growth since the late 1950s, interspersed with occasional contractions, as in 1968–70 and 1976–9 (see Table 5.1). This pattern of growth is not unusual or peculiar to Britain, and most major Western countries have seen a similar expansion in government spending (Else and Marshall, 1979, p. 11).

Percentage figures on the proportions of public spending since 1976 are outlined in Tables 5.2, 5.3 and 5.4. Each explores a different way of looking at the distribution of public spending within government. Table 5.2 divides expenditure according to economic categories which are broadly in line with our general list of policy products as public goods, public services and cash hand-outs.

Capital expenditure is the amount spent by government on new assets, such as buildings, land purchase, road construction, and it includes capital grants to the public and private sectors such as grants to universities, to housing associations, and for industrial investment. Current expenditure involves cash hand-outs and the day-to-day running and maintenance costs (heating, wages and salaries, telephone charges, etc.) of public services. The proportion of capital spending has declined more or less consistently since the mid 1960s and by 1981 it was in total some 40 per cent less than its 1974–5 level (Hood and Wright, 1981, p. 5). This is partly because, especially since the mid 1970s, attempts have been made to constrain public spending, and capital spending, being related to future services, has proved easier to cut. Cuts in current expenditures, involving immediate wage reductions, job losses and reduced services, benefits and pensions, are politically much more difficult to carry through.

As Table 5.2 illustrates, grants and subsidies make up a substantial and steadily increasing part of government spending. This is directly connected with the rise in the numbers of pensioners, of unemployed and of others who are dependent on government support. As people retire earlier, live longer or are increasingly without work, so the amount spent on government cash hand-outs increases. Because such expenditures are demand-determined, they are difficult to control, let alone constrain.

The distribution of spending between the various sectors of government is outlined in Table 5.3. In 1981–2 about 72 per cent of the money was spent by central government, 25 per cent by local authorities and 3 per cent by nationalized industries and public corporations.

TABLE 5.1   *Public Expenditure and ratio to GDP 1959–81*
(in 1979–80 prices)

Year	Public expenditure cost terms[a] £ billion	Year-on-year % change	Ratio of public expenditure to GDP
1959	39.6	–	33.4
1960	41.1	+3.8	33.2
1961	43.3	+5.4	33.8
1962	44.2	+2.1	34.2
1963	45.7	+3.4	34.0
1964	48.3	+5.7	34.1
1963–4	46.9		34.2
1964–5	48.7	+3.8	34.1
1965–6	51.6	+6.0	35.3
1966–7	54.7	+6.0	36.6
1967–8	61.6	+12.6	40.2
1968–9	61.0	−1.0	38.5
1969–70	60.8	−0.3	37.7
1970–1	62.4	+2.6	37.9
1971–2	64.2	+2.9	37.8
1972–3	68.6	+6.9	38.7
1973–4	74.4	+8.5	40.4
1974–5	83.6	+12.4	45.4
1975–6	84.1	+0.6	45.6
1976–7	82.5	−1.9	43.5
1977–8	77.1	−6.5	39.8
1978–9	81.5	+5.7	41.1
1979–80	83.5	+2.5	41.4
1980–1 provisional	85.9	+2.9	43.6

Source: Reproduced with permission from Pliatzky (1982) Appendix, p. 213.
Notes: a Calculated in terms of prices prevailing in 1979–80.

TABLE 5.2.   *Public expenditure (1976–82) by economic category*
showing percentage shares of total and overall total in
£ million cash[a]

	1976–7	1977–8	1978–9	1979–80	1980–1	1981–2[c]
Current expenditure						
wages and salaries	32.7	33.0	32.0	31.6	32.6	32.4
goods and services	16.8	17.8	17.6	18.0	18.1	18.6
grants and subsidies	33.3	36.1	36.8	36.6	36.6	38.0
Total current expenditure	82.8	86.9	86.5	86.2	87.3	89.0
Total capital expenditure[b]	17.2	13.1	13.5	13.8	12.7	11.0
Total public expenditure	100.0	100.0	100.0	100.0	100.0	100.0
in £ million cash[d]	53,380	56,789	65,475	78,521	94,279	105,677

Source: The Treasury, 1982.
Notes: a percentages rounded to nearest decimal point.
     b includes capital spending, capital grants and net lending.
     c estimated.
     d planning total: excluding interest and certain other minor payments.

It is notable that central government's share of spending has increased since 1976 as successive central governments have sought to restrain local authority expenditure. Prior to this the local authorities' share of overall spending had gradually grown from 23 per cent in 1953 to more than 30 per cent in 1975 (Else and Marshall, 1979, p. 15).

Table 5.4 shows spending divided according to policy programme and reveals that the main spending commitments are to social security, health and social services, education, and defence. In 1980–1 these four programmes accounted for more than 60 per cent of overall public spending. Since 1976 there have been some significant changes in the proportion of government spending committed to each programme — social security has taken a larger share, as has spending on law and order, while overseas aid and housing have declined in relative importance. These shifts within the overall package reflect partly demographic changes and partly the changing priorities of successive

TABLE 5.3　*Public expenditure (1976−82) by sectors of government showing percentage shares of total[a]*

	1976−7	1977−8	1978−9	1979−80	1980−1	1981−2 [b]
1. Central government (excluding lending to nationalized industries)	67.9	69.9	69.9	68.6	69.4	72.0
2. Local authorities	29.6	28.7	27.5	27.5	26.6	25.0
3. Nationalized industries and public corporations (including borrowings from central government)	2.5	1.4	2.6	3.9	4.0	3.0
Total public expenditure	100.0	100.0	100.0	100.0	100.0	100.0

Source: as for Table 5.2.
Notes: a percentages rounded to nearest decimal point.
　　b estimated.

governments. This latter point is brought out more clearly in figures produced by the House of Commons Select Committee on the Treasury and Civil Service which calculate expenditure changes in real or cost terms (that is allowing for inflation) and show that between 1980 and 1982, under a Conservative government, expenditures on defence and law and order rose by 1.8 and 6.1 per cent respectively, while those on housing, environmental services and education fell by 36, 7.4 and 2.1 per cent (Treasury and Civil Service Committee, 1982, p. x).

We may conclude this consideration of public spending by noting that the amount spent is substantial (amounting in 1981−2 to just under £1,900 per head of population), it tends to increase, and that its distribution is complex and varied. Spending figures provide a useful and relatively precise indication of the products of government. Yet, while they reveal the pattern of public spending, the bare figures tell us little about the considerations and manipulations that underlie their determination. The money available is limited and many demands are made upon it. Not all demands can be met. Some spending bids will lose out in the competition for consideration. Choice and priority are

essential. How, and by what criteria, are these choices made so that
resources can be divided between authorities, across categories of
spending, and within programmes?

TABLE 5.4   *Public expenditure (1976–82) by major programmes
showing percentage shares of total [a]*

	1976–7	1977–8	1978–9	1979–80	1980–1	1981–2[b]
Defence	11.6	12.0	11.4	11.7	11.9	11.9
Overseas aid and external relations	2.0	2.7	2.8	2.7	1.8	1.6
Agriculture	1.9	1.6	1.3	1.3	1.5	1.5
Industry, energy, trade and employment	5.8	3.9	4.7	3.7	4.4	5.3
Transport	4.4	4.0	3.7	3.8	3.7	3.7
Housing	7.1	6.3	5.7	6.0	5.0	3.1
Other environmental services	3.8	3.8	3.7	3.7	3.6	3.3
Law, order and protective services	3.1	3.1	3.1	3.3	3.4	3.5
Education	13.1	12.9	12.4	11.9	12.1	11.7
Health and personal social services	11.1	11.5	11.3	11.3	12.0	12.1
Social security	21.7	24.5	25.1	24.7	24.9	27.1
Other public services and common services	2.8	2.6	2.7	2.5	2.4	2.8
Scotland	5.7	5.8	5.6	5.6	5.6	5.4
Wales	2.4	2.3	2.3	2.3	2.2	2.2
Northern Ireland	3.0	3.2	3.2	3.1	3.1	3.1
Lending to nationalised industries	0.5	–	1.1	2.4	2.4	1.7
Total public expenditure	100.0	100.0	100.0	100.0	100.0	100.0

Source: As for Table 5.2.
Notes: a percentages rounded to nearest decimal point.
        b estimated.

In the rest of this chapter we consider two different ways of visualizing the activity of policy choice by using the labels of policy needs
and policy demands. Both reflect contrasting views of the purpose and
nature of policy making, and both raise questions about power. In the
following chapter we go on to consider, in detail, the process of expenditure policy making.

POLICY NEEDS

The notion that policy makers, when it comes to making choices, are guided by definitions of policy need has close connections with the technocratic and elitist views of policy making. The concept of need is much debated and requires clarification (Plant *et al*, 1980, Chapters 2 and 3). In everyday usage the term is often used by individuals as a way of indicating a desired or improved state of being. People may say that we 'need' more schools, more roads, more hospitals and so forth. Used in this sense it is not clear whether the term refers to what an individual desires as opposed to what he or she, or a particular section of society, requires in order to function fully and adequately. Desires and requirements are not the same things; as in the case of excessive wealth, many may desire it, few actually require it. Because of the varied usage of the term we adopt a specific meaning. Here need refers to what a third party feels an individual or set of individuals require: it thus refers to a standard imposed on individuals from outside. The distinction between this and its everyday usage can be illustrated by Culyer's analogy of a man in the desert who may desire water, but until someone else has made a judgment, cannot be said to need it (Culyer, 1976, p. 16).

The notion of needs is a highly valuative basis for policy choice. Defining what it is that people need is a matter of judgment, though the term misleadingly implies some kind of objective, absolute standard. In reality there are no universal definitions of need which are acceptable to all. All definitions involve assumptions about what it is that people require. For example, consider three widely used definitions of need. In the first place need might be defined in accordance with some notion of maximum standards, such as the best possible standards of education or health care. But such a definition is riddled with pitfalls. How does one define maximum standards? What is 'best' in the case of, say, education and health care? (See Illich, 1977, pp. 41–4.) And if we cannot define a maximum standard of provision how can we even begin to think about possibly achieving it? An alternative course is to take the opposite line and to define policy needs in terms of minimum standards. Hence it might be said that all individuals require a certain minimum level of housing provision, or weekly income, or formal education. Minimum standards are easier to define than maximum ones, and, therefore, in theory, easier to achieve. Yet the definition is in no sense objective. Apart from the obvious point that standards are likely to change, minimum criteria have to be determined on the basis of some values about what constitutes an acceptable minimum and from whose viewpoint. The third approach is to use comparative standards as a basis for defining policy needs. Comparing standards across and within countries on the grounds that similar populations should enjoy equivalent policy provision may seem a sensible way of proceeding, but making comparisons is not always easy. The information may be suspect or uncertain. Moreover, such comparisons inevitably raise highly contentious political questions about equality and the fair distribution of public resources (Forder, 1974, Chapter 3).

As these examples illustrate, there are no objective, absolute universal criteria for determining human needs. Even those basic requirements necessary for the maintenance of life, such as food, shelter and clothing, cannot be judged to be absolute human needs. On occasions even these essential, individual needs are sacrificed for wider collective definitions of need, such as in times of war or in the treatment of recalcitrant citizens, through punishment or deprivation. So we can see that the definition of need is inherently arguable. It is also political, for that which is defined as a policy need must reflect, at least in part, the interests of those who are doing the defining. Such definitions are bound to vary within and between different sections of the community.

Given our definition of need as a standard imposed by a third party and the highly subjective and political way in which needs are determined, three central questions arise. From what major sources do definitions of policy need emerge? How are such definitions justified and rendered acceptable? And whose definitions predominate?

There are many sources of need-definition. An important role is played by three major sets of personnel and institutions. Increasingly significant is the part played by experts: qualified specialists who are often members of organized professions. They are particularly influential in defining need in the social welfare fields: social services, education, health, and town and country planning (Wilding, 1982). But they also have a substantial part to play in other areas of government activity such as energy policy, policing and the maintenance of law. In all these cases it is the experts who to some large degree define what is required and is needed. In the case of the National Health Service, for example, medical practitioners through professional bodies (such as the British Medical Association) and the day-to-day administration of the service have become important arbiters of health care needs. They also have a significant say in the precise distribution of health service monies between, say, geriatric care as opposed to preventive medicine or mental health treatment (Cooper, 1975, Chapter 3; Culyer, 1976, p. 43).

The justification for this extensive role played by experts and professionals in determining need is to be found in the skills and the qualifications with which such experts can claim to be endowed and the willingness of non-experts to accept their claims, or their failure to counteract them effectively. It is often suggested that experts can take an objective and informed view of what it is that people require, using their specialized knowledge of a particular subject area. True, many important questions of policy choice appear to be primarily technical and hence, it can be argued, those with the relevant technical knowledge should settle them. A layman cannot decide the requirements for maternity treatment, transplant surgery, or radiographic equipment, nor judge priorities between them. Equally the 'man in the street', or even the informed politician, is not the best person to decide on educational standards and the precise content of the school curriculum. But these arguments presume that the major element in policy making is the gathering together of correct information and the appropriate kind of skilled personnel, and that it is this marriage of information and expertise which produces the 'best' possible solution. It is such rationalistic and technocratic ideas of policy making which in the end serve to justify the role of experts in defining policy needs.

A more traditional way of defining policy need can be termed 'partisan'. In this case notions of need are derived from the political ideas or broad philosophies held by policy makers. These may involve assumptions about the nature of man, society and the state, or, more precisely, about the proper role of particular government agencies. We call such approaches to defining need 'partisan' because they do not claim to be objective or neutral, rather they reflect a particular view of the world: an approach which is openly partial, involving a set of opinions about how things are and ought to be. The most obvious 'partisan' sources of policy needs are political parties and their key personnel. In the case of the Labour and Conservative parties, for instance, party philosophies or ideologies play an important, if general, part in shaping policy choice, not only within the party but also, when in office, within government. Under Clause IV of its constitution, the Labour party is concerned to achieve the 'common ownership' of the economy and the 'equitable distribution' of its benefits amongst the population. This ambiguous, yet broadly socialist, commitment has influenced the policy programme of successive Labour governments. The Conservatives are heirs to a varied philosophical tradition which emphasizes two major, and contradictory, strands of thinking. One is a liberal, free-market approach which lays stress on the need to minimize the role of the state and protect individual liberty, though mainly in the economic sphere. The other, a much older Tory tradition, stresses the benevolent role of the state and the importance of maintaining and developing the intricate web of social relations that exist between those who rule and those who are ruled (Harris, 1972, p. 16). These contrasting individualist and collectivist viewpoints exist side by side in the Conservative tradition. At different times, in the different circumstances of government and opposition, and amongst different sections of the party, one may dominate over the other in different areas of policy making. Each, however, offers general standards from which definitions of need can be derived.

'Partisan' definitions of need are not only obtained from the ideologies of the political parties. Personnel in other institutions such as government departments and some pressure groups have inherited and developed traditions of behaviour and thinking and particular institutional ways of looking at their policy worlds. Many government agencies, for instance, reveal what Lord Bridges once called 'departmental philosophies': particular and consistent ways of approaching their tasks which remain relatively constant despite changes in personnel (Bridges, 1950). The present Department of Trade has a strong free-trade position, reflecting a belief in the benefits of relatively unhindered international trade and an open home market. The Department of Industry, with a much more recent foundation and set of antecedents, has tended to favour government intervention in the market on behalf of industry, either in the form of tariff protection or of financial support. The Home Office has generally tended to be sympathetic to issues relating to individual morality but rather harsh on matters such as prisons and the treatment of offenders. The Foreign Office has, since the 1950s, tended to pursue policies concerned to limit the world role of the UK by emphasizing the Common Market and by cutting Britain's responsibilities and commitments further afield.

'Partisan' definitions of need can be justified on the basis that they are ethically right: that they reflect a set of moral assumptions which are correct, not in any empirical sense, but because those who hold with them believe they involve the 'best' conception of how things are and ought to be. A second ground for justification is that they are well tried and well accepted ways of operating. They have worked adequately in the past, have been tested and refined through application, and, hence, are a good basis for present and future actions. Finally, in the case of party political definitions of need, the grounds for their acceptance also rest on the argument of public support. Party programmes are placed before the electorate and, in theory, a democratic choice is made between one alternative and another. The party elected into government has thus had its definition of policy needs approved by the population. Of course this line of justification conforms very closely to the party government view, with its emphasis on the party manifesto and the electoral mandate to carry it through.

A further source for definition of policy needs involves the amalgamation of expertise and partisanship and is perhaps best illustrated by the network of advisory committees established by government to look into particular topics or to keep a watching brief on specific areas of policy. These committees have an investigatory as well as a policy-making function. They present evidence and make proposals and bring together specialists and more openly 'political', interested parties. The main committees involved are royal commissions, departmental committees and parliamentary committees.

Royal commissions are advisory committees which are formally appointed by the Crown, and are usually temporary, though there are a few permanent commissions such as the Royal Commission on Historical Monuments. Between 1900 and 1975 more than 150 commissions were established to consider a range of topics of varying importance including, in recent years, the police (reported 1962), the reform of trade unions (reported 1968), local government in England (reported 1969) and in Scotland (reported 1969), and the constitution (reported 1973). Since 1945 there has been a tendency to appoint fewer royal commissions, but with a broader scope and topic for consideration (Chapman, 1973). Departmental committees are appointed by ministers and may either be temporary or more permanent. Some of these committees consist entirely of civil servants and operate in secret, away from public scrutiny. Others are more public and draw together outside experts and representatives of particular points of view and interests. One survey identifies 123 "important" departmental committees appointed between 1900 and 1975, covering such topics as privacy (reported 1972), safety and health at work (reported 1972), and intermediate areas (reported 1969) (Butler and Sloman, 1975, p. 247ff). Non-legislative parliamentary committees are mainly concerned with controlling and supervizing the operations of government, but they sometimes put forward options for policy choice. The main parliamentary committees that do so are the Public Accounts Committee and the 14 select committees which were established in 1979 to monitor the work of particular government departments. These committees consider evidence from both experts and partisans when drawing together their reports and proposals: that on social services produced over 150 recommendations in its 1980 report on perinatal and neonatal mortality.

The amalgamation of expert and partisan sources through the operation of bodies such as committees and commissions can be justified on the grounds that their proposals are based on a wide range of information and evidence drawn from many sectors and viewpoints. A connected justification rests on the procedures involved and the fairness of the process of consultation. Committees and commissions generally call widely for evidence and attempt to consult at least the most obvious of the acceptable sections of opinion involved in an issue. Because of this wide sounding-out, the results of any inquiry are given some credence in that they suggest a degree of impartiality and neutrality. The convention of having, or appearing to have, a neutral chairman (often a judge or lawyer) adds to their credibility. Alternatively it may be suggested that by bringing together within the committee representatives of the major positions on an issue, all important interests are involved in and have some commitment to the recommendations that emerge. The justification here is one of achieving consensus and policy agreement, rather than fully informed or impartial policy making.

Our discussion of three major sources from which definitions of need are derived and the justifications for them further indicates the extent to which needs are essentially matters involving values rather than hard or agreed facts, and the degree to which they reflect particular sectional views. The latter point becomes especially pertinent when considering which definitions have the greatest influence on policy choice. In the business of choosing policy options, only certain sources of need are heard and make their mark. Other sources, definitions and interests are thereby less successful, while some may be excluded from consideration altogether. When we come to look at the issue of whose definitions play a part, we face what is in essence an exercise in power: the facility that one section has to ensure that its views and concerns predominate over others.

Which groups or sections have the power to impose their views when it comes to making policy choices? To this question there is no simple answer. One view is that the pattern of power is bound to vary significantly across different policy areas (such as education, employment and energy) mainly because the interests concerned and the relations between them will be distinct and peculiar to each area. Not only are different issues involved, but also different organizations, organized groups and personnel. This view has much in common with the pluralist perspective on policy making with its emphasis on the variability and diffusion of power. For instance, a pluralist view of health care would stress the importance of a number of potential need determiners, each vying for influence: the public, the patients, elected politicians and ministers, civil servants, general practitioners, hospital doctors, consultants, nurses and other clinical staff, and health service administrators. However, most studies suggest that the first two groups have at best only an indirect say in determining health care needs. Politicians and particularly ministers, especially in the Department of Health and Social Security and the Treasury, appear to have considerable influence upon the overall amount of finance committed to the service. In making these decisions they are closely advised by their departmental civil servants, who in turn depend on medical experts for precise definitions of health care needs. The role of experts is further enhanced when we consider who influences the precise pattern of health care expenditure. Here the experts are very influential with an important part being played by senior medical consultants and health service administrators (Cooper, 1975).

As the health care case suggests, the pluralist view of power cannot easily handle the domination of policy choice by experts' definition of needs. For when such situations apply, the implication is that power is concentrated in the hands of specialists rather than diffused amongst the community of policy makers. Such an analysis would suggest an elitist or technocratic, rather than pluralist, power structure.

Reflecting these technocratic and elitist perceptions of power, some critics of present trends have argued that experts and professionals have increasingly come to dominate need definition in many areas of government activity (Johnson, 1972, p. 9: Wilding, 1982). The 'man in the white coat' has, it is claimed, emerged as a powerful figure, and issues which are inherently political are turned into bogus technical matters from which the general public and their elected representatives are effectively excluded (Self, 1976). If this contention is justified and the role and power of experts has increased, then this development must in part reflect the growing complexity of government and the tasks which it undertakes. Providing and maintaining large-scale public services requires a degree of technical know-how. Conversely, partisan ideologies with their broad and generalized content increasingly appear irrelevant to some of the detailed and complicated problems faced by policy makers. Socialism, conservatism or liberalism provide painfully little guidance when it comes to making precise choices between spending priorities.

If the above analysis has any validity then the problem is two-fold: on the one hand, how to make partisan viewpoints more relevant to choices within the modern public sector; and on the other, how to control the experts and to make them accountable to the public and its representatives.

POLICY DEMANDS

The notion of policy demands as a means of determining policy choice provides an alternative and contrasting perspective to that of policy needs. According to this view, policy choices are a result of the pressures and requests for action which are placed upon policy makers. Thus, policies, instead of being based on a third party's assessment of what people might be said to need, are based on what an individual or group feel they should get.

Like needs, however, the term 'demands' requires clarification. We might begin at a very basic level by suggesting that all individuals, taken either as independent units or as members of collective groups, have wants. Perhaps an individual may want better housing, or to live free from atmospheric pollution, or to enjoy a certain standard of income. It is only when such wants are expressed with the ultimate intention or expectation of affecting the operations of public authorities, that they can be called policy demands. Not all individuals' wants are likely to be expressed as policy demands. Some will be ruled out initially by the individual as irrelevant to the operations of public authorities, as matters that in his or her view do not concern government. Other wants may be seen as relevant but excluded because they are judged by the individual concerned to be unattainable and not worth the effort likely to be involved in pursuing them. Perceptions of what is relevant and attainable will vary from individual to individual. Those who are least aware, least able to make use of, and least assured about the opportunities available to them seem the least likely to turn their wants into policy demands, no matter how legitimate, feasible and relevant these potential demands might appear to others.

There are many kinds of policy demands and many ways of expressing them. It is useful to distinguish two basic forms of policy demand which differ in terms of their content and the channels through which they are expressed. First, 'overt' demands which are expressed openly through such familiar channels as elected representatives, political parties, pressure groups, the media and direct contact with government agencies. Secondly, 'covert' demands which are less obvious in their outward manifestation. Covert demands are the expression of citizens' wants through the increase or decline in the use of policy products. The level of take-up of cash benefits, of usage of public services, or of obedience to rules and regulations are indications of demand. Grants available to industry and to house-owners for home improvements, for example, are not taken up by all who are eligible, nor are all personal pensions and tax allowances. Partly this may be because of ignorance of entitlements, and/or the lack of opportunity to gain access to them, and these would need to be investigated before conclusions were drawn about demands. But partly it may be that people simply do not want to use public policy products because they see them as irrelevant or inadequate. This may also be the case with many goods and services – the decline in the use of public transport being a clear example.

Covert demands have been little studied mainly because of the difficulties involved in isolating, identifying and measuring them. However, an awareness of their existence is important to any rounded understanding of demand expression. In some systems of politics, where the opportunities to express overt demands are curtailed, covert demand may offer the only, if rather crude, expression of public feeling.

In Britain, although opportunities exist to express overt demands through political parties, pressure groups, MPs, councillors, the media and so forth, there are still those who, through lack of knowledge or awareness or opportunity, do not make use of these overt channels. The only expression of demand from this 'silent' or 'excluded' population tends to be covert, however crude that measure may be. Hence the importance of covert demand, for it provides an indication, almost the only one, of what those who do not engage in the more open process of politics want and seek from government. In essence, to quote an old saying, silent citizens 'vote with their feet'.

Managing and Regulating Demands

When it comes to handling demands, government policy makers are faced with a number of problems. The first point to note is that there is a vast number and variety of demands placed upon government. For instance, according to Mrs Shirley Williams, an MP's average constituency correspondence is in the order of 200—400 letters a week, many of which contain demands for government action (Williams, 1980, p. 84). The activities of pressure groups provide a further example. In 1981 the number of major publicized demands for substantial government action made by the Trades Union Congress (TUC) and the Confederation of British Industry (CBI), as reported in *The Times*, numbered 37 and 46 respectively and covered such varied matters as industrial relations, open government, higher education, civil service pay, EEC tariffs and small businesses.

Because of the vast quantity involved, not all demands can be handled by government and it is essential to find some way of selecting key or worthwhile demands and aggregating similar demands together so that they can be fused into a more manageable total. Moreover, many demands are ambiguous and unclear, and sometimes they are even contradictory. This lack of clarity is obviously a problem when it comes to covert demands, but it also applies to more overt expressions. The vote can be taken as a manifestation of overt demand, yet it is never very clear as to what citizens are demanding when they cast their votes: whether their support is based on the whole of a policy programme or a particular part of it, or simply reflects a sense of identification with a particular candidate or party, or even revulsion for all alternative parties.

More concrete demands may be almost as difficult to make sense of. Prior to the March 1982 Budget, the CBI and the TUC publicized their views about what the Chancellor should do. Although they provided much detail, both sets of requests remained essentially unclear. The CBI wanted a £2 billion cut in the employers' National Insurance Surcharge, but they did not make it clear as to precisely how the consequential shortfall in revenue could be fully covered. The TUC package, though again quite precise, was also very uncertain on the revenue side. Because an element of ambiguity is present in all policy demands, government policy makers are unavoidably faced with the tasks of interpreting and clarifying the points which are put to them.

In the case of handling covert demands for certain policy products, a further problem arises when demands outstrip what is actually made available. Indeed, some have argued that there are certain public services, such as environmental protection and health care (especially in the areas of mental health and preventive medicine) where, in the absence of a clear and accepted definition of a 'clean environment' or 'good health', the public's capacity to absorb any amount of resources is more or less unrestricted (Powell, 1966, p. 28). A similar view is that the satisfaction of one demand can create further demands and so on *ad infinitum* (Wright, 1980, p. 145). Viewed from both these perspectives policy demand is potentially insatiable. An alternative notion is that demands for many public services, such as housing, schools, transport and, possibly, defence, are potentially finite in that there exists some agreement about the proper level of services and the sections most likely to use them, but such demands are way beyond available resources. The implication is that all demands cannot at present, or even in the immediate future, be satisfied, though in the fullness of time they could be accommodated (Pile, 1974, p. 4ff). Whichever of these arguments is accepted, what is revealed in all cases is a clear tendency for demands to outstrip supply. This excess of demand necessarily results in policy makers finding ways of limiting demands so as to keep them in line with the actual level of provision.

In sum, all government agencies are bound to be concerned with the management and regulation of the large number of demands placed upon them. This suggests that government has substantial and highly interventionist parts to play in demand politics. In effect policy makers are faced with two tasks: (1) selecting, aggregating, clarifying and interpreting overt demands, and (2) limiting covert demands. Both tasks have consequences for the type of demands that are influential and, consequently, successful in that they lead to action being taken.

Handling Overt Demands

In attempting to understand what is involved when it comes to selecting, aggregating, clarifying and interpreting overt demands, it is useful to visualize demand politics as a process involving a number of broad stages through which demands for policy action are progressively developed and transformed. The initial stage, as we have seen, involves the recognition by an individual or group of individuals of a want which, if considered feasible and relevant to the activities of government, may be articulated as a *demand*. Not all wants will be articulated as demands, nor will all demands be heard or acted upon. But some will move on to the next stage and become *issues* of political debate: matters of interest and discussion amongst either the general public or, more pertinently, influential sections of it. Some issues will progress no further, whilst others will be taken up by policy makers and given serious consideration. It is at this stage that issues can be said to have reached the *formal agenda* of politics: they are amongst the list of items which will actually be considered by a public authority. Not all of these agenda items will be resolved, only some will actually be carried through into the further stage of policy choice and, ultimately, action (see Cobb *et al*, 1976; Solesbury, 1976).

This notion of a demand process is in reality far more complex than we allow. Demands go through many subtle changes before they become issues. Issues are of many types and enjoy different degrees and levels of support. There are also numerous government agencies and some agendas are subsidiary to other agendas. However, the categories, though crude, do reveal the extent to which the procedure is selective. Certain types of demand succeed, while others fail to be taken up. Why is this?

The success of a demand appears to depend, on the one hand, on the attitudes of policy makers towards it and, on the other, on its ability to overcome certain organizational obstacles which can prevent or impede access to the agendas for policy choice. Taken together, policy makers' attitudes and the complexities of access go a long way to determining how far a demand will get, in what form and, in particular, whether it will be taken up by government. Selection and success is not arbitrary, it tends to follow established patterns.

Many demands are ruled out by policy makers because they are not considered acceptable or feasible. That is, in the judgment of a policy maker, they do not deal with matters which are the legitimate concern of government or which can be adequately acted upon by it (Hall *et al*, 1975, Chapters 3 and 15). Many ecological issues have suffered in this way – demands for perishable packaging materials and for the prohibition of lead in petrol for example. Successive governments have also been chary of introducing more stringent controls over pornography on grounds of problems of enforcement and intrusion into individual morality. Indeed questions of individual conscience are almost always avoided by governments, and laws on such matters as abortion or homosexuality stem from initiatives taken by backbenchers through Private Members' Bills. Policy makers are also loathe to intervene in important areas of economic activity such as the Stock Exchange, banking system and other financial markets.

Attitudes of policy makers sometimes depend on the party political complexion of a particular government. For instance, Conservative policy makers tend to regard the issue of trade union reforms as more acceptable than do their Labour counterparts. Many of those involved in policy making, however, are not partisans. The bulk of personnel in government are full-time officials and, unless we stick rigidly to a conventional or party government view of policy making, it is clear that their attitudes towards what is acceptable are bound to be reflected in the flow of issues and demands taken up by the agencies in which they work. Though different individuals, particularly within different agencies, will hold different judgments about what is acceptable (see the section on departmental philosophies on p. 118 above), in general it seems that demands or issues involving fundamental changes either in the structure of government or the economy are, in normal times, very likely to be judged least acceptable, especially by those agencies most likely to be affected by them (Schon, 1973, pp. 31–3). This in part reflects a predictable defensive attitude and it conforms to our earlier incremental notion of the behaviour of policy makers.

Acceptability and feasibility, however, are not only judged on the basis of the content of the issue or demand. Factors relating to the manner in which a demand is expressed and the source from which it comes are also important in determining policy makers' attitudes towards it. Some channels for expressing demands are far more acceptable than others and consequently are afforded greater attention. Certain pressure groups, for instance, have a close relationship (often called 'consultative status') with government departments. The British Roads Federation has links with the Ministry of Transport, the TUC and the CBI with the Department of Employment, and the National Farmers Union with the Ministry of Agriculture, for example. Such groups are almost incorporated into the structure of government itself, as emphasized in our elite pluralism view of policy making. Other groups, such as Friends of the Earth and Transport 2000, tend to be considered less valuable by policy makers. Equally, demands which are expressed through the 'normal channels' of parliamentary and pressure group lobbying are likely to be deemed more acceptable than those which are expressed through less conventional means. Direct action, such as demonstrations and public campaigns, may be questioned and, if lacking in effective public support, rejected largely in response to the tactics used to press them (Saunders, 1980, pp. 231–7). Clearly policy makers' judgments about what is acceptable, both in terms of the content of the demands made and the behaviour of those expressing them, will greatly influence where they look and what demands they hear. Such judgments will not be based on purely factual premises nor are they likely to be wholly neutral or detached. They will reflect the values, beliefs and opinions of policy makers.

Closely linked with policy makers' attitudes are structural or organizational factors which can either help or impede the success of a demand and determine whether it leads to action. Government agencies can be regarded as being at the centre of a system of communication in which, in the demand model, the channels or lines of contact are from various publics to policy makers. Some demands or messages never gain expression through any channel, but, amongst those that do, some may not be heard at the receiving end either because of a technical breakdown in the communication (the line may not function adequately or the message may be indistinct or incorrectly broadcast) or because those who receive the message may inadvertently misunderstand and/or misinterpret it. But the situation is more complex than our simplified communication system suggests, for there are a great many channels, messages and receivers. Moreover some channels are better, and some receivers more important, than others. On top of this it has to be recognized that there are, within government, subsidiary channels and receivers which are subordinate to some higher or more important link or set of policy makers. Clearly a message (a demand or issue) has to proceed all the way up the line from one subsidiary agenda to another, if it is finally to be acted upon. It can fail at any one point or be reshaped and altered.

If we apply the above notions to central and local government, it is possible to isolate certain individuals who have the opportunity to influence the flow of demands. Some civil servants and local government officers will have an important part to play in deciding which demands get through, and what shape they will be in, if and when ministers, MPs, and councillors (in Cabinet, Parliament, council chamber and committee) come to make a final, formal decision. Indeed, looked at from the point of view of demand politics it is difficult to deny that officials do, and by necessity must, play a significant part in the making of policy. Of course, others also affect access and the flow of demands: MPs, for instance, as well as councillors and pressure group spokesmen and occasionally others, such as journalists and academics. Nevertheless officials, especially senior ones, because they are inside the machine and control its day-to-day operation, are bound to be in a very strong position.

One way of visualizing the part played by these key individuals is to regard them as barriers which have to be overcome if a demand or issue is to progress. Some act as 'doormen' or 'gatekeepers' in that they actually control access to an institution or an agenda or set of important policy makers. These tasks can often be fulfilled by quite lowly and apparently unimportant personnel; receptionists in local authority social service departments can greatly influence applicants' chances of gaining access to qualified social workers (Hall, 1974). Equally a minister's private secretary, usually a young civil servant with high potential, can influence the flow of requests placed before the minister. It has been suggested by Crossman that secretaries to the Cabinet, who are amongst the country's top senior civil servants, can influence the flow and content of items appearing before the Cabinet, or before ministers or other officials (Crossman, 1975, pp. 103 and 582). The same point has been made about permanent secretaries and other top civil servants acting either collectively or individually (Haines, 1977, Ch. 3; Williams, 1972, Ch. 5). Whether this happens to the extent that Crossman and others suggest is debatable, but there can be no doubt that for all senior civil servants and top local government officers the opportunity to intervene exists and, because of the pressure of business, such initiative must at times be exercised. After all the minister or committee chairman cannot deal with every matter that comes into the department; if he did he would soon be overwhelmed by detail. So his staff must select what goes before him and, in the absence of precise guidelines, they are bound to determine their selection on the basis of *their* judgments about what their political superiors need to see. Civil servants are said to rely on 'knowing the minister's mind', his or her particular interests and pet policy concerns. Issues relating to these will certainly go before the minister, other matters may be given less priority (Heclo and Wildavsky, 1981, pp. 131–2).

As well as preventing and controlling access, career officials, elected politicians and others may also filter and reinterpret. Filtering involves breaking a demand or issue into parts, allowing some parts access and the opportunity to go forward, while blocking others. Interpreting involves the recasting or reconstruction of a demand or issue so that it becomes subtly different. For example, a demand for nursery school places for the under-fives might be interpreted or passed on as a suggestion for more public grant aid to private nursery schools. It is probably in the business of filtering and interpreting demands that career officials make their most important contribution to determining policy choice. It may be done inadvertently and without any sense of malevolence and sinister purpose, but it is unavoidable and it places in the hands of officials a considerable and important power.

If any demand is to succeed it has to overcome these institutional and personnel barriers. Its progress is somewhat akin to negotiating an obstacle course: at any obstacle it can be stopped, filtered or reinterpreted. Moreover there is not usually one set of barriers to overcome but a hierarchy of control points which need to be successfully negotiated if the demand is to be acted upon. It follows that the higher up this hierarchy a demand emerges, the more chance it has of success — hence the important position held by those who are already ensconced within the structure of government, such as career officials and elected politicians, as well as those external pressure groups that have close contact with key individuals and points of access in government.

The impression that emerges from this analysis does not entirely conform to the conventional view of policy making with its emphasis on the central role of parliamentarians and councillors, their responsiveness to citizen demands, and the clear distinction between career officials and elected politicians as administrators and policy choosers respectively. A consideration of the management and regulation of overt demands suggests a model of policy making more in line with our bureaucratic and technocratic views, with some elements of 'elite pluralism' reflected in the part played by a few influential and incorporated pressure groups.

Limiting Covert Demands

The need to limit covert demands applies especially when demand for services or cash benefits is well in excess of what is actually made available. Limits on demand are generally achieved through the simple mechanism of controlling supply. In essence the demanding public have to make do with what is provided, and their demands have to be fitted into this pattern. Supply rather than demand determines the level of services. Given limited resources, not everyone can have all his demands fully satisfied so some means or basis has to be found for distributing the limited amounts available. What happens, in effect, is that goods and services are *rationed*.

Limiting the consequences of excess demands through rationing the supply of public goods and services and cash payments can take a number of forms, each of which has implications for the pattern of demand expressed, and also, though we do not analyse this until Chapter 8, for the way in which policy products are finally distributed. One approach is to apply a free-for-all, with no formal restriction on access or supply and with the pressure of demand determining outcomes. This tends to result in those with better access, information, connections and know-how getting the lion's share of the policy products available. The less advantaged, and possibly the most needy sections of the population, lose out.

A second approach designed to ensure a fairer distribution of limited resources is to introduce some definition of eligibility as a means of distinguishing those most in need. Many cash benefits such as Family Income Supplement, rent and rate rebates and free school meals, are only granted to those whose income is below a certain level. The two main problems of using what is commonly called a 'means test' are (1) defining eligibility and (2) determining who should or should not be considered eligible. The definition of eligibility raises questions about which criteria will be used as a basis for making a judgment and who will do the defining – problems very similar to those already discussed in the case of defining policy needs. The difficulties involved in determining who should be considered eligible will partly be overcome once eligibility is defined, but there will still be problems when it comes to dealing with exceptional, marginal or unusual cases (see Chapter 7 on discretion).

Queuing for use of services or cash hand-outs is another way of rationing. Because resources cannot fulfil all demands, in certain areas of policy provision the public must wait in order to gain access. With luck, in time, present demand will be fulfilled, though by then new expressions of demand will have taken their place in the queue. Queuing is a fairly common phenomenon in health care where the waiting list for hospital inpatient treatment has remained almost constant at between 450,000 to 500,000 since the creation of the NHS in 1948

(Cooper, 1975, p. 23). Queuing is also present in many other areas of public provision including special educational facilities, social services and environmental improvement. There are three important questions to ask about a queue: how long is it? how quickly is it moving? how much internal mobility is there within the queue? The last question is particularly pertinent, for some in the queue may be in greater need than others and this requires some way of assigning priorities. Yet how are these priorities to be determined and how will they operate? There tends to be dependence on the specialists' decision as to urgency. Alternatively, mobility may be enhanced for some because they have more resources than other members of the queue. For instance money may buy a patient more immediate access to a consultant or, by 'going private', the patient may avoid the queue altogether. Queue jumping and avoiding are fairly frequent practices, but the ability to indulge in them is open only to those who have the right knowledge, opportunities and resources.

Demand can also be rationed through various administrative restrictions which, by making access difficult, limit the use of public goods, services and payments. Many payments require the initial filling in of long and complex forms. In 1976 in only one of the London boroughs could a claimant apply for a rent and rate rebate on one form. Twenty others required the filling in of two forms and in the remaining 12, three or more forms were needed. Some facilities have restricted opening times, others are located in awkward or out of the way places. Cuts in council spending, for example, often mean that public libraries are open for fewer hours outside the normal working day. The consequence is to restrict access and reduce potential demand. Again the same points apply as above: some, because of the resources available to them, will find it easier to overcome these restrictions than will others.

Limiting covert demands through rationing is likely to produce unintended consequences which can affect the distribution of policy products, a subject which we consider in Chapter 8. Here our concern is with the difficulties of interpreting the nature and extent of policy demands when a rationing system is in force, particularly when knowledge and access are important factors in determining take-up of policy products. It is clear that detailed studies into the relatively uncharted area of covert demand, though essential, face severe practical and research difficulties. In broader terms, however, it is apparent that, in order to understand the process of covert demand more fully, we need to develop an appreciation of precisely which sections of society have greater opportunities than others of gaining access to those policy products distributed through rationing.

NEEDS, DEMANDS AND POWER

Policy choice involves distinguishing between a variety of apparently equally pressing alternatives. As a basis for choice, needs and demands raise very different issues for discussion. Taking a broad perspective, both approaches reflect deep theoretical notions about the nature of politics. The notion of needs has elitist implications with emphasis on a third party deciding what is 'best' for others. It implies a role for government which is active and interventionist, where the main direction of influence is from those in positions of authority downward to the citizenry. We saw that, in its modern guise, it is often technocratic with a bias towards policy choosers who can claim some form of expert knowledge and technical skill. By contrast, the notion of demands seems to imply a conventional or even pluralist view of the political system in which influence is dispersed and inherently democratic and moves upwards from the populace to those in authority. Those who make choices are thus seen as being reactive to pressures upon them, and policy products reflect the wishes of the citizenry.

While, in theory, the concepts of need and demands are, respectively, elitist and democratic, in practice the contrasts between the two perspectives are not so distinctive. In the first place when it comes to the actual making of policy, needs and demands are usually intertwined. Most policy choices are a consequence of a mixture of moral and partisan viewpoints, expert advice, external pressures and the operation of interests internal to government. Usually the formation of a policy involves the mixing of all these elements rather than the isolation of any particular one. Secondly, both approaches tend to converge around the issue of power. Needs, as we have argued, reflect interests, and demands have to be managed and regulated. Seen from this perspective, the needs approach is not inherently more elitist than its demand counterpart, nor are demands necessarily more democratic. Both involve the selection of some possible bases for choice and conversely the rejection of others.

This issue of power has arisen intermittently, and we can conclude by considering some of its features as they have been revealed in the preceding pages. In the light of the argument in this chapter, the understanding of power is not simply to be seen as a matter of analysing who influences policy choices, but, more substantially, it refers to which, and whose, needs and demands succeed as a basis for actual policy choice and, conversely, which and whose needs and demands fail. Power thus has both a positive and a negative side: what is chosen and what is rejected, or not even considered. Certainly there can be no rounded analysis of power without a consideration of both these dimensions (Bachrach and Baratz, 1962).

We have also recognized that the ability to influence policy choices is not wholly a reflection of the political resources (political skills, money, organization, etc.) enjoyed by a particular set of need definers or section who are pursuing a demand; it is also a matter of access and opportunity. Some sections seem to have greater access and opportunity to pursue their ends than do others. This casts doubt on the pluralist notion of power as diffuse and balanced and suggests instead that elite pluralism may offer a more accurate picture of the process of policy choice.

The pattern of access and opportunity, however, does not exist independently of those who are in positions of authority and can control key points of entry to an institution and the flow of information that forms the agenda for policy choice. As we have seen, this places those who collect and interpret policy information (be it derived from definitions of needs or from demands) in a potentially influential position, and suggests a view of power closest to the technocratic or bureaucratic viewpoints. The exclusion of certain demands or issues and definitions of policy need and the deliberate shaping of policy choices is, we have argued, unavoidable given the pressure of demands placed upon public agencies and the variety of definitions of need which come before them. One idea, akin to the administrative dispersion and diffusion view, holds that this process of exclusion and shaping is totally random and arbitrary and that it lacks pattern and intent. An alternative view is that there is some continuity in the kinds of demands or issues and definitions of need that are taken up for serious consideration. After all, it can be argued, personnel seem likely to share certain attitudes about what is acceptable, while organizational factors may tend to facilitate certain types of access and certain types of communication to the detriment of others. Moreover, if particular sets of preferences can be assumed to operate, the structures and forces shaping them also become matters of interest. These arguable points are deeply interesting and they tend to lead towards the consideration of elitist and ruling-class views of policy making. Both emphasize the shared values and perspectives of those in positions of power, and the tendency to exclude or even suppress those demands and definitions of need which are contrary to the interests of the elite or dominant class.

So power has a negative and a positive side. It involves selection and exclusion and is concerned with access, opportunities and attitudes. Some scholars have talked about a 'bias in organizations' which facilitates and encourages, through variations in physical access, the development and success of some influences to the detriment of others (Schattschneider, 1960, p. 71). Of course, any bias is not strictly wholly organizational; it is also, as our discussion suggests, reflected in the values shared by key personnel about what is broadly acceptable. This 'bias in attitudes' may be regarded as fortuitous and coincidental, or it can be seen as a product of the conditioning created by policy makers' career structures, or their professional training, or their social background. As we shall see in the following chapter, it is possible to visualize a third form of bias which can be located in the actual operation of the machinery of policy making itself. There may be a built-in bias towards certain kinds of outcomes, regardless of the opportunities for access and the attitudes of personnel.

TOPICS FOR DISCUSSION

1. Select a contemporary (central or local) government policy. How and why did it get onto the agenda for policy decision?
2. Why is it that some demands for policy change are more successful than others?
3. Choose a policy area and consider (a) the problems involved in defining need, and (b) whose definitions of need should predominate in making policy choices.
4. In what ways do senior civil servants influence the management of policy demands?
5. Are needs and demands really distinctive?

KEY READING

A clear account of the notions of needs and demands can be found in

Culyer (1976), Chapters 2 and 3, while the issue of demands is also handled in Hall *et al.* (1975), Part 2. On power begin with Bachrach and Baratz (1962) and then turn to M. A. Crenson, *The Un-Politics of Air Pollution* (Johns Hopkins University Press, 1971), Chapters 1 and 7. Some useful material on the civil service is to be found in H. Young and A. Sloman, *No Minister* (BBC, 1982) and P. Kellner and Lord Crowther-Hunt, *The Civil Servants* (Macdonald, 1980), Chapter 9. On the handling of issues and the role of officers in local government have a look at Saunders (1980), Part 2.

REFERENCES

Bachrach, P. and Baratz, M. S. (1962) 'Two faces of power', *American Political Science Review*, Vol. 56, pp. 947–52.

Bridges, Lord (1950) *Portrait of a Profession*, Cambridge University Press.

Butler, D. and Sloman, A. (1975) *British Political Facts 1900–1975*, Macmillan.

Chapman, R. A. (ed.) (1973) *The Role of Commissions in Policy Making*, Allen & Unwin.

Cobb, R., Ross, J. and Ross, M. H. (1976) 'Agenda building as a comparative process', *American Political Science Review*, Vol. 70, No. 1.

Cooper, M. H. (1975) *Rationing Health Care*, Croom Helm.

Crossman, R. (1975) *The Diaries of a Cabinet Minister*, Vol. 1, Hamish Hamilton and Jonathan Cape.

Culyer, A. J. (1976) *Need and the National Health Service*, Martin Robertson.

Else, P. K. and Marshall G. P. (1979) *The Management of Public Expenditure*, Policy Studies Institute.

Forder, A. (1974) *Concepts in Social Administration*, Routledge & Kegan Paul.

Haines, J. (1977) *The Politics of Power*, Hodder and Stoughton.

Hall, A. (1974) *The Point of Entry*, Allen & Unwin.

Hall, P., Land, H., Parker, R. and Webb, A. (1975) *Change, Choice and Conflict in Social Policy*, Heinemann.

Harris, N. (1972) *Competition and the Corporate Society*, Methuen.

Heclo, H. and Wildavsky, A. (1981) *The Private Government of Public Money*, Macmillan, 2nd edn.

Hood, C. and Wright, M. (eds) (1981) *Big Government in Hard Times*, Martin Robertson.

Illich, I. (1977) *Limits to Medicine*, Penguin.

Johnson, T. (1972) *Professions and Power*, Macmillan.

Pile, Sir William (1974) 'Corporate planning for education in the Department of Education and Science', *Public Administration*, Vol. 52, No. 1.

Plant, R., Lesser, H. and Taylor-Gooby, P. (1980) *Political Philosophy and Social Welfare*, Routledge & Kegan Paul.

Pliatzky, L. (1982) *Getting and Spending*, Basil Blackwell.

Powell, E. (1966) *Medicine and Politics*, Pitman.

Saunders, P. (1980) *Urban Politics*, Penguin.

Schattschneider, E. E. (1960) *The Semisovereign People*, Holt, Reinhart and Winston.

Schon, D. (1973) *Beyond the Stable State*, Penguin.

Self, P. (1976) *Econocrats and the Policy Process*, Macmillan.

Solesbury, W. (1976) 'The environmental agenda', *Public Administration*, Vol. 54, No. 4.

Treasury (1982) *The Government's Expenditure Plans 1982–83 to 1984–85*, Cmnd. 8494–1, HMSO.

Treasury and Civil Service Committee (1982) *The Government's Expenditure Plans 1982–83 to 1984 85*, House of Commons Paper 316 (1981–82), HMSO.

Wilding, P. W. (1982) *Professional Power and Social Welfare*, Routledge & Kegan Paul.

Williams, M. (1972) *Inside No. 10*, Weidenfeld and Nicolson.

Williams, S. (1980) 'The decision makers', Royal Institute of Public Administration, *The Experience of Government*, RIPA.

Wright, M. (ed.) (1980) *Public Spending Decisions*, Allen & Unwin.

6

Dividing Resources:
the Politics of Public Expenditure

Spending money is relatively easy. Planning, controlling and, perhaps, curtailing that spending is altogether more difficult. Yet for all governments spending and restraint need to go hand in hand simply because, as we have seen in Chapter 5, expenditure requirements tend to outstrip supply. Successive British governments have been faced with the problems of managing and determining the division of public spending and it is to these problems that we now turn.

Determining the division of public monies is arguably one of the most important of the constant, annual tasks that governments undertake. However, as we shall see, relatively few people are involved and the procedures whereby decisions are reached are somewhat obscure and more or less closed to public scrutiny. In order to penetrate this vital and secretive aspect of government, the material in this chapter is organized into two main parts. Initially, the machinery and procedures of public expenditure politics are examined with special reference to how these have developed and how they have been operated within both central and local government. In the second part of the chapter we concentrate on the play of power. Consequently, we consider not just how decisions are made but who influences them and what forces help to shape them.

MACHINERY AND PROCEDURES

The process of reaching overall expenditure choices usually follows a systematic and a set format. Of course, small-scale decisions about specific spending programmes are being made more or less continuously at all levels of government. However, these have to fit within a larger framework of broader decisions about overall expenditure and its distribution. Since the early 1960s, in both central and local governments, procedures have been introduced with the intention of making the division of overall expenditure both more organized and more coordinated. Since their initiation, these procedures have been developed (and greatly altered) in the light of practice and in the context of changing economic and political circumstances. In order to understand the nature of expenditure politics, it is essential to consider this wider economic and political context.

The Context of Expenditure Politics

Since the early 1960s the machinery of expenditure politics has had to adapt in line with the changing nature of the UK economy and the varied political objectives of successive British governments. In the 1970s the British economy ceased to expand at its previous pace (albeit well below the level of Britain's major competitors) and moved into a period of low and almost no growth. This period of economic stagnation had, by the end of the decade, become one of absolute decline as the size of the economy actually contracted (Lomax, 1982, p. 10). In a declining economy the opportunities to expand expenditure are few and government personnel are likely to be concerned with spending restraint. As we shall see, expenditure politics adapted to this background of economic stagnation and decline by increasingly emphasizing the problems of controlling and holding down public spending.

On the political front, different governments have pursued the expansion of public spending, while others have sought its contraction, and all have wished to encourage spending on certain favoured programmes. As we have seen in Chapter 5, from the late 1950s until the 1970s public expenditure grew cumulatively as a proportion of GDP. Conservative and Labour governments pursued expansionary expenditure policies, especially in the fields of social welfare (pensions, health, education, housing) and industrial development. During this period, spending growth was justified on the grounds of an expanding economy and the right of the public sector to pre-empt the fruits of that expansion for the public good (Donnison, 1982, p. 20). The 1970–4 Conservative government, under Mr Heath, pledged to roll back the public sector and to cut expenditure, but failed to do so and the real value of public spending went on to reach an all-time peak in 1974–5. It was the 1974–9 Labour government that began in earnest to attempt to control and contract public spending. Even so, these governments did not cut across-the-board, but attempted to defend and expand spending on employment and industry (Burch and Clarke, 1980, p. 26). The 1979 Conservative government entered office with a clear commitment to cut public spending, though it was also committed to expansion in at least two areas: defence, and law and order.

As we can see, economic pressures and political objectives combined towards the middle of the 1970s to produce an expenditure context emphasizing constraint. The concerns of policy makers in the late 1950s, 1960s and even early 1970s, had been how to plan the future distribution of rising public spending, but by the mid-1970s the focus had moved to constraining and cutting spending in a declining economy. By the late 1970s the dominant issue had become one of determining which sections would bear the brunt of the cuts, rather than which would benefit most from expansion.

Expenditure Politics in Central Government

Origins and Intentions. Prior to the early 1960s the machinery for dividing public expenditure operated on a year-to-year basis. Little attempt was made to link resources to revenue and to plan expenditure over the long term, even though most expenditures were committed for periods of more than one year. Following the report of the Plowden Committee in 1961 (Treasury, 1961), a new system was established and this has formed the basis of the machinery for public spending decisions which has operated ever since.

The intention behind the 1960s reforms was to achieve a means of planning expenditure in relation to the resources available and the priorities of government. Originally the system was designed to allow a five-year view of expenditure to be taken, with expenditure plans being decided fairly firmly for at least two to three years ahead and tentatively projected for a further two years. Each year the expenditure programme would be looked at, and the projection for years four and five adjusted in the light of changing circumstances and commitments. This 'forward look', 'rolling programme' was complemented by a medium-term forecast of the likely or assumed development of the economy over the planned period. By thus relating plans to economic prospects, expenditure decisions and the resources to cover them could be kept in line. Finally, the system was intended to allow the priorities of government to be specified and decisions on spending were expected to conform to these, while persistent attempts were to be made to monitor and assess what was actually provided and, hence, assure that results were in line with intentions.

An important feature of the original post-Plowden system was that expenditure was to be considered in volume rather than in actual cash terms. That is to say that plans, though expressed in money terms, really related to the standard or level of services provided, such as the numbers of hospitals built, roads provided or teachers trained and employed, and not the amount that was actually spent. This was done by calculating all figures in constant prices so as to allow for inflation. Obviously under such a system, if assumptions about future costings and prices are wrong, then the cash actually spent will be out of line with original projections. Plowden was really about planning the amounts of public goods and services rather than about controlling the amounts of money actually spent. This proved to be a fatal weakness.

Thus, in theory, the post-Plowden system was intended to allow for the long-term planning of expenditure in relation to resources and priorities, and to provide some means of evaluating the consequences of spending in line with original intentions. As such it conforms closely with our rational view of the behaviour of policy makers, with an emphasis on full information and the establishment and achievement of objectives. Further, by making the procedures of expenditure politics more technical, it hints at a technocratic solution to the problem of dividing money resources.

Operation in Practice. Since the early 1960s, the operation of the post-Plowden system has centred upon the preparation of an annual public expenditure survey by the Treasury and the major spending departments. An important part is played by the Public Expenditure Survey Committee (PESC), which involves senior Treasury officials and the Principal Finance Officers of the major central government departments. It has the task of organizing and coordinating public expenditure activities in central government. This emphasis on organization and coordination, rather than on planning and monitoring, is perhaps the central feature of the post-Plowden system in practice.

Coordination has been achieved across both space and time so that the PESC-related machinery involves all central government spending across the whole of the public sector and the full development of expenditure decisions throughout the financial year from April to March. Increasingly the spending derived from central government of local authorities and nationalized industries and public corporations has been more fully integrated into central government expenditure procedures. In 1975 a Consultative Council on Local Government Finance in England and Wales was established so as to enable the representatives of local government to play a fuller and more integrated part in the annual discussions leading to the settlement of the Rate Support Grant (RSG) (Treasury, 1978, p. 3). More recently the annual review of nationalized industries' investment programmes and financing has been more closely integrated into the overall annual expenditure process and has, at least since 1981, been dealt with under the auspices of a Cabinet subcommittee chaired by the Prime Minister. These expenditure plans for local government and nationalized industries and public corporations are drawn together with those covering central government and published as a White Paper, originally in November/December of each year, though since 1980 publication has been held back until the following spring, sometimes coinciding with the Budget.

The machinery is organized around an annual timetable of events. The publication of each expenditure White Paper marks the beginning of the coming year's expenditure planning exercise. Taking the previous year's total and projections as a starting point, discussions take place before and during May amongst senior Treasury officials and departmental civil servants about the likely out-turn of planned expenditure in the current year and the opportunities for making changes. In June the PESC produces a series of projections of the possible future development of expenditure which are laid before the Cabinet, or one of its subcommittees, for consideration (Layfield, 1976, p. 400). The PESC expenditure projections were initially supplemented by a Medium-Term Assessment (MTA), as envisaged by Plowden, though since 1980 this has been abandoned in favour of a Medium-Term Financial Strategy (MTFS). In the light of these two pieces of information, ministers and their civil servants begin a series of negotiations with the Treasury about the exact nature of the final package. This period of departmental bids, counter-bids and haggling usually lasts until November/December, when the final proposals are ratified by the Cabinet.

The system has worked as a useful means of coordinating expenditure decisions across government and throughout the financial year. Of course, it originally sought to do far more than this by planning ahead, relating expenditure to resources and monitoring results. Consideration of the fulfilment of these more ambitious tasks fully reveals the extent to which, in practice, the system has been adapted and developed in ways very different from what was either originally intended or attempted. The most important changes in the system took place in the mid-1970s against the background of a stagnating economy, and in direct response to three major weaknesses revealed in the operation of the post-Plowden machinery.

The first weakness concerned the inherent difficulty of producing realistic forecasts of the future state of the economy. Time and again the Medium-Term Assessment proved too optimistic, especially as far as the expected rate of economic growth was concerned. Consequently expenditures were decided which were later to prove out of keeping with the real level of activity in the economy, and this tended to push the growth in public expenditure beyond the rate of economic expansion. It was partly because of this unreliability that the 1979 Conservative government introduced the Medium-Term Financial Strategy which, rather than being mainly concerned with what was likely to happen in the economy, established target limits for the growth of the money supply and public sector borrowing. The MTFS thus serves as a framework for and constraint upon the whole exercise of determining the division of expenditure. A second weakness was the consistent inability of governments to establish detailed priorities and objectives and hence to create a way of sensibly relating resources to expenditure plans and ensuring the effective monitoring of spending. Third and finally, because of the emphasis upon volume (i.e. goods and services purchased) rather than cash (i.e. money actually spent) the system tended towards overspending whenever inflation, and therefore costs, was rising more quickly than had been expected. This became particularly marked in the early 1970s when actual spending overshot planned levels by an average of 5 per cent in each of the years up to 1974–5 and then reached a peak by overshooting planned levels by 8 per cent or £6.5 billion (Wright, 1980, p. 101).

Taken together, these three weaknesses meant that public expenditure was neither being properly planned nor was it fully under control. In order to remedy the situation, important reforms in the machinery were initiated from 1975–6 onwards. Cash limits were placed on particular blocks of expenditure so that, in normal circumstances, no more than the cash amount specified could be spent, regardless of the level of services provided for in the plan. This system has now been extended to cover about 60 per cent of all government expenditure

(Treasury, 1982, p. 7). Other reforms include a more efficient and immediate way of gathering information on a monthly and quarterly basis about the actual level of spending as it takes place, and a 'contingency reserve' fund which is the absolute cash amount allowed for any unexpected expenditures in the year ahead. At much the same time the five-year plan period was attenuated to four, with firm decisions only being made for the year ahead. For 1980 and 1981, the plan period was further reduced to what was effectively a three-year basis and in 1982 plans were detailed only for the coming year. 1976 also saw the beginning of expenditure planning in cash as well as volume terms, and from 1981–2 onwards all annual reviews of expenditure have from the outset been discussed purely in terms of the cash that would be available and since March 1982 have been published in this form (Treasury, 1981(b)).

These developments have undermined the original principles on which the post-Plowden system was founded. The changes that took place in the 1970s constituted a move from resource planning to a system more strictly based on cash controls. Moreover, since 1979 the PESC machinery itself has been used as a means of attempting to curtail the size of the public sector whereas previous expenditure cutting exercises were *ad hoc*, being operated outside the formal expenditure machinery. As can be seen, the transformation of public spending procedures, especially in the late 1970s, was both substantial and significant and as a consequence the system has moved from expenditure planning to control, to contraction.

We can illustrate the contemporary operation of central government expenditure machinery by examining the 1981–2 expenditure round. As always, the political and economic context is vital to understanding what took place. On the political front, an important section of the Conservative government leadership remained committed to pursuing a policy designed to reduce inflation by controlling the amount of money and activity in the economy. Related to this was a desire to reduce both the size of the public sector and the Public Sector Borrowing Requirement. This policy implied further large cuts in public spending — already during its first 18 months in office, the Conservative administration had attempted to cut public expenditure on at least five occasions. Though supported by the Treasury, the Chancellor of the Exchequer, the Prime Minister and some of the major economic ministers, this policy of cuts had previously drawn some resistance from other ministers and their departments, and in November 1980 they successfully resisted £1 billion of the £2 billion cuts in planned spending being sought. This reversal appeared to undermine the government's central economic strategy but, rather than alter the policy, the Chancellor stood firm and reasserted his approach in the March 1981 Budget. This reassertion of Treasury will implied substantial further cuts in the coming expenditure round (partly in order to make up for the failure to act in November 1980) so as to bring the strategy back on course.

These political events took place at a time when, after nearly two years in office, the government's economic policy was showing few signs of success. Though inflation was beginning to fall slowly, the economy was in absolute decline and overall output had dropped by 3 per cent since 1979 and by more than 15 per cent in the manufacturing sector. Unemployment had reached the 2.5 million mark and the rate of company liquidations and bankruptcies was rising fast. It was against this background of a divided government and a difficult economic situation that the 1981–2 expenditure round took place.

As usual, the PESC public spending options were finalized in May 1981 and placed before the Cabinet in June along with the Treasury's revised Medium-Term Financial Strategy, which had already been outlined in the March Budget. By July it was apparent that, because of unforseeable increases in demand related expenditure (such as unemployment pay and social security payments), overspending by certain government departments, and the likelihood of overreaching the targets set for the PSBR, substantial cuts of around £4 billion in planned spending would be needed. At this stage the bargaining between the Treasury and departments began and it quickly became clear that, in the face of resistance from sections in the government, there was little chance of carrying through the proposed cuts on the scale envisaged. In September, the Prime Minister acted to change the situation by sacking three senior ministers who were critical of the Treasury's approach and replacing them with ministers likely to be more sympathetic. Nevertheless, achieving the cuts remained difficult and, following a further Cabinet retreat in October 1981, a novel piece of machinery in the form of a small committee under the chairmanship of the Home Secretary, Mr Whitelaw, was established. This committee interviewed each Cabinet minister individually in an attempt to gain further concessions, but with limited success. In November it was replaced by a 'Mark 2' subcommittee under Mrs Thatcher. By such means the Treasury viewpoint made some progress, though the eventual scale of cuts in planned expenditure (at £1 billion) was far less than had been originally sought. The totals thus agreed were briefly announced in December and published in detail in the expenditure White Paper at the time of the Budget in March 1982. At this point, and on the basis of these figures, the next annual round began for 1982–3.

The 1981–2 case illustrates the degree to which expenditure procedures have shifted from planning to contraction and from the long to the (often very) short term. The cuts being discussed were for the following year and, in some cases, such as some of the spending of the Department of the Environment, for the current year. Overall it supports the view that both 'forward looks' and gauging the consequences of spending have been progressively sacrificed to the need to find immediate cash savings. It seems that rationality has proved elusive and the approach to expenditure policy in practice has been more in keeping with an incremental strategy involving small-scale expansions or contractions in existing programmes. Furthermore, as we shall see when we consider the play of power in expenditure politics, the move to contraction has weakened the technocratic and civil service domination of expenditure decisions, and allowed a far more overtly political and partisan contribution to be made.

Expenditure Politics in Local Government

It is difficult to generalize about expenditure politics at the local level. In England and Wales alone there are 456 different local governments each with unique traditions, social, economic and political characteristics, and particular ways of operating (Stanyer, 1976, Ch. 3). The fact that no two local governments are exactly alike means that, in order to examine the machinery of public spending at the local level, it is essential to consider individual cases. Consequently the procedures adopted in three selected authorities are examined in the following pages. However, there are some points of general similarity which affect most local authorities, and it is worth considering these beforehand. In order to limit the range of the topic we have restricted our remarks to local governments in England only.

We saw in Chapter 3 that all local governments depend upon central government for some of their finances. A large part of local authorities' current 'revenue' expenditure is derived from central government's Rate Support Grant and much of the rest is in the form of specific grants for particular projects and services and subsidies for the provision of council housing. Local authorities' capital expenditure is partly financed by loans sanctioned by the centre. Because of this close involvement by central government, all local governments are to some extent constrained in terms of the expenditure decisions they can reach (Danziger, 1978, Ch. 2). Moreover, when it comes to conducting their own expenditure policy making, local governments have to relate to the central government's expenditure cycle (Layfield, 1976, p. 398). The announcement of the RSG in December of each year and, from 1982, the grant-related expenditure assessments for each authority in July, are fixed points around which all local authorities have to operate.

In addition to the influence of central government, in recent years many local authorities have changed their methods of organization and practice (Stanyer, 1976, Ch. 11). These changes have been subsumed under the label of 'corporate management' whereby local authorities, instead of operating a series of relatively independent committees overseeing separate service departments, have introduced overarching committees to help coordinate and integrate the activities of the council. Most local authorities now have policy or executive committees (or their equivalent) and many have also established finance and manpower committees. These committees operate across the structure of the local authority and usually consist of either the leading members of the council or the chairmen of the departmental committees, advised by some senior officers. This relatively common corporate approach has produced some similarities in public expenditure machinery.

These similarities, resulting from central government influences and reforms of local authority structures, make it possible to generalize cautiously about certain features of the annual expenditure cycles in the so-called 'typical' local government. Usually the procedures for calculating estimates for the coming year begin in the autum of the previous year in the form of a report to the finance or policy committee on capital spending, drawn up by officers in the finance department. Little further can be done, especially as far as current expenditure is concerned, until the central government makes its RSG subsidy known, usually in December, though bids for capital and revenue spending may be put forward by the various service committees and departments. In January the officers produce a further report on options for capital and revenue expenditure in the coming year in the light of the bids that have been made and of the various levels of rate that would be needed. It is at least at this point, often earlier, that the policy or finance committee attempts to set certain financial targets and requests service committees to tailor their demands to fit within them. After bargaining and negotiation throughout February the final totals are reached and agreed by the policy committee, the rate is recommended and the whole package is then put forward before the full council for approval in March.

A central feature of this procedure is the important part played by the finance officers and the members of finance and policy committees in overseeing and setting the terms of the discussion as well as in coordinating and controlling the exercise. The annual cycle at local level is noticeably shorter than in central government. The key period is from December to March. Of course, the notion of a 'typical' local authority is misleading for some attempt to plan expenditure over a two- or three-year period. Others try to relate objectives to resources and even to monitor the consequences of expenditure. Indeed, since the late 1960s this kind of rational approach to public spending has been more widely accepted, though in recent years the necessity of curtailing expenditure may have tended to undermine long-term planning (Hinings *et al*, in Wright, 1980). However, an even more varied picture emerges when we turn to look at recent expenditure cycles in three different local authorities.

Manchester City (Metropolitan District) Council: Deciding Spending for 1980–1. The key to understanding expenditure choices for the financial year 1980–1 in Manchester was the domination of the Council by the Labour Party. More than 70 of the 99 councillors were Labour and they tended to meet separately prior to committee and council meetings so as to reach an agreed position. The Council was organized into 14 main committees. Their membership reflected the political balance of the council and most were connected with a particular Department such as Direct Works or Education. These 14 included coordinating committees for finance and policy, and a Budget Resources Committee (BRC). The latter was vital to the expenditure machinery. It consisted of all committee chairmen, plus eight members from the finance and the policy committees. This committee met in private and had executive powers to enable it, if necessary, to force spending decisions on other committees. All committees were advised by the relevant senior officers who attended their meetings, with the Town Clerk and City Treasurer being especially involved.

The establishment of the 1980–1 expenditure estimates started in

1979 against the background of a newly elected Conservative government seeking expenditure reductions and a Manchester City Labour Party determined to limit the consequences of any cuts. The City Labour Party consisted of delegates from the 33 wards in the city and was consulted by the Council Labour Group. In March and September 1979 the City Labour Party first adopted and then reaffirmed a policy of no cuts in services.

The expenditure cycle began in earnest in the late autumn of 1979 when officers submitted to their committees estimates of their own department's expenditure plans. These consisted of all committed expenditure for the coming year and a separate improvement plan to cover new developments. After discussion and amendment at committee level, these were drawn together by the Treasurer's Department in the form of a report which was submitted to the BRC in January 1980 following the November 1979 announcement of the RSG settlement. This showed that committee decisions implied a rate increase of 49 per cent. This was unacceptable to the BRC which agreed a 30 per cent increase and cut of £13 million in the submitted estimates. Each committee was then asked to achieve a particular level of reduction. In February the City Labour Party publicly opposed the 30 per cent proposal and proposed less substantial reductions and a 35–40 per cent rate increase. Initially it seemed that the Labour Group on the Council had accepted this policy, but following a series of informal meetings between the Town Clerk, the City Treasurer, the Leader of the Council, and the Chairman of the Finance Committee, the BRC met in private and proposed a rate increase of 29 per cent. In March some members of the Council Labour Group attempted to alter this proposal. They were unsuccessful and the expenditure proposals were then accepted by the full Council, with twelve Labour members voting against them and one abstaining.

Wirral Borough (Metropolitan District) Council: Deciding Spending for 1981–2. The organization of the Wirral Borough Council on Merseyside in 1980–1 reflected a strong corporate approach with business divided between six main committees of which one, the Policy and Resources Committee (PRC), played a leading role. This committee consisted of the key members of the other committees and was also advised and supported by the Finance Committee. The membership of all committees reflected the political balance of the Council in which Conservatives held 37 of the 66 Council seats. Members of the majority Conservative group usually met prior to committee meetings in order to reach an agreed view. The initiative for many spending proposals came from the officers, but only after consultation with committee chairmen.

The Conservative dominated authority was committed to the government's policy of cutting local government expenditure and, in June 1979, the Council had adopted a minute which strictly limited any future expansion. During 1980 it became clear, especially following the autumn announcement of the RSG settlement, that further restraint would be needed of the order of about a 5.6 per cent reduction on current expenditure if the rate increase was to be kept down in accordance with party policy. Moreover, it also became evident that, without some reduction, the Wirral Council would be more than 10 per cent above the government's assessment of what it needed to spend, and this could lead to a further loss of financial support under 'penalty clauses' which were being introduced in new legislation.

The expenditure cycle really began in late September 1980 when the PRC established principles to guide the estimating activities of the Council. These took into account the likely effect of inflation and emphasized the need to constrain spending. In October officers in the departments drew up a range of estimates and economies for each section and this was drawn together by the PRC into a summary budget. From late October to December, committees considered these budget options and drew up a list of priorities. By December 1980, in the light of the RSG announcement, the summary budget indicated a large overspend and the PRC instructed each committee to propose economies of 6 per cent. The committees were informed by officers of the Finance Department where cuts could or should be made, and their proposals were submitted to the Finance Committee in early February 1981 before being considered by the PRC later that month. It was the PRC at this meeting which decided which of the economies was acceptable and its proposals, including a 15 per cent rate increase, were approved by the full Council in March 1981.

Crawley Borough (Shire District) Council: Deciding Spending for 1981–2. The Crawley authority covers Crawley New Town and is one of the district councils within the West Sussex county area. In 1980 it had a Labour majority, numbering 18 out of 26 seats. Council business took place through four main service committees and these were coordinated and overseen by a central Management Board. The membership of these committees reflected the party-political balance of the

Council, and all chairmanships and vice-chairmanships were held by Labour councillors. The Management Board (MB) was Labour dominated with only one 'opposition' member and it had the power to reject, and refer back for alteration, estimates it did not approve. The Labour Group was highly cohesive, being small in number, and it had close connections with local trade unions and ward parties. Members usually reached agreement in private before committee and council meetings.

In the RSG settlement announced in November/December 1980, Crawley found itself being called upon to make cuts in 1981–2 of about £1.5 million to a total spending of £3.4 million, or risk losing its full Rate Support Grant income of £400,000. In effect the Council was being asked to cut more than three times the amount it expected to receive. This situation arose as a consequence of the central government's new block grant, and its assessment of Crawley's required level of spending, which was deemed to be much lower than its existing expenditures. As a consequence, compared with the previous year, the RSG was to be reduced by 60 per cent.

The expenditure cycle began in the late autumn with the service committees putting forward estimates for future spending. These were drawn up by the officers in the various departments and amended by the committees. In December 1980, following the announcement of the RSG, officers suggested to the Management Board savings of 7 per cent. This was rejected by the Board, and, following a meeting of the Labour Group and consultation with ward parties, committees were instructed to prepare estimates on the basis of the previous year's policies, with the expectation that any shortfall would be covered by an increase in the rates. In January and early February 1981, the main lines of policy were determined in private meetings of the Labour Group and towards the end of the month, the Management Board met to discuss a spending programme of £5.3 million for 1981–2. In March this was approved by the full council despite strong reservations on the part of the Council's officers. The policy meant that Crawley would not receive any RSG for 1981–2 and the burden of expenditure fell fully upon the rates, which were increased by 97 per cent. This increase enabled Crawley to stand still and avoid any reductions in services.

Conclusion. Our three case studies reveal the variety of expenditure politics at the local level: the different types and structures of committees involved; the varieties of party systems and connections between local party organizations and the council; and the variations in dependence on central government funding through the RSG. The case studies also reveal important similarities in such matters as budget timetables, officer involvement (especially when initiating and advising on spending proposals), and in the bargaining between policy and finance, and spending committees. Clearly central government's role is significant, but it does not always get its way, and other pressures can often outweigh its influence at the local level.

In many ways the machinery of public expenditure in local government has undergone similar changes to that at the centre. The longer term planning approach, which was popular in the 1960s and early 1970s, appears not to have been sustained in the late 1970s and 1980s. This shift from attempted rationality can be partly accounted for on the grounds that both central and local government have developed in the same context of economic stagnation and, more recently, decline. But it also reflects the extent to which the spending activities of local government are shaped by the actions of national government. Moreover, our case studies suggest that the notion of officer dominance and technocratic government at the local level (Elcock, 1982, Ch. 5), is, at least in the field of expenditure politics, increasingly less easy to substantiate.

THE PLAY OF POWER

Expenditure politics provide a telling illustration of the operation of power, for the very act of dividing limited financial resources is liable to be contentious, simply because there is seldom enough money to go round. Hence some sections win and some lose. But who wins and who loses? Who is influential and who is not?

In the rest of this section this play of power is analysed in two ways. Initially, power is examined in terms of those biases in the workings of expenditure politics which help to shape the pattern of influences determining overall spending priorities. This takes up the bulk of the section, but we also consider power by examining out-turns (or results) of expenditure policy making, especially as revealed in the distribution of funds amongst the various categories of spending outlined at the beginning of Chapter 5. Studying results tells the observer something about which sections involved in expenditure politics are successful, while looking at biases says more about who is directly involved and who has the opportunity to exert influence.

Biases in Expenditure Politics

In order to carry out business, personnel in all government organizations need to select materials and issues to handle. Selection tends to be made on the basis of set procedures and established ways of doing things. In effect government personnel operate in a partial manner (in that they cannot do all things and must concentrate their efforts), and tend to be predisposed or inclined towards certain types and sources of influence at the expense of others. These biases towards certain issues and certain influences were noted in Chapter 5 and were seen to apply to two features of the operation of government agencies.

One set of biases can be located in the viewpoints or general attitudes of government personnel, and especially those key personnel who are in positions to control and shape the handling of an issue. Such attitudes involve a particular 'cast of mind' as to what is feasible and acceptable, and they may be held consciously or unconsciously and acted upon deliberately and intentionally or automatically and unknowingly. Balancing these biases in attitudes is a second set of biases which are built in to the structure of the organization itself. These can include matters relevant to the location of the organization such as the ease of approaching it and gaining entry to it; its pattern of communication and contact both internally and with outside organizations; and its working procedures such as its hours of operation and methods of handling material. These structural biases can affect what matters are taken up by the organization, how they are handled and with what speed. They ensure and enhance the expression of certain influences upon policy making at the expense of others which either fail to gain entry or are filtered out.

Realizing that there are biases in attitude and structure focuses attention on the issue of who has access to and who is involved in policy making, and thus is one way of approaching the issue of power in expenditure politics. But in addition to these biases, it is also possible to distinguish those that have been built into the actual operation of the machinery of expenditure politics and which tend to produce certain kinds of expenditure policy making. So if the question of biases is to be handled thoroughly, attention must be given, not only to problems of access and involvement, but also to the results of those operational biases which arise through the actual working of the machinery for making spending choices. Even then we will need to interpret our findings in the light of the views of power and policy making outlined in Chapter 2.

Access and Involvement. Different individuals, sections and groups have different degrees of access to and involvement in expenditure politics at both the national and the local government levels. It is possible to distinguish three groups of key participants who set the tone and determine the direction of spending policy: those who initiate and organize the proceedings; those who are involved and drawn in to expenditure policy making; and those who are consulted.

At the national level, initiating and organizing participants consist of about 50 senior Treasury officials who are primarily concerned with expenditure matters, the Chancellor of the Exchequer, sometimes the Prime Minister and especially the Chief Secretary to the Treasury on the ministerial side, and the principal finance officers from the various departments who, together with senior Treasury officials, make up the membership of PESC. Other Cabinet and junior ministers may also intermittently fulfil organizing and initiating roles, especially in those instances when the Cabinet's Future Economic Strategy Committee attempts to take a view on the overall package of public spending before the annual cycle begins. Within local government the initiative usually comes from officers within the Treasurer's or finance department, often in response to central government guidelines. However, organizational responsibility tends to be shared with the chief executive and tends to involve the political leaders of the council and senior committee chairmen. Moreover, as our case studies in Manchester and Crawley suggest, in some authorities the organization of expenditure policy, once introduced, falls into the hands of the leaders of the dominant party or even the party group or local party.

Involved participants usually take part in the expenditure process at the behest of initiating and organizing participants, and they do so on an intermittent rather than persistent basis. At the national level they include departmental officers who are concerned with expenditure planning and policies within their departments and, at the ministerial level, those ministers not involved in organizing the proceedings are usually drawn in on discussions concerning spending in their own departments. The Cabinet, as a body, does not usually discuss spending decisions in detail until very close to the December climax of the cycle, though it often looks at broad spending strategy in the summer. In local government, depending on the exact organization of the authority, involved participants tend to be senior officials from spending departments, members of council committees and, in some instances, other members of the dominant party group.

Consulted participants are informed but not usually closely or directly involved in making overall spending choices. Often they are told what has happened after decisions have, in effect, been reached, though their views may have been taken into account in reaching those decisions. At the national level they include the local authority associations, which are consulted about the setting of the RSG; senior personnel in nationalized industries and public corporations, who place their spending plans and investment needs before government; and Parliament, which does have an opportunity to discuss published spending plans and, in theory, though hardly ever in practice, to reject all or part of them. Backbench members of the governing party may also be consulted, usually when the Cabinet itself is split and the various factions require allies. Generally, when a Cabinet is united the number of consulted participants is few. Consultation at the local level appears to follow a similarly restricted pattern. In 1980–1 Manchester City Council informed local authority trade unions of its plans, and senior officers and chairmen held meetings with representatives of the local chambers of trade and commerce and the trades council. In Crawley, local trade unions and party branches were consulted, whereas in the Wirral business interests as well as party opinions were taken into account. In the main, however, it appears that consultation is limited, and most discussion takes place within the authority, with the full council and the opposition usually playing a negligible part.

Our discussion of access and involvement reveals two features of expenditure politics. First, it tends to be secretive, with business conducted in private away from the scrutiny of the public and many of their elected representatives. This seems especially the case at the national level, though in recent years, particularly in 1976–7 and from 1979 onward, accounts of Cabinet and ministerial discussions on expenditure have been extensively leaked to the newspapers. Second it seems that very few people have direct access to, and are closely involved in, the essential decisions which determine overall spending priorities. Perhaps no more than 200 key participants are directly involved at national level and perhaps 20–40 in a local authority. Amongst those directly involved, an important and persistent part is played by senior civil servants and officers especially in Treasury and finance departments. Some politicians also play an essential part, such as the Prime Minister, the Chancellor of the Exchequer and the chairmen of local authority finance and policy committees. Of course it does not follow from this that those who are directly involved necessarily act without any regard to wider pressures and interests. Lack of direct access is not the same as lack of representation. This is a point to which we return in our conclusions.

Biases in Operation. While limits on access and involvement have led to secretive policy making involving few participants, the way in which expenditure politics is organized has itself tended to propel spending decisions in certain directions. In effect the machinery has produced a kind of self-momentum which has had consequences for the manner in which spending decisions are reached as well as for their content.

A recognized feature of most expenditure procedures is that present decisions start from existing commitments carried over from the previous round (Wildavsky, 1975, pp. 216–19). Though starting anew each year (or 'zero based') budgeting has been tried in some local authorities, it has never proved wholly successful and, given that many resources are committed over the long term, it is unlikely to work in many instances. This tendency to build on the past means that alterations in spending totals usually deviate only marginally, up or down, from the existing situation. As pointed out in Chapters 2 and 5, spending decisions are usually incremental rather than root-and-branch and radical. Because central government machinery has been operated on the basis of past totals rolled forward over a planned period, it has tended to conform to and exacerbate this accepted incremental pattern. Moreover, the machinery, particularly at the national level and especially prior to 1976, served to impel expansion in public sector spending. This was not always intended, but the use of volume figures and overoptimistic economic forecasts helped to encourage ever higher levels of public spending by avoiding the real costs involved. After 1976 almost the opposite seems to have happened as, following the introduction of cash limits, spending on some programmes fell below targeted levels. The cutbacks achieved in 1976–7 and 1977–8 were partly a consequence of unforeseen effects of the new cash controls (Wright in Hood and Wright, 1981, p. 23). In 1981–2 the cash limited expenditures of central government were underspent by 1.8 per cent, while those of local authorities were 14 per cent below target. It might be said that the built-in impulsion to expand spending has been replaced by a built-in predilection to contract it. A similar phenomenon can be seen at the local level, especially in those authorities, such as Manchester, which discuss expenditure in terms of two sets of figures: existing commitments and 'improvements'. Allowing for 'improvement' suggests there is a willingness to entertain and accept expansion.

The machinery also assures an important position to those who initiate the annual proceedings — civil servants and officers in Treasury and local finance departments and their ministers and committee chairmen. The PESC projections (and until the late 1970s the Medium-Term Economic Assessment) served to set the direction and tone of the debate and placed finance departments, as the originators of these proposals, at an advantage in that policy making tended to be on their terms and on the basis of information provided by them. Critical officials, civil servants, ministers or local authority committee members have often found it difficult to question the statistics and halt the momentum of the exercise. Within central government, in recent years, the Treasury's position has been further strengthened by placing an extra Treasury Minister in the Cabinet and through such devices as cash limits and tighter expenditure checks. Increasingly the Treasury's traditional concern to control the amount of money spent has become more and more dominant. A similar strengthening of finance departments and policy committees has taken place within many local authorities. In addition, the machinery is increasingly biased towards central government interests and influences. In effect the determination of overall spending totals has become more and more managed and controlled from Whitehall.

The move towards strengthening Treasury and local finance departments in a period of economic stringency has not necessarily led to a more coordinated approach to spending decisions. The departmental nature of central and local government has tended to work against any attempt to impose binding priorities, even in the face of attempts at cutback in the late 1970s and early 1980s. Departments continued to fight their corners and to protect their spending power. This departmentalism is inherent in the organization of British government and it gives a particular complexion to expenditure politics emphasizing haggling, bargaining and marginal change (Heclo and Wildavsky, 1981, Chapter 1). In some local authorities, departmental conflicts may have been weakened by the move to more overtly corporate types of organization, but, even in these instances, beneath the corporate superstructure departmental influences remain.

These biases in the operation of the machinery lead expenditure discussions along certain pathways. They obstruct an economically rational approach, and can also help to produce unforeseen results as in the case of the expansion of spending in the early 1970s. Those who operate in the world of expenditure politics thus find that their opportunities to influence spending choices are constrained and shaped by these built-in biases.

Expenditure Out-Turns 1979–82

Having examined who is involved and how the machinery operates, we now consider the actual out-turns of expenditure. We do this by analysing the categories amongst which central government expenditures have been distributed and concentrate especially on the period since 1979 which, at least on the surface, has been one of public spending constraint. Looking at those categories of spending which are diminished when cuts are made or attempted can help the observer to pinpoint some of the major interests and forces that are successful (or unsuccessful) in expenditure bargaining.

It is important to realize that, despite frequent attempts to constrain public spending since 1979 (see p. 144 above), the level of spending in real terms has continued to rise. It has been estimated that in 1981–2 expenditure was (in real terms, allowing for inflation) some 5 per cent higher than in 1979–80, and some 7 per cent higher than had been planned in March 1980 (Treasury and Civil Service Committee, 1982, p. vi). Despite this overall increase, significant cuts were made within particular categories of spending.

Taking the broadest 'economic' category of public expenditure, the weight of recent cuts has fallen on capital as opposed to current spending. The reductions have been quite dramatic so that in 1980–1 capital spending was nearly 40 per cent less in real terms than in 1975–6, and future plans suggest a further weakening (Treasury, 1982, p. 13).

The burden of cuts has also fallen disproportionately on local authorities. In each of the three years from 1979, total central government expenditure grew while total local authority expenditure declined. Indeed, since 1975 total central spending has increased by around 8 per cent, while local authority spending has fallen by more than 16 per cent (Treasury, 1981a). This drop in local spending is connected with the changes in capital spending already noted: cuts in capital spending have also fallen most heavily on local authorities. In addition, government has failed to cut its own current programmes to the same degree as local authorities. At the same time the capital investment programmes of nationalized industries and public corporations have been severely constrained.

This pattern of selective cuts is also reflected in the alterations to individual expenditure programmes since 1979. The major increase has been in social security funding, though there have also been significant increases in expenditure on defence and law and order. By contrast, the major decreases in expenditure have been in the areas of housing, industrial support, education and transport. The increases in social security spending were demand-determined, a direct product of the rising numbers of pensioners and unemployed entitled to receive pensions and benefits. Such demand-determined expenditure is, as we stressed in Chapter 5, relatively difficult to control and constrain. The changes in spending on defence, law and order and industry reflected the policy priorities of the government. Cuts in housing and transport were in part a result of central government's failure to cut its own current spending with the consequential shifting of the burden on to the capital spending on housing and transport, administered by local authorities.

The post-1979 picture of cuts, both real and attempted, serves to underline some of the points already made about the setting of overall spending totals in Britain. It confirms especially the extent to which choices are made on short-term criteria with a tendency to seek the easy option as in the case of cuts in capital spending. We may also note the increasingly centralized, central government-based nature of the proceedings. Those at the centre who organized and were involved in the working of the expenditure machine fared relatively well and spread the costs of contraction beyond the confines of their own jurisdiction to local authorities and nationalized industries capital spending. The clear impact of political will was also evident, as shown both in the attempt to reduce public spending in total and in the priority given to certain programmes. Interestingly this exercise of will was not successful as far as overall expenditure totals were concerned; it did not lead, as intended, to a contraction of spending in real terms. Indeed the 1979–82 period provides a neat example of the extent to which the exercise of power by particular governments has, in the end, been constrained and shaped by those biases of attitudes, structure and operation which have characterized expenditure politics.

CONCLUSION

Public expenditure politics provides a telling illustration of the problems and features of policy choice. The attempt to establish criteria of need and to pursue economic rationality, as exemplified in the post-Plowden reforms and the development of a planned approach, was modified in practice, especially in the face of a declining economy. The original idea of planning expenditure in relation to priorities and available resources became transformed, particularly after 1975–6, into a means for controlling and even contracting public spending. At the same time the influence of the Treasury and of local authority finance departments was heightened, and simple accounting principles came more and more to dominate matters of expenditure choice. This move to control was also signified in the gradual development of central government's domination over the area of expenditure policy making. This, in turn, may have had the added consequence of shifting the burden of constraint from central to local government. A further feature of expenditure politics in the context of economic decline has been a weakening of the technocratic nature of the exercise and a marginal strengthening of the partisan, party political contribution.

While technical definitions of need and priority appear to have fared badly, the role of public demand in determining expenditure choices is open to interpretation. Our discussion of the 'play of power' revealed how secretive and confined the process of setting overall spending targets has tended to be. We noted that those who are directly involved are few in number and that limits on access and involvement prevent many from participating. Moreover those who are involved are very much constrained by the tendencies or biases within the machinery of expenditure politics itself. These further complicate the patterns of influence created through access and involvement. On one interpretation, this evidence can be taken to indicate an exclusive and closed system of policy making substantially cut off from, and relatively unresponsive to, outside pressures. Alternatively, on the basis of the same evidence, it can be argued that the few who are directly involved are subject to, and operate in response to, other wider, indirect pressures. Ministers, for instance, may push up overall spending in order to bid for votes or the support of key sections of the community, and at least some government spending programmes have been produced in response to the demands of powerful pressure groups.

The picture of power is not, therefore, straightforward, and there are aspects of many of the views outlined in Chapter 2 which can be applied to an explanation of expenditure policy making. As we have already mentioned, central and local government schemes for long-term expenditure planning may be regarded as technocratic, in that they lead to the creation of complex and esoteric procedures with the consequent need for specialists. The related bureaucratic viewpoint is also relevant and is supported by the influential part played in expenditure choices by Treasury civil servants and local authority finance officers, especially in the years prior to 1976. A pluralist perspective can offer some insight into the way in which public demands and external pressures influence spending choices. In explaining recent developments, a party government viewpoint would have some relevance in that partisans have tried, with more determination than previously, to pursue their objectives, though this has not always been done in response to party thinking or prompting. The features of secrecy, confined numbers of participants and centralization suggest the possibility of an elite or even a ruling-class explanation of expenditure politics.

All these views — party government, technocratic, bureaucratic, pluralist, elite and ruling-class — imply that in the end some sectional, group or class interest predominates. But our discussion of the biases inherent in the operation of the policy machinery suggest an alternative explanation. Namely that there is a kind of self-generated momentum in spending policy which belies attempts at direction and control. In such a Kafkaesque world of unforeseen events and unexpected consequences the administrative dispersion and diffusion view of policy making seems appropriate. Yet even the failure to achieve spending plans can also be seen as a reflection of the influence of certain key interests and their ability to resist the application of such plans. Such a conclusion implies an elite pluralist view of policy making, perhaps emphasizing the ability of public sector interests to resist cuts in financing and staffing.

Clearly each of these viewpoints has some insight to offer, but noticeably there is one view — the conventional — which appears to have limited relevance. As we have seen, Parliament, the council and the public through their elected representatives are seldom consulted. This conflicts with an important function traditionally ascribed to elected bodies such as Parliament and local councils: that of holding executives to account and scrutinizing their decisions. Our analysis suggests that the ability of elected assemblies to do this is severely limited.

Determining policy priorities is only one step. Power is not simply a matter of what is decided, but also of whether it can be carried through. The important policy decisions are often made after plans and intentions have been finalized, in the course of actually trying to carry them out. This vital and neglected topic of policy application is considered in the next part of the book.

TOPICS FOR DISCUSSION

1. Why has it proved so difficult to cut back public expenditure?
2. Is public expenditure both impossible to plan and beyond control?
3. Does central government control local authority spending?
4. What does the process of public expenditure politics reveal about the operation and distribution of power in government?
5. Do public expenditure policy decisions reflect the influence of demands or of needs? What needs, and whose demands?

KEY READING

The machinery of expenditure politics at the national level is clearly outlined in Treasury (1978), while Danziger (1978) provides an analysis of budget processes in particular local governments. The essays by Wright and by Greenwood and Hinings in Wright (1980), as well as in Hood and Wright (1981) are up to date and informed. Insight into the politics of expenditure policy making within the Treasury can be found in Heclo and Wildavsky (1981).

REFERENCES

Burch, M. and Clarke, M. (1980) *British Cabinet Politics*, Hesketh.
Danziger, J. M. (1978) *Making Budgets: Public Resource Allocation*, Sage.
Donnison, D. V. (1982) *The Politics of Poverty*, Martin Robertson.
Elcock, H. J. (1982) *Local Government*, Methuen.
Heclo, H. and Wildavsky, A. (1981) *The Private Government of Public Money*, Macmillan, 2nd edn.

Hood, C. C. and Wright, M. W. (1981) *Big Government in Hard Times*, Martin Robertson.

Layfield, Sir Frank (1976) Department of Environment, *Report of the Committee on Local Government Finance*, Cmnd. 6453, HMSO.

Lomax, D. (1982) 'Supply-side economics: the British experience', *National Westminster Bank Quarterly Review*, August.

Stanyer, J. (1976) *Understanding Local Government*, Fontana/Collins.

Treasury (1961) *The Control of Public Expenditure*, Cmnd. 1432, HMSO.

Treasury (1978) 'The management of public expenditure', *Economic Progress Report*, Supplement, October.

Treasury (1981a) *The Government's Expenditure Plans 1981–82 to 1983–84*, Cmnd. 8175, HMSO.

Treasury (1981b) 'Public expenditure: planning in cash', *Economic Progress Report*, November.

Treasury (1982) *The Government's Expenditure Plans 1982–83 to 1984–85*, Cmnd. 8494, Vol. I, HMSO.

Treasury and Civil Service Committee (1982) *5th Report: The Government's Expenditure Plans 1982–83 to 1984–85*, House of Commons Paper 316 (Session 1981–82), HMSO.

Wildavsky, A. (1975) *Budgeting: A Comparative Theory of Budgetry Processes*, Little Brown.

Wright, M. W. (1980) *Public Spending Decisions*, Allen & Unwin.

PART IV

APPLYING POLICIES

7

The Products of Government:
Carrying out Intentions

The division of public expenditure is central to the work of all governments, and a minister's 'success' or 'failure' in obtaining resources is said to affect his reputation within his department. Much time and effort is spent, in Cabinet, in Cabinet committees, and in meetings between senior civil servants, in negotiating financial allocations; the same is true in local government. In Chapter 6 we considered public expenditure policy decisions and traced the development of techniques such as the PESC.

It is arguable how far these techniques have been successful. In 1971, government forecast a growth in public spending of 12 per cent (in real terms) by 1974–5. By 1975 the actual increase was 28.6 per cent representing an additional expenditure of no less than £5 billion over that planned (Heclo and Wildavsky, 1981, p. XXI). This pattern of public spending exceeding targets has continued, and figures in Chapter 6 revealed its extent since 1979. In other policy areas there are also abundant examples of policies which do not get carried out as planned or intended. 'The houses that will never be built' was a headline in *The Guardian* on 1 December 1978. The article began:

> Britain's 400 housing authorities were yesterday advised to speed up their house-building programmes over the next two years after the Department of the Environment confirmed that 35,000 homes out of the 100,000 planned for this year will never be built.

Political scientists have, until recently, curiously neglected the carrying out of policy. The traditional emphasis in textbooks has been on the formulation of policy and on the roles of Parliament, government departments, parties and pressure groups in creating new policies. There has been an implicit assumption that policies, once decided upon, are put into action by some near-mechanical process.

The advent of policy studies has changed this. Our Policy Approach in this book emphasizes the processes and products of government. We are as much interested in the carrying out of policy products as we are in the acquisition and division of resources. In this chapter we focus on the products of government and concern ourselves with the carrying out of those products, whether they be rules and regulations, goods and services, or transfer payments. We go on, in the next chapter, to consider the consequences for citizens of the application of policy products. This distinction between carrying out and consequences (or policy impact) is an important one (Van Meter and Van Horn, 1975). An Act of Parliament is an example of a policy product. The ways in which it is carried out, and problems which arise in carrying it out are our concern in this chapter. Its impact on society (whether or not this is as originally intended) we consider in Chapter 8.

In framing this distinction we have deliberately avoided the term 'implementation'. As a concept it lacks clarity, for it is frequently used to include both the carrying out and the consequences. It is also often said to start only when a policy or programme has been formally ratified, whereas in Chapter 1 we argued that such a chronological separation from policy formulation is unreal and possibly misleading. Some policies do not need formal ratification, but simply emerge from statements of intent or from practice in the field. The movement of resources towards community care or preventive health are examples. Furthermore, the separation suggests that, once 'implementation' gets under way, there is no more policy making, whereas the processes are inseparable. Community care, for example, is 'implemented' by health and local authorities, but they see themselves as taking policy decisions in an attempt to meet governmental objectives. Thus, 'one man's policy is another man's implementation'.

The study of the ways in which policies are carried out is important to both academic political scientists and active practitioners of politics. Political scientists have become increasingly concerned with the concept of power and the making of policy decisions, but have sometimes assumed that the task of applying those policies is purely technical or administrative. It has been left to other academic disciplines such as sociology, social administration and law, to point to the importance of discretion. Freedom to decide as they see fit is given to those who are carrying out policy products, and is necessary even in the case of what appear to be the most simple tasks. Indeed, it is arguable that every decision taken, however trivial, involves discretion – or it is not a decision at all, but merely an entirely predictable and programmable event (G. Smith in Adler and Asquith, 1981, pp. 47–8).

The interpretation of government policy products involves discretion being delegated to particular people deemed capable of acting as interpreters. Adler and Asquith distinguish three types of discretion – professional, administrative and lay – each having its own problems (Adler and Asquith, 1981, Ch. 1). Professional discretion is traditionally given to doctors to diagnose and treat the ill, teachers to teach, and chief constables to organize policing systems. This is in line with the technocratic view of policy making discussed in Chapter 2. It results in professionals having a considerable amount of autonomy; consequently large areas of public policy are subject to limited or minimal public control and are, in effect, determined by professionals (Wilding, 1982, Ch. 2). Doctors, for example, decide what is or is not an illness needing treatment. This is not the clear-cut technical issue that it may seem. Some years ago, American psychiatrists concluded that homosexuality was a disease. They did so by show of hands in a vote at their annual congress!

Administrative discretion has always been both more rule-bound and more open to challenge. Ombudsmen, for example, can investigate only the administrative actions of teachers and doctors, and not their professional work. Politicians and lay members of statutory bodies tend to focus their attention on administrative issues, rather than on the professional content of a policy, and demands for tighter rules and procedures are the normal response to tragedies such as baby battering. Administrators can be sacked or moved to other work much more easily than can professionals: indeed, periodic movement from job to job is normal in the civil service. The rationale for administrative discretion was given in Chapter 2, in the discussion on the bureaucratic power view of policy making.

Lay discretion is found in tribunals, magistrates' courts, local authorities and statutory bodies. 'It rarely poses a threat to professional or official domination or control' (Adler and Asquith, 1981, pp. 30–1), because lay bodies tend generally to accept and act upon the professional and administrative advice they receive from their officials, who in turn seek to present a united front. A local or health authority's 'team' of officers is well aware that its collective and individual discretion is likely to be maximized by its presenting an agreed set of recommendations. Of course, during its search for consensus, which involves some individual loss of autonomy, the team will take into account the likely reactions of the lay members to any recommendations. The importance attached to these 'anticipated reactions' as a measure of lay influence is apparent, but is particularly hard to assess or research.

What is clear is that government does not always get its way, that its power is limited. The constraints which operate on government during the formulation of policy may also influence the carrying out of that policy. Concepts of power, authority and values are just as appropriate here as earlier. A deliberately narrow but detailed study of the limits of administration concludes that administrative factors are seldom the critical limitation affecting the application of policy and that 'many contemporary "administrative" problems lie basically in schizophrenic social and political attitudes' (Hood, 1976, p. 206). For academics, then, the carrying out of policy is important because it is a critical process.

The practitioner of politics would not dispute any of this. He particularly wants explanations of what are commonly viewed as failures to carry through policy. Many industrial and economic policies, for example, have apparently not been successful in the last 20 years, so practitioners have become increasingly concerned with the factors affecting the success of policy and of its application. They need, in particular, to know whether the policy is inappropriate, or whether problems of applying it account for the policy failure. If the latter, are those problems soluble and can the process of carrying them out be improved? After all, obtaining 'power' is of little value if that power cannot be effectively exercised, and a knowledge of the limits of power should help to ensure that a realistic political agenda is pursued. Seemingly good ideas are of little use if they can never be put into effect.

For scholars and practitioners alike, this is an important subject. To help unravel its complexities, we propose first to review the means of carrying out policies before going on to consider their effectiveness.

THE MEANS OF CARRYING OUT POLICIES

In order to get their policies carried out, governments attempt to modify, regulate and control human behaviour. Put bluntly, like that, it is immediately apparent that problems will inevitably arise. None of us likes to feel 'controlled', yet we are. For much of the time this is accepted, perhaps without even being noticed — most of us drive on the left automatically and only complain (or even think about it) when we arrive in Calais or St Malo. Normally, awareness of policies is only manifested when policy changes are being considered: we can safely predict that controversy over the enforced wearing of car seat belts will quickly lessen, as was the case with the then controversial introduction of compulsory crash helmets for motorcyclists, regular MOT tests on vehicles, and the breathalyser.

In part, then, the carrying out of policy is related to control. How does government attempt to control its citizens? If an individual cannot hope to oversee (seeing or hearing) more than a dozen or so other individuals, is it realistic for government to attempt to regulate and control the actions of millions? How does it do this? Aren't breakdowns in control inevitable?

The control machinery available to government can be described in three ways. The first, and most general, approach is from the point of view of the sanctions used. Second, there are the methods of control which are operated. A third approach is to consider the nature of the policy product on the grounds that the machinery for one type of product may not be appropriate for other types. We consider each in turn.

Sanctions

The key distinction is between negative and positive sanctions. Negative sanctions usually involve the threatened or actual use of force, including imprisonment, withdrawal of a licence to drive, compulsory service in the forces or work in the community, and even dismissal from work. The direct nature of negative sanctions provides a clear and unambiguous link between the action of government and its application to the citizenry.

Negative sanctions both restrict and modify behaviour. People are prevented from doing certain things, and do other things because they fear the consequences of not doing them. However, though they can be used to change behaviour, they do not necessarily change attitudes, and this is an important weakness. Indeed, negative sanctions can generate widespread hostility which, in turn, reduces the degree of support for the regime or government. Classic examples include the

French 1939—45 Resistance, underground dissident movements in the USSR, and the activities of the IRA in Northern Ireland.

In contrast, positive sanctions seem, at first sight far more desirable in that they are behaviour inducing. They involve persuasion and bargaining, the objective being to get citizens to do things because they are convinced that they are in their best interests. Positive sanctions are indirect: government shapes the environment in which citizens live and hence shapes the values of citizens. Superficially, they seem to be the mark of a free society, to build up regime support, and to accord with the pluralist view of policy making.

In practice, positive sanctions are not quite as ideal as this analysis suggests. A key drawback is that, because they operate indirectly, their success in shaping behaviour is less certain than was the case with negative sanctions. Thus they dilute the authority of the regulator, because he has to make concessions or bargains in order to achieve his objectives. Take, for example, government policy on improving the quality of the housing stock. Successive governments have long preferred positive sanctions such as improvement grants to the negative approach of compulsory repairs on pain of heavy fines or imprisonment. But the low take-up of grants and the poor state of many houses suggests that the use of positive sanctions has not worked as well as had been hoped (Berthoud and Brown, 1981, pp. 188—9).

Other features of positive sanctions which some find unsatisfactory relate to the techniques which may be used to induce particular forms of behaviour or sets of attitudes. Censorship of news and opinions is understandable during international conflicts like that in the Falkland Islands in 1982, but is unlikely to disappear entirely when peace is restored. Certainly, propaganda and persuasion play a part in governments 'selling' public policies to their citizens. Government has established a large-scale public relations machinery of press officers attached to each ministry and specialist departments like the Central Office of Information. It seeks, usually successfully, to ensure that its message is relayed by the media and through its own publications. Its public pronouncements are supplemented by private briefings of journalists, one group of whom (known as 'the lobby') meet ministers and the Prime Minister's Press Secretary literally every day. Newspapers conventionally refer to 'Whitehall sources' or 'sources close to the government' (Tunstall, 1970).

Patronage is another controversial technique. A place in the Honours List, appointment to the magistracy or one of the many statutory bodies, or selection as a member of the Cabinet may be used to influence the attitudes and values of some citizens, or reward people for supporting the regime or government. But patronage can be interpreted more broadly and can go beyond these examples, in that quite junior public officials can effectively decide who obtains, or benefits from, public policy products. Doctors' receptionists, for example, can ration health care by deciding who does and does not see the doctor (Foster, 1979). Their techniques may encourage citizens to cooperate, to queue in an orderly manner, or to refrain from complaining for fear of subsequent victimization.

Form of Control

Not all policy products are expressed in a clear and unambiguous manner, and not all are legally enforceable. It is indeed a common fallacy that all government policy is enshrined in Acts of Parliament and that parliamentary approval is necessary before policy changes can be brought about. Most aspects of foreign and economic policy, for example, are introduced without legislation. So, too are some social policies — community care and preventive health care are two instances.

Those policy products which do conform to criteria of clarity and legality we can label *formal*. Parents must ensure that their children receive education. If they do not they can be taken to court and, if absence from school continues, their child could be taken into care. Cars must satisfy regulations about the number and size of lights, and owners must have a vehicle excise licence. These are examples of formal controls.

On close investigation, we find far fewer formal controls than many would expect. Most rules involve a degree of ambiguity and most legislation has to be interpreted when it is being carried out. 'Rules' which do not receive any formal ratification, or maybe even scrutiny, are developed. These can be variously titled standards, conventions, codes of conduct or guidelines. Such controls we call *informal*. They embrace encouragement by ministers to health authorities to develop community care services, guidance to junior immigration officials on what questions may be put to potential immigrants, codes of conduct on picketing, and criteria for the award of discretionary payments by supplementary benefit officers. Parliamentary or local authority scrutiny of this type of informal control may be limited to instances of public controversy as happened, for example in 1981 when allegations of virginity testing at immigration centres were made. For the most part, however, these informal controls are developed by those carrying out policy and not by top politicians.

The distinction between formal and informal controls is a valuable one, but is not clear-cut. Many policy products are carried out through a combination of the two. Unfit housing is an example. Parliament has authorized local public health officers to declare houses 'unfit for human habitation' when they fail to meet ten criteria listed in legislation (Buxton, 1970, p. 123). The interpretation of the ten, and the weight to be accorded to each, are matters of local decision. What constitutes 'dampness' or 'lack of natural light'? Even though appeals to the minister are possible, there remains considerable variation from area to area.

The distinctions we have made so far in this section — positive and negative sanctions, formal and informal controls — cannot, then, be regarded as watertight or mutually exclusive. It is best to view them as categories devised to aid analysis and as ideal types which fall at the ends of a continuum (T. Sharpe, cited in Adler and Asquith, 1981, p. 95). Usually one element tends to be dominant in any particular policy application, but others will also be apparent. The advantage of categorization is that it enables us to construct a diagram within which we can classify policy areas, particular types of policy initiative, or regimes. This we do in Figure 7.1.

Like all attempts at classifying the infinitely varied world of politics, the diagram can be criticized as crude. Yet we believe that it does offer some useful insights into the problems of carrying out policies, and into why it is that controls and sanctions are often not applied fully or effectively. In particular, the amount of discretion that lies in the hands of officials is pinpointed and we contend that discretion is a major reason for policy failure. On the other hand, the diagram also indicates problems which arise when discretion is limited. In the top left quarter, we see the combination of formal and negative systems. This can produce policies that fail to take proper account of local needs and changing circumstances and that are highly unpopular and so carried out by use of force or directives. Citizen allegiance to the regime and its policy products may be undermined.

By contrast, the bottom right quarter illustrates the mixture of informal and positive systems. Those who carry out policies have great powers, but at the cost of their not being fully accountable for their actions, which will not necessarily meet the objectives of the original policy makers. And treatment of individual cases will vary from official to official, from place to place, and from day to day. At some point this begins to conflict with what J. T. Winkler describes as 'the predominant interpretation in Britain for many years...that one of the defining characteristics of the liberal state was the rule of law, not men' (in Adler and Asquith, 1981, p. 83). Possibly worst of all is the bottom left quarter combination of negative sanctions and informal controls. In such 'petty tyrannies', harsh and unpredictable behaviour by uncontrollable and unaccountable officials result in neither allegiance to the regime nor the effective carrying out of policy.

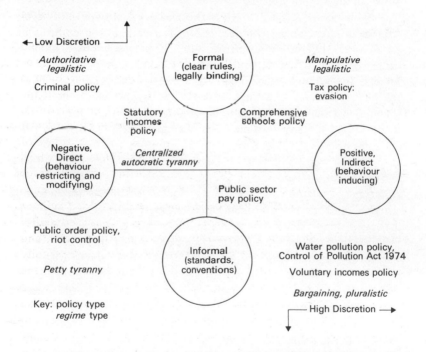

FIGURE 7.1 *Controls, Sanctions, Regimes and Policy Types*

Winkler goes on to claim that 'a large number of people, in a large number of different ways, are concerned about the growing size, power, secrecy and discretion of the state' (p. 133). Certainly, we can discern a trend in Britain towards the informal/positive mix of controls, with its emphasis (see Figure 7.1) on discretion and bargaining. Indications include increased use of delegated legislation, of laws which deal with standards, conventions and guidelines rather than with precise rules (recent examples are the Health and Safety at Work and the Control of Pollution Acts), and of conciliatory and bargaining agencies (such as the Race Relations and Equal Opportunities Commissions). The shaping of policy outcomes is placed more and more in the hands of those we have traditionally called administrators. This may be unavoidable in a complex world of large-scale interventionist government. It does, however, raise some key constitutional issues. Who, in effect, decides policy? To whom are such policy makers accountable? How can they be controlled?

At this point we need to view the means of carrying out policies from a different angle. Our discussion of sanctions and controls has raised several interesting problems, but their precise nature is likely to vary according to the particular policy product under review. This is because the methods used to carry out policies will not always be the same. In particular, the main types of policy product identified in Chapter 1 (rules and regulations; goods, services and transfer payments) each have their own methods of application.

Type of Policy Product

Rules and regulations. These clearly require techniques for detecting whether rules are being broken, and machinery for ensuring that they are maintained. Hence, public authorities are concerned with surveillance and enforcement. Their officials 'police' the carrying out of rules and regulations.

Some 'policemen' administer or apply rules and regulations, others watch over or inspect the activities of officials or private citizens responsible for this administration or application. The first type includes, among others, the 96,000 inland revenue and customs and excise officials identified in Chapter 4, social security officers, and (of course) our 100,000 policemen. Concerning the second type, no fewer than 54 inspectorates were identified in a recent study, of which 44 had no other tasks but inspection and surveillance (Rhodes, 1981, Appendix 2). These 44 embraced 18,000 staff, the largest being 5,570 environmental health officers and 4,110 building control inspectors, both employed by local authorities. Among the best known are the 452 Her Majesty's inspectors of education, 41 fire brigade inspectors and

630 auditors of local authority accounts (the 'district auditors' who, for example, surcharged and drove from office the councillors of Clay Cross in 1973 for excessive subsidization of council house rents). Chronologically, the oldest is the (one person) anatomy inspector, founded in 1832, and the youngest (1975) the five diving inspectors.

In addition to machinery for enforcement and surveillance, the carrying out of rules and regulations also involves determining the precise and proper application of a rule. Universal rules have to be applied to particular circumstances, and there will sometimes be ambiguity or uncertainty. Mechanisms for interpretation are therefore necessary.

Sometimes those who police also interpret; in other instances 'judges' or 'referees' are introduced to interpret or arbitrate between conflicting views about the meaning and pertinence of a rule. In a particular policy area, there may well be a combination of the two types with the initial interpretation being made by a 'policeman' but appeal to a 'judge' being possible, as in the case of the rateable value of a property where the district valuer has to justify his decision before a tribunal if the owner is dissatisfied. Indeed, another trend in Britain has been the development of a large-scale system, of 'administrative law' to arbitrate between conflicting interpretations of rules and regulations (Hill, 1976, Ch. 7). Today tribunals handle many thousands of cases, but some of the advantages they were said to have over the official legal system are in doubt. Often hearings have become quite formal, and the uses of precedent and of legal representation have grown (Donnison, 1982, pp. 45–6). One study has also doubted the impartiality of chairmen of Supplementary Benefit Tribunals (R. Lister quoted in Adler and Asquith, 1981, p. 31).

The legal system, too, is concerned with interpretation, though it also has important enforcement functions. The English concept of individual case law, guided by precedent as interpreted by judges, gives those judges an important role in the carrying out of policy. 'Judges make law through the development of the common law and through the process of statutory interpretation: what an Act of Parliament means' (Griffith, 1977, pp. 15–16). Like Lister, Griffith is also concerned about impartiality. He claims to detect a judicial conception of 'the public interest' which upholds the activities of the state, property rights, and 'certain political views normally associated with the Conservative Party', and cites numerous cases in support of this thesis (Griffith, 1977, pp. 169–70, 175–6, 182, 195, 200). Whether or not he is correct, it is apparent that the judiciary is becoming increasingly involved in political issues both through court cases and through the appointment of individual judges to hold inquiries into events in which social or economic judgments need to be made: Lord Scarman's Report on the 1981 Brixton riots is a recent example (Scarman, 1982).

Because rules and regulations necessarily require surveillance, enforcement and interpretation by people close to, or with subsequent knowledge of, their point of application, the exact results will vary according to the context. Precise prediction is not possible. This implies a dilution in the control of those higher in the policy-making hierarchy, and the possibility that policy will not be carried out as originally intended. It also raises questions about the attitudes and values which are brought to bear on the application of policy, and about the public accountability of quite lowly officials who are in effect shaping policy through the sum of their decisions. This weakens the conventional view of policy making, with its emphasis on the accountability of the formal institutions of government.

Goods, services and transfer payments. An important aspect of these policy products has been covered in the previous section in that all such items, and particularly transfer payments, require rules and regulations which specify their proper distribution in society by indicating levels and standards of policy products and individual entitlements to services and cash benefits.

Additionally, there needs to be a machinery for organizing and distributing these policy products. Large-scale public goods and services require large-scale machinery. If the services provided are at least to approximate to the levels intended, such machinery requires three sets of characteristics: command and organization; communication and information; and planning and provision. We consider each in turn.

A common 'ideal type' of command and organization is through a hierarchy of officials in which subordinates respond to the orders of their seniors. The classical pyramid has each senior responsible for a number of subordinates. Thus, an assistant secretary in the civil service may be one of five or six working to a particular under secretary; and a section head in a local authority department has several clerical officers under him. The under secretary and section head, though very different in status, salary and level of responsibility, perform basically similar tasks. They must, again, in theory, receive and interpret orders from their seniors, clearly articulate their own commands, ensure that these are intelligently received, and monitor the activities of their subordinates to ensure that these match their commands and that feedback about the application of those commands is being received.

Effective command structures, then, imply the existence of some means of gathering and communicating information. Information is needed about the operations of the organization and the detailed application of policy if those in command are to monitor progress and issue new orders designed to ensure that actual and intended provision of services are closely related. Good information and effective communication help to ensure that policy products are fully carried out.

Thirdly, the raw materials of the policy product must be provided, and plans must be made for their continued provision. However good the command structure and communication and information system, a service cannot be provided without adequate resources. The health service is dependent upon doctors, nurses, medical equipment and buildings; transfer payments come from money in the bank or Giro. Ideally, the right resources must be available at the right time and in the proper form, and resources must be committed in advance through careful planning. A 600-bed general hospital, for example, is likely to take about a decade to complete, and construction needs to be in sequence with roads, kitchens and boilerhouses preceding nurses' homes and laboratories. Wards and outpatient facilities come later. When completed, the hospital will need a constant supply of money, manpower, drugs and equipment. Planning all these events is a complex technical exercise. It also has major political implications, for it commits future policy makers to provide the necessary resources. Perhaps it is not surprising that some policy programmes do not get carried out as intended, and that delays and modifications to plans are common.

In Chapter 2 we explored the rational view of policy making and commented that it had become very fashionable in the 1960s. The need for planning was an aspect of rationality which particularly appealed to academics, politicians and senior advisers. The Fulton Report on the civil service (1968) called for 'planning units' in each ministry, but these were never appointed (Booth, 1982, pp. 198–9). Planning systems – plans for particular services, often drawn up by local authorities and statutory bodies at the request of ministers – did, however, mushroom. More than 20 were established in the 1970s, but they were badly co-ordinated with each having its own timetable, procedures and data base (Glennerster, 1981).

This fragmentation of planning partly reflects the overall structure of government. The administrative diffusion and dispersion view of policy making emphasized that a consequence of fragmentation was difficulty in actually getting things done. In practice, few goods and services are provided by a single command structure, and responsibility for some transfer payments (rate and rent rebates, for example) is also divided. To put it starkly, few ministers are ultimately in command of the goods they promise. Housing ministers do not build or repair houses, the Department of Education does not run schools, and the health and social services are not provided by the Department of Health and Social Security.

The consequences for the carrying out of policy are considerable. Each separate agency will have its own objectives, timescales and relationships, and conflicts between agencies are likely from time to time. To this must be added the inevitable human element in that, within a single hierarchy, people will not always work well together. Competition for promotion, petty jealousies, failure to respond to requests from unpopular colleagues, and human errors mean that, to use our own ideal-type language, commands will not always be 'clearly articulated' and 'intelligently received'. The longer the hierarchy, the greater the potential problem, for at each level, messages are in effect interpreted and filtered. Commands passing down the organization and data passing up it are both affected by this process of filtering.

These features of fragmentation and of human behaviour come together to make the carrying out of policy difficult. Government policy of improving services for the mentally ill offers a good example. Due to resource limitations, organizational problems and personal attitudes, the policy worked slowly:

....the reorganisations of the health and social services in the 1970s have left mental health services fragmented among an extended network of public agencies. Policy leadership is attenuated by the existence of many tiers of management between central government and the staff involved in service delivery; and by the significant role at the periphery played by professionals claiming discretion over key aspects of service provision. In addition, the large hospitals which form the core of the old pattern of services are commonly regarded as highly resistant to change (D. Towell in Barrett and Fudge, 1981, pp. 183–205).

Sadly, the 1982 reorganization of the NHS has done little to reduce this organizational fragmentation, and resources remain scarce.

For analytical purposes, we have categorized three ways of studying the means of carrying out public policy products, according to the sanctions used, the nature of controls, and the type of product. Though this is, we believe, helpful as an aid to analysis, we must again emphasize that, in practice, such categories are not always distinct. A particular programme is likely to embrace many of their features: transfer payments, for example, involve several types of sanction and control, and embrace a number of policy products.

Our review of the methods of carrying out policy has touched on some of the problems which can arise. We have suggested that it is by no means inevitable that policies get applied in the manner intended. If this is so, and we believe that there is strong supporting evidence, then an important aspect of academic study is to consider the effectiveness of the carrying out of policy. We do this by looking, first, at what can go wrong, and second, at why things go wrong.

THE EFFECTIVENESS OF CARRYING OUT POLICIES

What can go wrong?

It is already clear, that, when it comes to carrying out policies, there are bound to be problems. The idea of full or complete application at the very least assumes the existence of a perfect system of administration and crystal clear policies, but in the world of everyday, practical politics, neither of these conditions is likely to apply. It seems virtually certain that something will go wrong.

Broadly, there are three possibilities. There may be a failure to carry out policies, long delay, or consequences which were unintended. In all three instances any evaluation of the degree of success in carrying out the policy must be based on the objectives of that policy. Unless we know what was intended, we cannot judge whether or not a policy has succeeded. Unfortunately, however, we have already found out that objectives are commonly unstated, ambiguous or even in conflict with one another. They range, as we saw in Chapter 2, from broad political to general and specific policy objectives and it is difficult to disentangle them. Judgments about effectiveness can only be made on the basis of stated objectives, and confidence in any judgment must depend on both the rigours of the analysis and the extent to which there are clearly stated goals.

Total failure to carry out policy, our first possibility, clearly arises when a government loses power and its successors repeal a policy not yet carried out. Local election results have led to the cancellation of decisions about changes in bus fares, council house rents, and the employment of private contractors to run municipal services such as refuse collection. Nationally, three post-war Labour governments legislated to reduce profits made from land ownership, but Conservative successors reversed the policy before it was fully carried out (Barrett and Fudge, 1981, pp. 65–86). Conclusions about failure to carry out policies are relatively clear-cut in such cases.

More difficult is to disentangle broad from specific policy goals, for the former can lead to the creation of new policies for largely symbolic reasons and a specific policy failure can be claimed as a symbolic policy success. For example, in 1981, the Conservative government announced its intention of forcing a local authority to hold a referendum if it wished to raise the level of rates between its annual budgets. This led to a major political row. Many Conservative politicians viewed the policy as an unacceptable attack on the traditional financial autonomy of councils, and threatened to oppose it. The government retreated, withdrew its Bill and replaced it by another containing different proposals for dealing with councils which were, allegedly, overspending. Was there a policy failure here? Certainly, the referendum plan was never carried out. On the other hand, the broader objective of restricting local governments' financial autonomy may still have been met by the second Bill, and the referendum plan can be seen as merely symbolic of the government's determination to clip councils' wings.

Our second possibility relates to delay. Of course, what is or is not an excessively long time in carrying out policies involves judgment, for scarcely ever do stated objectives give a clear timescale. Whilst Acts of Parliament and statutory instruments come into force on a particular date, they are frequently little more than enabling measures, bare bones on which the flesh is later added. It would, for example, be unrealistic to expect the 1974 Control of Pollution Act to lead to clean rivers immediately, for industry must be given time to improve its methods of processing waste by-products. On the other hand, by 1982, certain sections of the Act had still not been brought into operation and seemed to be in abeyance, and other sections vested considerable discretion in the hands of officials, some of whom acted slowly (Richardson, 1982). Other examples of delays which seem to be longer than had been intended might include the raising of the school leaving age to 16 (in the 1944 Act, carried out 28 years later), and the continued existence of urban areas still not in smokeless zones despite the 1956 Clean Air Act (Scarrow, 1972).

Thirdly, policies may be carried out but with unforeseen or unintended consequences which, at least in part, are contrary to the original policy objectives. Governments seek to modify human behaviour, but cannot necessarily predict accurately human response to policy products. Weaknesses in their analysis are usually apparent with hindsight. It now seems obvious that the restriction on office building in London in 1965 through the introduction of office development certificates, would cause rents and developers' profits to rise, yet the opposite seems to have been one of the aims (Wehrmann, 1978). Also in 1965, the Rent Act sought to give security to private tenants and to keep their rents down. This led to a reduction in the amount of rented accommodation and to the introduction of devices not covered by the Act, like service charges which, to a tenant, effectively meant a rent rise (Banting, 1979, pp. 62–5).

Housing policy is riddled with examples of unintended consequences. General improvement areas (GIAs), introduced in 1969, were intended to help the urban poor. In GIAs grants towards house improvement were set at a high level (up to 90 per cent of the cost at one time), and councils could undertake environmental work to improve the local quality of life still further. Two major unintended consequences resulted. First, some of the urban poor could not afford to pay even their modest share of the costs (Lambert *et al*, 1978, Ch. 5). Secondly there was an incentive, particularly in London, for prosperous middle-class households to move into such areas. Areas like Barnsbury, Fulham and Canonbury rapidly became 'gentrified' as existing citizens were persuaded to move out. Long-standing working-class communities were broken up (Lambert and Weir, 1975, pp. 366–73; Lansley, 1979, pp. 228–36).

Our discussion of the three types of policy failure, separated for purpose of analysis but in practice often overlapping, has produced a considerable amount of further empirical evidence in support of the thesis that policy is unlikely to be carried out as intended. The earlier material, on sanctions, controls and policy products, introduced mainly conceptual evidence (such as the idea of a perfect administrative system) relevant to the same thesis. We now gather together many of the threads contained in these earlier sections by asking the final question: why is it so difficult to carry out policies as originally intended?

Why is it difficult to apply public policies?

Again, it is convenient to isolate and itemize, even though in a particular case a mix of factors will probably apply. We identify seven main reasons which emerge from the earlier discussions.

First, there is the problem, common to most policies, of *ambiguity*. We have already seen, both in this chapter and in Chapter 2, that there are three types of policy objectives; that objectives may be unclear, unstated or even incompatible with one another; and that it is only comparatively recently that governments have begun to state explicitly (some of) their policy objectives. Partly, the problem of clarity is linguistic. Language is imprecise and words can change their meaning over time. The concept of 'unreasonable' behaviour by a local educa-tion authority, for example, was expected, by those who formulated the 1944 Education Act, to apply to relations with individual parents. In 1976 the Education Minister sought to apply it to a whole policy when attempting to prevent Tameside Borough Council from reinstat-ing grammar schools. The courts found against the Minister, but not because the 'unreasonable' clause could not apply to general policies (Griffith, 1977, pp. 126–9).

Lack of clarity in stated policy objectives is also partly deliberate. For political and administrative reasons, it is almost always convenient to have room to manoeuvre and to avoid taking too precise a position on a particular issue. Far better to outline a general strategy than set specific targets, as in the case of the policy of reallocating health care resources in favour of underprovided regions. No clear timescale has been set and individual policy decisions which run counter to the strategy can be explained away as mere hiccups (an argument made in 1982 in justification of poorer regions having to find more resources than overprovided ones to meet health workers' pay claims).

Incompatible stated objectives were apparent when local govern-ment was reformed in 1974. Two aims were to introduce a 'clear-cut' system and to keep responsibility 'as close to the people as possible'. The first suggested that services like transportation should be run by a single local authority, the second that some aspects might be provided by one authority and others by another (strategic planning, for example, is best over a wide area but decisions on planning applications could be taken locally). This incompatibility was apparent during debates on the 1972 Local Government Act, with the clear-cut objective frequently taking a back seat and a complex system being the result (Wood, 1976, pp. 185–7).

Ambiguity affects accountability. Institutions particularly concerned with accountability – parliamentary select committees, ombudsmen, major interest groups, the judiciary – frequently face difficulties in establishing who is responsible for particular policy decisions, what is the nature and extent of that responsibility, and what were the aims of the policy, when seeking to judge success, or legality.

A second area of difficulty lies in *relating general rules to particular situations*. Circumstances vary from case to case, yet a rule has to be applied. This process of application may involve a rule being refined or reinterpreted to suit the particular circumstances. A succession of detailed decisions can modify the original policy. A January 1982 regulation, for example, insisted that goods in shops be labelled according to their country of origin. An immediate problem facing local trading standards officers was how to label goods made up from materials from several different countries or goods assembled in Britain from imported components. Their interpretations may result in many largely imported goods being labelled 'Made in Britain', which is not what the policy makers had in mind.

Interpretation of policy products is normally delegated to those at the point of application, as in the case above where local officials effectively decide on how best to carry out a policy. We pointed out when discussing discretion on p. 170, that a consequence is that government's powers are limited. In particular, policy will not always be carried out as originally intended because those exercising discretion believe that policy to be inappropriate without modification, or because it is so unclear as to leave those intentions in some doubt. In the latter instance, those with discretion are effectively full-blooded policy makers.

The third problem is one of *enforcement*. Enforcement officers lack the capacity to 'police' all the potential points at which policies and rules can be undermined or broken. In Chapter 4 (p. 93) we saw that each year only 3 per cent of tax returns from the self-employed are examined thoroughly, and that the average VAT outlet is inspected only every five years. Other enforcement agencies (categorized on pp. 176–7) face the same logistical problems.

Two consequences follow from this excess of potential rule breaking over and above the capacity to prevent it. First, 'policemen' often depend on information received from the public. Second, they are necessarily forced to concentrate their limited resources in particular areas which *they* consider to be priorities for surveillance and enforcement. Both consequences result in differential enforcement, and make the attitudes and values of informers and 'policemen' significant determinants of enforcement activities. Public values may condone income tax evasion more than fraudulent claims for social security benefits, for example, with the result that the benefits system is more rigorously policed than are tax returns. The values of 'policemen' will cause them to concentrate on some parts of policy at the expense of others. The police service itself offers excellent examples. Some forces actively seek out drug offences, homosexuality, pornography and prostitution, but not necessarily because these are greater in their areas than elsewhere. The Chief Constable of Greater Manchester publicly stated his intention of leading a drive against such crimes and deployed a plain clothes squad to observe public conveniences for cases of gross indecency. Effectively the police had decided, on the basis of their judgments or prejudices, where to detect crime. Because of these two consequences, a consistent approach to enforcement and surveillance is, therefore, not possible.

Fourth, *the future is uncertain.* Policy has to be carried out in circumstances different from those which existed when it was first debated, and those changed circumstances cannot be accurately predicted. The 1974 local government reforms were designed during a period of prosperity and a growing public sector, and the new structure was geared to growth which never took place due to the onset of the economic recession. Professor Donnison faced similar problems on appointment as Chairman of the Supplementary Benefits Commission: the traditional framework of assumptions about the economic and social structure of society was being eroded, with consequences for anti-poverty policy (Donnison, 1982, pp. 18—26). At the very least, fine tuning of policies is necessary from time to time; in other cases whole policy products may become obsolete. Inbetween these extremes are cases like the proposed expansion of teacher training and obstetric health care facilities where policies needed to be halted or reversed when the birthrate dropped sharply from 1972. The relevance of economic policy also had to be dramatically reappraised in the 1970s when massive increases in energy costs changed the Western economic system almost overnight.

From these examples, it is clear that some changes make whole policies inappropriate. Our point in relation to the carrying out of policy is that *all* changes affect the application of policy and can mean that policies are not carried out as intended, and that those responsible for carrying out policies have more influence than had been expected. The growing mass of discretionary social security payments, for example, so overwhelmed local offices in the 1970s that 'they invented their own rules of thumb', such as giving a grant only every six months, or freely giving up to £20 but investigating claims for more. Claimants in some offices were 10 or even 20 times more likely to succeed than those elsewhere, a result quite contrary to the policy of equitable treatment (Donnison, 1982, p. 44).

A fifth area of difficulty stems from *problems of managing large-scale organizations and operations*. When discussing the idea of a 'perfect' organization on pp. 178—9, we became aware that, in practice, perfection is an impossibility even when all concerned are genuinely seeking to work together efficiently. This is doubly the case when there are people involved who do not support policies they are supposed to be carrying out. Lord Scarman found that some junior London policemen were racially prejudiced, though the senior officers were not, and that such prejudice 'does manifest itself occasionally in the behaviour of a few officers on the streets' (Scarman, 1982, para.4.63). This, of course, is quite contrary to public policy on race relations. Chapman cites numerous civil service examples of activity being deliberately delayed by using a range of devices and ruses (Chapman, 1979, Part I).

We also identified fragmented responsibility as an organizational problem of the large modern state. In a study of a programme to bring jobs to the long-term unemployed of Oakland, California, an attempt was made to quantify the consequences of fragmentation. The project involved 15 different groups, 30 major decision points and 70 separate agreements. The authors calculated than an 80 per cent probability of agreement (which they considered to be very high) would make the chances of completing the whole project less than one in a million! To obtain a 50—50 chance of completion, each agreement needed a 99 per cent probability of acceptance (Pressman and Wildavsky, 1973, pp. 102—10). It is tempting to conclude that one answer is to consolidate organizations so that one and not 15 groups would be involved in a programme. Consolidation, however, involves the creation of large bureaucracies with their own internal weaknesses. It can also mean a reduction in accountability and local responsibility. The 1974 amalgamations, for example, arguably took local government further away from the people. One analysis is that this was against the interests of working people because power became concentrated in the hands of highly paid officers and the few lay people with the necessary time, usually middle-class professionals or business people (Dearlove, 1979).

Sixth, the successful application of public policy frequently depends on *citizen compliance*, and this is variable. In Chapter 3 we identified support as the key resource of the state. In Britain, the use of coercion and fear to obtain support is unusual, and government relies on willing cooperation through positive sanctions and indirect controls (see Figure 7.1), particularly in the case of social policies. A consequence is differential obedience. The extent to which citizen compliance is central to the carrying out of policy can determine the fate of that policy, for take-up of policy products will vary (see Chapter 8). For example, council houses are modernized by local authorities whether or not tenants wish for such changes, whereas private houses are only modernized when occupants choose to modernize. Citizen compliance is not a key factor in the first case; it is crucial to the second.

The seventh, and final, factor is the *policy timetable*. Elected politicians' primary concern is with the short term. They hold office for only four years in the case of councillors and, at the longest, five if Members of Parliament. Members of statutory bodies tend to be appointed for between two and five years. Calculations show that ministers last, on average, for less than three years, and in the 37 years since the Second World War, there have been nine different Prime Ministers. It is, therefore, realistic to speak of the 'political timetable' as being one of 3–4 years.

The timetable for carrying out policy, however, is frequently far longer. Construction work may be necessary; training or retraining could be a factor; complex systems of administration might need to be established; it could be desirable to give the public advance warning of, and time to get used to, policy changes. Hence, over many years, there is a need to develop and maintain a momentum if a new policy is to be successfully applied. Local government reform took nine years, the overhaul of the social security system still had 'unfinished business' after five years (Wood, 1976, pp. 176–80; Donnison, 1982, pp. 53–4 and Ch. 7). The short-term interests and considerations of top politicians can cause problems for those responsible for carrying out policies when their timescale does not coincide with the political timetable. Policies for the development of hospitals, motorways and airports have all been modified during their application, and delays due to reductions in the allocation of resources are almost folklore.

Our aim in this section has been to identify common reasons why public policies are carried out only with difficulty. In any particular case study, a mixture of the seven factors is likely to apply. They are not mutually exclusive, and have been itemized both to aid analysis of particular cases and to indicate that there are, indeed, formidable barriers to be overcome before public policy is applied to society in the way policy makers intended.

CONCLUSION

The importance of studying the application of policy is now apparent. The conventional view that, once ratified, policy more or less looks after itself, clearly has no credibility. Delays and modifications can so severely reshape policy products as, in effect, to replace them: the carrying out of policy is itself policy making. This means that a good deal of power lies in the hands of those responsible for carrying out policy. Sometimes these people are citizens, whose compliance can be a prerequisite of success. Often they are public officials in large-scale organizational hierarchies and, as such, they are 'irresponsible'. This does not mean that they deliberately behave in an irresponsible manner. It does mean, however, that it is hard to make the system accountable. Controlling the behaviour of often very junior and lowly paid officials (such as clerks in social security offices, doctors' receptionists) is a difficult enough task for their immediate superiors, let alone for ministers, councillors and members of statutory public bodies.

Another group of officials who carry out policies are much more senior and have achieved a status which makes them just as difficult to control. A tradition of deference to professionals and to senior administrators means that their word tends to be accepted and that, in the case of professionals, they set their own standards and are judged by their peers rather than by lay people. Thus, only doctors can prevent other would-be doctors from practising. Again, the question of accountability arises, for it is arguable that doctors in effect run the health service; that teachers decide on levels and standards of education.

Accountability, then, is a major concern which emerges from our consideration of the carrying out of policy. Some of the views of policy making discussed in Chapter 2 now seem less appropriate, notably the conventional, the party government, and the pluralist approaches. The notion of stages of policy making contained in the rational view also conflicts with our conclusion that policy is continuously made, and that policy making cannot be separated from the application of policy. On the other hand, the administrative dispersion view is compatible with our analysis of the effect of fragmentation of responsibility on the carrying out of policy, incrementalism with our contention that policy is constantly being remade, and the bureaucratic power and technocratic views with the evidence about large-scale organizations and about discretion.

It is tempting to use the seven factors identified as barriers to policy application in order to come up with a set of conditions for the effective carrying out of policy. Hood does this, and so do Sabatier and Mazmanian (Hood, 1976, Ch. 1; Sabatier and Mazmanian, 1979). The latter list five conditions for 'effective implementation', including clear objectives, lack of ambiguity, the skill and commitment of implementers, the support of groups and politicians, and the continuation over time of the priority given to the policy. To these we can add from our own analysis and from other studies, the desirability of minimizing the number of decision points, the need for adequate resources, and the importance of establishing good monitoring techniques.

This prescriptive approach is something of an academic's 'recipe book'. Its weakness is that it lists conditions that are 'precisely those which empirical evidence suggests are not met in the real world' (Barrett and Fudge, 1981, p. 18). We are close to viewing the carrying out of policy as the near-mechanistic approach which we condemned as unrealistic at the start of the chapter. It is much more than a technical process of applying a clear set of rules and objectives. We go on in Chapter 8 to confirm that the way in which policy is applied can be an important factor in determining its impact on society.

TOPICS FOR DISCUSSION

1. How can discretionary powers be effectively controlled?
2. Examine the arguments for and against the use of formal controls and negative sanctions.

3. How do (a) public authorities and (b) teachers attempt to regulate student behaviour? With what degree of success?

4. In what sense and in what ways do police create crime and social workers produce social problems?

5. What factors determine whether or not citizens comply with public laws, rules and regulations?

6. How can the carrying out of policy be improved, and with what consequences for both government and citizens?

KEY READING

A useful survey of discretion is Adler and Asquith (eds) (1981). The issue of control in a bureaucracy is discussed in A. Dunsire, *Control in a Bureaucracy* (Martin Robertson, 1978) Chapters 3 and 4. On the surveillance and enforcement of rules see Hill (1976), Chapter 7, and Griffith (1977). The problems of providing goods and services are reviewed in Pressman and Wildavsky (1973), Chapters 5 and 6. Hood (1976) summarizes some of the problems of applying policy in his concluding chapter. So do Barrett and Fudge (eds) (1981) in Part One of a book which contains several useful empirical case studies.

REFERENCES

Adler, M. and Asquith, S. (eds) (1981) *Discretion and Welfare*, Heinemann.

Banting, K. (1979) *Poverty, Politics and Policy*, Macmillan.

Barrett, S. and Fudge, C. (eds) (1981) *Policy and Action*, Methuen.

Berthoud, R. and Brown J. C. (1981) *Poverty and the Development of Anti-Poverty Policy in the United Kingdom*, Heinemann.

Booth, T. A. (1982) 'Economics and the poverty of social planning', *Public Administration*, Vol. 60, No. 2.

Buxton, R. J. (1970) *Local Government*, Penguin.

Chapman, L. (1979) *Your Disobedient Servant*, Penguin.

Dearlove, J. (1979) *The Reorganisation of British Local Government*, Cambridge University Press.

Donnison, D. V. (1982) *The Politics of Poverty*, Martin Robertson.

Foster, P. (1979) 'The informal rationing of primary medical care', *Journal of Social Policy*, Vol. 8, No. 4.

Glennerster, H. (1981) 'From containment to conflict? Social planning in the seventies', *Journal of Social Policy*, Vol. 10. No. 1.

Griffith, J. A. G. (1977) *The Politics of the Judiciary*, Fontana.

Heclo, H. H. and Wildavsky, A. B. (1981) *The Private Government of Public Money*, Macmillan, 2nd edn.

Hill, M. J. (1976) *The State, Administration and the Individual*, Fontana.

Hood, C. C. (1976) *The Limits of Administration*, John Wiley.

Lambert, C. and Weir, D. T. (1975) *Cities in Modern Britain*, Fontana.

Lambert, J. *et al.* (1978) *Housing Policy and the State*, Macmillan.

Lansley, S. (1979) *Housing and Public Policy*, Croom Helm.

Pressman, J. L. and Wildavsky, A. B. (1973) *Implementation*, University of California Press.

Rhodes, G. (1981) *Inspectorates in British Government*, Allen & Unwin.

Richardson, G. (1982) 'Policing pollution: the enforcement process', *Policy and Politics*, Vol. 10, No. 3.

Sabatier, P. and Mazmanian, D. (1979) 'The conditions of effective implementation', *Policy Analysis*, Autumn.

Scarman, Lord (1982) *The Scarman Report: The Brixton Disorders, 10–12 April 1981*, Penguin.

Scarrow, H. A. (1972) 'The impact of British domestic air pollution legislation', *British Journal of Political Science*, Vol. 2, No. 3.

Tunstall, J. (1970) *The Westminster Lobby Correspondents*, Routledge & Kegan Paul.

Van Meter, D. and Van Horn, C. E. (1975) 'The policy implementation process: a conceptual framework', *Administration and Society*, Vol. 6, February.

Wehrmann, G. (1978) 'A policy in search of an objective', *Public Administration*, Vol. 56, No. 4.

Wilding, P. (1982) *Professional Power and Social Welfare*, Routledge & Kegan Paul.

Wood, B. (1976) *The Process of Local Government Reform 1966–74*, Allen & Unwin.

8

The Consequences of Government: Outcomes and Impact

Governments seek to affect the behaviour and lifestyle of citizens by modifying the distribution of resources in society. This much we have already ascertained in earlier chapters. But there we tended to focus on what government does, rather than on what people get in the way of policy products (with the notable exception of the case study of taxation in Chapter 4). It is this issue to which we now turn.

It is commonplace to hear or read about politicians' claims of policy 'success'. Speeches and public pronouncements, often drafted by senior officials with a personal interest in and responsibility for a particular policy area, are peppered with a seemingly impressive array of statistics purporting to show that policies are working as planned. Governments wish to be seen to be in control. The 1979 Conservative government, for example, pledged itself to reduce the number of civil servants and overall level of public expenditure and will naturally publicize data which indicates success and play down any evidence which suggests otherwise.

Earlier chapters have demonstrated the concern of politicians and officials with levels of expenditure, particularly in an era of world-wide economic recession. Much time is spent on policies about the acquisition and distribution of resources, and the carrying out of public policies. As political scientists we should be equally concerned to study the consequences for citizens. We need to ask (and hopefully, answer), questions about policy impact. Is the nation healthier or better educated as a consequence of government policy? Have all groups in society benefited from defence, law and order and social policies? Dye's analogy makes the point: 'we cannot be content with measuring how many times a bird flaps its wings, we must assess how far the bird has flown' (Dye, 1978, p. 312). Our contention is that the Policy Approach demands that attention be given to the outcomes of policy products as well as to those products themselves; that spending or staffing levels provide us with only a limited view of the consequences of public policy.

Questions about policy impact are usually much easier to ask than to answer. Evaluating the consequences of government is not simply a matter of obtaining precise statistics. Judgments have to be made about matters like the timescale over which to assess a policy. One policy may be affected by another, or by changes in the behaviour of society (better health, for example, may be a consequence of dietary and sanitary improvements as well as of modern medicine). Accurate evidence may be difficult to obtain because impact is what is felt and experienced by individual citizens who could find it hard to measure their feelings or even to recall their earlier lifestyle before the introduction of the particular policy being evaluated.

There are, then, considerable methodological problems to be overcome in the study of policy impact. And when we go beyond mere analysis and seek to evaluate policy we become confronted with another series of problems which may be termed moral and ethical. Analysis may show that new policies achieve certain sorts of change within society. Sexual behaviour, for example, may alter partly as a consequence of the availability on the NHS of free contraception. Evaluating the success of that policy involves making judgments about the desirability of such changes. Abstract notions of justice, fairness or equity arise when policies relating to poverty, employment, housing and law and order are assessed.

If there are these apparently enormous problems, why study policy impact? We see three reasons why such studies are essential, and are critical of the way in which many political science texts ignore the subject. First there is a pragmatic reason. It is important to ensure that governments get value for money, that policies are being carried out as intended and at reasonable cost. Secondly, there is a democratic reason. The conventional view of policy making emphasized the accountability of governments and policy makers. Their actions are based on certain (not always clearly stated) objectives, and the study of policy impact in part is designed to test whether or not these objectives have been achieved. Thirdly there is a moral reason. In order to assess or compare the performance of governments, we must be able to judge the extent to which citizens, and particular sectors of society, have been treated fairly or equitably, unfairly or inequitably.

For these reasons we believe studies of policy impact, however difficult they may be to undertake, to be one of the most important (and most neglected) tasks facing political scientists.

We now propose to separate two distinct approaches to the study of policy impact. First, we look at studies of the effectiveness of policy, at whether or not a policy has worked, is working, or is likely to work, and at reasons for any policy failure which is observed or predicted. From this we go on to consider studies of the distribution of policy products — who benefits and by how much? In both cases our aim is to discuss methods of study and to review studies that have been made. Our concern is to outline the factors to be considered when calculations or assessments of policy impact are made, the problems involved in making such assessments, and the conclusions reached by researchers about the consequences of public policy for the citizen.

THE EFFECTIVENESS OF POLICY

A fundamental distinction between effectiveness and distribution is that distribution can be measured and assessed without any knowledge of the aims of policy. Effectiveness, however, can only be assessed in relation to a set of objectives. A new car is effective if it matches the manufacturer's performance specification in terms of factors like acceleration, comfort, fuel consumption and maintenance costs. All are charted in the publicity material, and usually in a precise way. Public policies commonly lack such detailed objectives against which they can be judged and few are likely to be stated clearly in policy statements. Earlier, examples were given of unclear, unstated and even conflicting objectives.

In both this and the section on distribution we follow a two-part approach, looking both at public policy across the board and at particular policy areas, or even specific programmes. The latter more specialized and detailed approach may offer the greater chance of precise measurement of policy impact, but it is important to bear in mind that policies cannot realistically be viewed as discrete, separate entities. Collectively they make up a jigsaw, for each piece is affected by the shape and composition of other pieces. Hence the importance of looking at the whole of the puzzle as well as at the individual components.

Assessing Effectiveness Across All Policy Areas

In theory effectiveness across all policy areas can only be assessed against a set of overall policy goals. Rarely do governments produce such a set, though the advent of 'planning' and of interest in rational systems of policy making has led to a few examples. We consider two: the National Plan and the Social Report.

The 1964–70 Labour government drew up plans, while in opposition, for a restructuring of responsibility for the economy. One criticism had been that the Treasury was too concerned with short-term policies to be able to pursue long-term growth, something to which Labour was committed. The structural response was the creation of a separate Department of Economic Affairs, to be responsible for economic planning. At its head as Secretary of State was its most enthusiastic proponent Mr (now Lord) George Brown and among his main aims was the production of a National Plan which would challenge the Treasury 'tradition of making economic policy and industrial activity subject to all the inhibitions of orthodox monetary control' (Brown, 1972, p. 104). The plan, published in 1965, contained a set of economic goals, including the annual rate of growth of the economy (some 4 per cent) and the extent of investment in sectors such as manufacturing industry, as well as a specific timescale.

The National Plan turned out to be an example of ineffectiveness. Within a year of publication it was largely abandoned, when the government responded to an economic crisis by devaluation and cuts in public spending. Later the Department of Economic Affairs was wound up. From its outset, however, the plan had been criticized as being too concerned with setting target figures: its authors devoted time to 'arithmetic and presentation' rather than to *'policies* for faster growth' (Brittan, 1971, p. 317 – author's italics). By 1967 a document of little more than historical interest, the National Plan remains the first substantial and coherent British example of an across-the-board set of economic (but not social) objectives. It set targets by which economic performance and the effectiveness of government economic policy could later be judged. In a much more limited way, todays Medium-Term Financial Strategy (see Chapter 6) performs a similar function.

Another approach, pioneered in the USA, is the idea of a Social Report containing statistical indicators of policy achievement, and objectives or targets for future social policies. This came about in the 1960s as a reaction against the emphasis on measures of economic performance as indicators of social wellbeing, and a new fashion known as the 'Social Indicators Movement' was born (Carley, 1981, p. 1). Academics sought to develop groups of measurements which gave an accurate overall picture of the quality of life, and to integrate separate measures in an overall Social Report. One such system was made up of as many as 477 separate indicators (Carley, 1981, p. 49).

Social reporting rapidly received international recognition. Between 1970 and 1976 no fewer than 30 countries published documents on the state of society and quality of life, Britain leading the way with its annual *Social Trends*. Most of its 13 chapters reflect particular policy areas and, in addition, there are usually some general articles on developments in social indicators. In 1975 and 1980, for example, two looked at the inner city. The first concentrated on the problem of delimiting areas of deprivation while the second included a valuable section on difficulties of monitoring inner-city policies as well as an assessment of recent social and economic changes in those areas (Holtermann, 1975; Allnutt and Gelardi, 1980).

The theory of social reporting—the establishment of targets against which policies can later be judged for effectiveness—does not always accord with practice. *Social Trends*, for example, gives a good picture of the social state of the nation and allows us to quantify improvements in features like infant mortality rates and the ownership of consumer durables, but it does not list precise targets at which social policy is meant to be aiming. Indeed, government does not appear to have such targets across the board, though they may exist for some individual policy areas and experts may recommend them as in the case of five-year targets, recently outlined for preventive health (McCarthy, 1982). Claus Moser, head of the Central Statistical Office, sees a need to concentrate future research in social statistics on the identification of better performance measures and of clearer sets of policy objectives. He admits that *Social Trends*, published by his department, is a series of tables, rather than an integrated set of social accounts, and that value judgments are decisive in the choice of what indicators to use and what to discard (in Bulmer, 1978, pp. 210–12).

Choice of indicators can seriously affect analysis and conclusions. We must constantly watch for 'value judgments hiding behind a facade of statistical neutrality' (Carley, 1981, p. 64). All social reports are likely to contain a section on housing conditions, for example. In

Britain it is traditional to use Census material on the lack of a bath or indoor toilet as indicators of unsatisfactory housing. Yet consumers of housing are just as, or more, concerned with factors like noise insulation, friendly neighbours, or proximity to parks, buses, shops or jobs. The impact of housing policy, involving widespread demolition of Victorian terraces and their replacement by impersonal, expensive blocks of flats has, on the one hand, dramatically reduced the number of houses lacking baths and toilets but, on the other, often led to personal unhappiness and the breakdown of community spirit. The traditional indicators ignore these social consequences.

Social reporting remains in its infancy, with work still needed on indicators, targets and the criteria by which they are selected. There is criticism that the system is biased in favour of liberal reforms and social welfare policies, as targets usually imply a need for resources to be allocated to those areas (Dye, 1978, pp. 324–6). Perhaps because of this, academics seem more interested than policymakers, who rarely make use of social reports 'except perhaps as background data' (Carley, 1981, pp. 121–4). Policymakers may also be reluctant to use material which suggests that the impact of public policy has not matched the claims and aspirations of politicians. Social reports are quite likely to show this; so, too, are studies of individual policy areas.

Assessing Effectiveness within Particular Policy Areas

Traditionally, the assessment of policy success or failure has been impressionistic and anecdotal, and there is a need for the 'systematic objective evaluation of programmes to measure their societal impact and the extent to which they are achieving their stated objectives' (Anderson, 1975, pp. 132–3). We distinguish between assessments which are made during or after the application of policy, which we call policy evaluation, and assessments made before policy is applied, which we call policy experimentation.

Policy evaluation, then, is a judgment on what has gone before or what is taking place. Systematic evaluation involves studying and identifying the target group at which the policy is aimed, the consequences of the policy both for that group and for other groups in society, and the extent to which those consequences match the policy's objectives. All three elements present problems.

The first element, the target group, is not always easy to identify, particularly in the case of policy areas involving private information about individual citizens. The take-up of free school meals, of rent and rate rebates, and of some tax allowances, for example, can only be estimated because we have imprecise knowledge of the full extent of the population eligible to receive such benefits. The exact target group for housing improvement policies, or health care facilities may be equally imprecise. Secondly, the consequences of policy are hard to identify, particularly when the policy has an impact generally on society. A consequence of clean air zones may be better health (which could also have resulted from other policies such as health and safety at work legislation), but may also be higher prices as industrialists pass on to consumers the additional costs of installing machinery which minimizes atmospheric pollution. Thirdly, measuring these consequences against the original policy objectives is made additionally difficult by the frequent lack of clear objectives.

Given these severe methodological difficulties it is perhaps not entirely surprising to find that a great deal of policy evaluation is crude and unsystematic. Evaluation by political parties and pressure groups is naturally subjective; that by Parliamentary Select Committees and official Committees of Inquiry and Commissions is traditionally heavily dependent on 'evidence' given to it by politicians, public agencies and pressure groups, 'evidence' which is largely opinion. It is only since the mid-1960s that such inquiries have been given any research resources, and these remain extremely limited (L. J. Sharpe in Bulmer, 1978, p. 305). The 1960s also saw the ideal of a more rational system of policymaking take a strong hold. As we saw in Chapter 6, much effort went into the creation of new machinery and processes for resource allocation, notably the PESC (Public Expenditure Survey Committee). In conjunction with PESC came the introduction of PAR (Programme Analysis Review), a technique intended to examine the value and consequences of particular programmes (Self, 1972, pp. 270–2), but which concentrated on resource allocation and expenditure levels rather than on policy impact and evaluation. Probably the best known new institution has been the Central Policy Review Staff (CPRS, commonly known as the 'think tank') which has produced, though not always published, reports on several policy areas including race relations and housing programmes. However, much of its work has focused on the machinery of government rather than on policy. Reports such as those on central–local relations and British representation overseas are scarcely in the field of policy evaluation.

Most policy evaluation has stemmed from individual initiative, usually by academics. Consequently, there are some policies about which we know a good deal (clean air zones, aid for the victims of thalidomide), and others about which we remain quite ignorant. The evaluation of the educational impact of middle schools, sixth form colleges, and even comprehensive schooling remains primitive, partly because of continued disagreement about the objectives of education. One-man operated buses, with slower service times, were not fully appraised until 1981 (Boyd, 1981). The same year, Challis attempted to measure the outcomes of social service departments' involvement in the care of the elderly. After both reviewing the literature and outlining his own original research he concluded that outcome measurement remains 'at an early stage of development' (Challis, 1981).

To sum up, policy evaluation remains fairly unsophisticated, but increasingly interests academics. At least we are now aware of key problems, such as unclear objectives, unspecified target groups, the identification of all consequences of policy change, and statistical measurement. Technical problems will continue to be tackled by academic research. But changes in policy design which would enable better policy evaluation are likely to be difficult to obtain.

Effectiveness within a policy area can be tested in advance of the general application of a proposed new policy through the technique of policy experimentation, derived from the idea of a scientific experiment. The scientific model requires a laboratory situation. A hypothesis is tested on a selected group of people with another similar group acting as a 'control'. Both groups are monitored by observers over time, the results for each group are compared, and the policy is either applied universally or rejected as inadequate or unsatisfactory. In Figure 8.1 we give one of the best known of American examples. Clearly, at least in theory, there are great advantages to be gained from the type of experiment undertaken in New Jersey and Pennsylvania. It offers the best possible opportunity to measure policy impact, it is economic in that costly proposals need only be introduced when thoroughly tested, and it allows the full range of consequences of a new policy to be identified. Against this, however, there are some serious ethical and practical disadvantages to be considered (Dye, 1978, pp. 326–30).

The ethical drawback is the argument that it is, in principle, wrong to withhold public services from the control group. Depending on the nature of the experiment, that group may be denied money (as in the

---

The US Graduated Income Experiment 1969–72

Proposition:	'given a guaranteed annual income, by how much, if any, would recipients reduce their work effort.'
Population:	Sample of 1,300 families in five cities in New Jersey and Pennsylvania all with able bodied males in the labour force or capable of entering it. Sample divided into experimental and control groups.
Experiment:	Experimental groups covered a range of guaranteed income levels from $1,650 to $4,125 p.a. Each group was subject to one of 8 different rates (e.g. 30 per cent, 50 per cent, 70 per cent) at which their income supplements were reduced as their total income exceeded their guaranteed income.
Data Collection:	All sample reported incomes regularly and were interviewed every three months over a three-year period.
Results	Revealed little difference between experimental and control group.

FIGURE 8.1   *Policy experimentation: an example*

graduated income example), schooling, health care, protection from pollution—possibly with a significant effect on their quality of life. An experiment can literally be deadly, as in the case of one involving cardiac patients in Bristol. The hypothesis was that post-operative care at home was more satisfactory than in hospital: testing it presumably meant putting some patients' lives at risk (Cooper, 1975, p. 57).

Serious practical drawbacks include the likelihood that people will behave unnaturally or abnormally when they are aware of being observed, and that the results might be different if conducted over a wider area or a longer timespan. Experiments usually are short term but policies may not emerge or be observable during the test period. In addition, results may be manipulated either by the inventors anxious to prove successs or by politicians keen to proceed with, or abandon, the proposed new policy. Another notable American experiment was 'Head Start' under which earlier and better schooling for the very young was offered in certain areas of acute social deprivation. Those monitoring the experiment were unimpressed, concluding that there were only 'limited lasting effects', but the political popularity of the programme ensured its continuation and the allocation of additional resources (Anderson, 1975, pp. 147–51). Finally, monitoring is both essential and costly. Reluctance to spend money on it can mean that it is unsystematic and anecdotal rather than scientific and rigorous. Defects could include experimental and control groups which are too small, an unsuitable location selected purely on grounds of convenience, or the collection of too little data.

Many of the best known British experiments have been attempts to tackle social deprivation. The two most documented are Educational (later changed to Social) Priority Areas (under which additional resources go to schools in depressed industrial areas) and Community Development Projects (designed to combat the high incidence of multiple social deprivation by tackling the total personal needs of individuals, families and communities). Both illustrate some of the practical problems of experimentation mentioned above, and both involved offering services to some people, but not to others with similar circumstances (though in neither case was there much discussion of the ethical consequences of the experiments).

EPA and CDP projects were monitored by academics. From the outset the experimental areas were monitored more closely than control areas—indeed there were quite inadequate control groups (Rutter and Madge, 1977, Ch. 4). Even more serious was the 'wide range of loosely formulated objectives' for 'the lack of clearly stated goals or concepts has proved a major obstacle for the conduct of any formal evaluation' (S. W. Town in Bulmer, 1978, Ch. 8). Town went on to report that the five education authorities undertaking the EPA experiment gave little or no authoritative backing for any initiatives, that some schools were resistant, and that in any case if there were educational consequences they would only appear after many years. He found the 12 CDP projects to include several in which the local authorities and public agencies were hostile, and that each of the 12 developed its own unique approach which made comparisons difficult. Some concentrated on improving the uptake of benefits, others on self-help schemes, or on sponsoring social and environmental projects. Some concluded that poverty was an inevitable consequence of capitalism and called for wider structural reform of the economy (a radical solution unacceptable to government!).

Policy experimentation seems attractive and, in the narrow sense of introducing a new policy in a few areas or for a limited number of people, has been increasingly used in Britain. Recent examples include Enterprise Zones and Urban Development Corporations in certain inner-city areas to stimulate economic recovery (Home, 1982, pp. 123–35), and an Enterprise Allowance scheme introduced in five areas in 1982 and extended country-wide in 1983 before evaluation was completed. This pays £40 per week to unemployed people seeking to set up in business. But none are properly scientific. They, and the earlier examples of EPA and CDP, tend to lack one or more of the essential features of a full experiment – a control group, closely defined objectives, adequate monitoring arrangements. Their use indicates, instead, a new, more cautious approach to policy making – which places an emphasis on 'looking before you leap', but lacks the rigour needed for proper evaluation. It reflects partly the shortage of money due to recession and partly lessons being learned from the post-war experience of 'policy disasters' such as highrise housing, Concorde, and expensive defence and land-use planning decisions (for the latter see Hall, 1980).

THE DISTRIBUTION OF POLICY

Public policy involves a redistribution of resources between areas, individuals, social groups, industries and other organizations. We saw, in Chapters 3 and 4, how government gathers in resources from society, and in Chapters 5 and 6, how it decides to divide these resources between policy programmes or products. Our concern in this section is to consider the consequences of that division on society: who actually gets what?

Ways of assessing the distributional impact of policy fall under two broad heads – listing and social accounting. Listing means that benefits distributed by government are listed, each is given a value, and the values are apportioned amongst recipients. We can then add up the total received by an individual, age group, social class or whatever. Social accounting stems from the fundamental criticism that listing is one-sided in that contributions to the resources being distributed are not considered. Benefits need to be balanced against costs. Hence social accounting involves drawing up a personal balance sheet to arrive at the *net* benefits received. It considers the impact of, for example, the tax system outlined in Chapter 4 as well as of policy products, and follows from our model of the Policy Approach outlined in Chapter 1. As Figure 1.3 on page 14 shows, the Approach incorporates what is taken in by government and what is handed out by government, and sees the two as being related. The model, of course, simplifies in order to illustrate a general idea. In practice, listing and social accounting are complex exercises, and we can identify five problems of assessing distribution common to both.

First, they start from an assumption that benefits, and costs, are recognizable entities. In practice it is extremely hard to define, demarcate and locate costs and benefits. For example, some costs can also be seen as benefits, depending on one's standpoint. The major cost of the NHS is wages and salaries, but these are actually a benefit to the more than one million staff who have a job. Again, benefits of health care are often judged in terms of costs of provision, but a large pay rise for bureaucrats may add nothing to the level of patient services offered, and could even reduce these as funds are found to meet the new salaries (M. O'Higgins in Sandford *et al*, 1980, p. 35). Even more fundamentally, Ivan Illich challenges the whole nature of organized medical care as a benefit, claiming that doctors are a cause of ill-health and that better health has resulted not from their activities but from improved diets, housing conditions and public health actions to reduce pollution and vermin (Illich, 1977, Part I). Whilst he exaggerates (Horrobin, 1977), by, for example, ignoring important medical developments such as hip joints, heart pacemakers and kidney transplants, his argument has some merit. An equally radical attack on the alleged benefits of education can also be mounted by suggesting that its prime purpose is not to inform and enlighten, but to indoctrinate, socialize and repress individual initiative. Thus, a commonly recognized benefit becomes a cost!

The problem becomes even more complex when it comes to locating and assessing the importance of intangible benefits and costs. Achieving social status, a sense of wellbeing, or personal security may be as important a benefit to some as receipt of a cash payment or use of a public service. Public participation in policy making may be viewed as an important benefit, but is not easy to recognize (voting is, but political debate is not, for there is no single definition of what constitutes political debate. Does a chat in a pub?). It is arguable that such benefits and costs may be no less important than tangible ones. We ourselves described the acquisition of support as the key resource of government in Chapter 3.

The second problem follows from the first. If we assume, and it is an assumption, that it is possible to define and locate costs and benefits we are then faced with the problem of valuing them. Ideally, a numerical or financial measurement is needed. Even with tangible costs and benefits this is difficult, and we will see later that statisticians have yet to agree on the extent of individual benefit gained from services like defence, which give a collective benefit. Intangible and symbolic policies aimed at regime or government support (such as public participation, race relations and equal opportunities) are even harder to value. Yet their importance is that they symbolize 'what society aspires to be', and modern politics may be as concerned with 'who feels what' as with the traditional idea of 'who gets what' (Dye, 1978, pp. 315–6). The implication of this is that the student of policy distribution is faced with an almost impossible task.

The three remaining problems raise tricky technical issues of measurement, but are less fundamental than the first two. The need to create 'accounting units' in order to group our 56 million citizens was discussed in Chapter 4. Broadly three ways are commonly used: by occupation or social class, by geographical location, and by demographic characteristics such as age, sex or household size. The choice may affect any findings about distribution – a comparison of policy products in the North and the South, for example, is dependent on geographical definitions: does the North start at Watford, Watford Gap (on the M1, near Rugby) or Water (a village in Lancashire)?

Fourthly, a timescale for measurement is needed. The distribution of policy products may be assessed in the short, medium or long term and the choice may be important, for the distributional pattern can change over time. The immediate impact of the policy of selling council houses, for example, is an increase in the level of owner-occupation and an extra source of income for local authorities. But some argue that in the longer term there will be a housing shortage, a need for expenditure on new council houses to replace those sold, and dissatisfaction among tenants in poorer council accommodation who can no longer aspire to a better quality council house as those are the type that will have been sold (Murie, *et al*, 1980).

Finally the reliability of information on which lists or social accounts are based can be a problem. In Chapter 4 we pointed out that information is not wholly impartial or accurate, and its source and presentation always needs to be examined carefully. Distributional studies often rely on data from the annual Family Expenditure Survey. This exercise involves 7,000 households recording every item of expenditure for a fortnight. We know that such records are not entirely accurate. The Central Statistical Office has to correct the responses on drinking and smoking where under-reporting is apparent (Central Statistical Office, 1982, p. 97). Inevitably, there is other over- and under-reporting on items which are less checkable. In this case the basic data need to be questioned, but in other cases it is the presentation which is biased. During the course of the 1982 pay dispute in the NHS, for example, the Secretary of State asserted that an increase of 47,000 staff between 1979 and 1981 (of which 34,000 were nurses) was 'evidence of the government's policy to maintain real growth' (DHSS, 1982). His presentation ignored the fact that a reduction in the working week of nurses from 40 to 37.5 hours had been carried out and that this necessitated the employment of many extra nurses. His 'real growth' was in public expenditure, not in impact on the patients.

These five problems are clearly formidable — indeed some might be tempted to argue that they make distributional studies an impossibility. We repeat that such studies are essential. They are an important way of evaluating government — its performance and the consequences of its policy product. We also believe that they are worthwhile. Agreed, some factors cannot be measured, but an attempt to analyse distribution on the basis of the more tangible benefits and costs can be made. Our point, in detailing the problems at length, is that the assumptions and methodology of any study need to be clearly laid out and critically examined before any conclusions are drawn from it. The five problems are a checklist for the reader.

In considering the work done on distribution we again separate studies of single policy areas from those which look across the whole range of policy products. In this case it is convenient to look at single policy areas first.

Distribution within Particular Policy Areas

Studies of the impact of particular policy products such as health care or education are invariably listings rather than social accounts. They tend to look only at who gets what and not at who has paid what.

Julian Le Grand has undertaken some of the best work in this field.

He measures distribution within four areas of social policy – housing, education, health care and transport. His aim is to test to what extent these social policies achieve 'social and economic equality'. Though he is setting up abstract or detailed principles as a basis for measurement, he does believe that notions of equality have been important in policy decisions about providing free or subsidized social services. He does not claim that governments necessarily pursue equality as their main goal, but suggests that it has been 'a major justification for a massive expansion of government activity' (Le Grand, 1982, p. 8). He also notes that there is a widespread belief that public expenditure on social policies 'benefits primarily the less well off' (Le Grand, 1982, pp. 13–15).

Le Grand, then, is using his own hypothesis rather than governmental objectives. As we pointed out earlier, this is perfectly acceptable in the case of distributional studies as these aim only to measure what is happening in society. Judgments about effectiveness, on the other hand, need to be based on policy objectives.

Five separate definitions of equality are established: equality of public expenditure, of final income after redistribution, of use of services, of costs of users, and of actual outcomes (people's health or housing conditions). In the case studies as many of the five as can be are applied to available data on the policy area. The results are, to say the least, thought provoking. In the case of the NHS, for example, three of the five concepts of equality (of use, cost and outcome) are tested. None has been realized. On use 'the better off appear to receive more health care relative to need than the less well off' while costs are 'greater, the higher the social group'. Outcomes also cause him concern for 'inequalities in health do not seem to have diminished since the inception of the NHS' (Le Grand, 1982, Ch. 3).

These challenging conclusions have been echoed elsewhere in other recent work on health care. Maynard found that most European health care systems, like ours, have failed in their quest for greater equality of both health and health care provision (Maynard, 1981). That this is embarrassing to policy makers is clear from the reception given to the Black Report in 1980. This four-man expert committee found marked inequalities between social classes in both health and the use of health-care facilities. The Report called for the establishment of a comprehensive anti-poverty programme, as well as changes in priorities within the NHS (Townsend and Davidson, 1982, Chs. 6 and 7). The government released only 260 copies, and these could not be purchased at its bookshops. The Minister, in an introduction, questioned the research and described the conclusions as unclear and unrealistic, in a clear attempt to manipulate the results. In 1982 the Report was published commercially.

We have concentrated on the distributional consequences of health policies, because evidence about health and the use of health care facilities is clearer than that about most other social policies. Le Grand's other three case studies result in equally critical conclusions about distribution. He uses four of his five concepts of equality when considering education and finds that 'the provision of free education has created neither equality of use, cost, public expenditure nor outcome. Indeed, it is possible that in some cases *it may actually have promoted greater inequality*' (Le Grand, 1982, p. 79 – our italics). A fascinating detailed study of the London Borough of Newham offers some support for this view. It examines patterns of provision in the borough's secondary schools and finds that, among other things, educational costs varied between schools by more than 100 per cent with lowest spending being on schools with the most deprived children (Tunley *et al*, 1979).

This pattern of distribution emerges again in Le Grand's studies of housing and transport and leads him to conclude that 'the strategy of promoting equality through public expenditure on the social services has failed' (Le Grand, 1982, p. 132). His solution is the creation of policies to tackle inequalities of money income (also part of the Black Report strategy), with the tax and cash benefits systems as key tools. These we go on to consider in the next section, on the overall distribution of policy products.

All the studies discussed above have had to cope with the five methodological problems which we raised on pages 204–6. As well as illustrating technical issues about the reliability of data, choice of a timescale and division of society into accounting units, they also reveal the more general, but basic, problems of identifying costs and benefits and of dealing with the spillover consequences of one policy on another.

Identifying a benefit, for example, raised difficulties in the study of education. Le Grand made an 'arbitrary' decision that staying on after the age of 16 constituted use of a service, while educational performance (notably exam results) constituted outcomes. In the case of housing he could not make any distinction between use and outcome (Le Grand, 1982, pp. 15–16). The boundaries of a policy area were also far from clear. No generally agreed criteria exist to guide researchers as to whether or not a study of health care policies should include anti-pollution programmes and environmental health services. What is clear is that consideration of the NHS alone constitutes the narrowest possible of definitions, and that spillover effects and external influences are inevitable, but hard to identify and quantify. Educational policies for example, are affected by policies on youth unemployment and industrial training, which are the responsibility of different ministers. On a more general level there are those who see education as benefiting, not just pupils and teachers, but the whole of society. Spending on educational provision is described as an 'investment in the future', but the wider benefits are hard to assess.

One consequence of these problems of identifying benefits and coping with spillover effects is that distributional studies of particular policy areas can always be criticized as narrow. Yet their value in providing a detailed snapshot of the benefits gained from policy products is apparent. In addition, they raise important questions about the performance of government which deserve wider consideration. Such consideration can be given in studies of distribution across all policy areas.

Distribution across All Policy Areas

The case study approach using the listing system, typified by Le Grand's work, has been criticized as narrow. The definitions of policy areas are restricted, monetary benefits such as rates and rent rebates or social security payments are not considered, and the studies limit themselves to benefits received without considering costs or balancing them against benefits. But their conclusions do give cause for concern. The idea of a welfare state is based on the notion of redistribution, yet Le Grand found that most public expenditure on social policies is distributed in a manner that broadly favours the high social groups. Is this because Le Grand has overlooked the role in redistribution of a progressive tax system (discussed in detail in Chapter 4) and cash benefits?

The Central Statistical Office regularly looks at the relationship between taxes or contributions paid and benefits received from policy products. The method of calculation is straightforward. To an individual's original income (OI) is added any other direct cash payments (DCP) such as child benefit, and from the total is deducted any losses due to direct taxation (DT). The resulting net figure, termed disposable income (DI), or money in the pocket, is then reduced by the amount paid in indirect taxes (*IT*) such as Value Added Tax or duty on petrol, but supplemented by an estimated cash amount equal to any subsidies (notably for housing) and benefits in kind (*SBK*) received from the state (schools, hospitals). We are then left with final income (*FI*). The formula is thus:

$$OI + DCP - DT = DI - IT + SBK = FI \text{ (CSO, 1982, p. 109).}$$

The formula may be straightforward, but calculation of its component parts certainly is not. The CSO results are inevitably somewhat rough and ready, and lack the precision of the narrower case studies considered earlier. In particular, the CSO is a prisoner of three serious weaknesses in the information on which the study is based. These relate to the household expenditure figures and to the allocation between households of government income and of public expenditure (see Field *et al*, 1977, pp. 185–200 for a detailed critique of the CSO's methodology).

Inaccuracies in the Family Expenditure Survey have already been discussed. Over- and under-reporting are inevitable, but cannot always be compensated for by statisticians. The sample (6,944 in 1980) is not a complete cross-section of households. Greater London is under-represented as are households headed by someone elderly, self-employed or with children. Within a household it is not possible to allocate to individuals expenditure on joint benefits such as heating and lighting, so individual wealth or poverty cannot be assessed (CSO, 1982, p. 109).

Gaps in the allocation of government income and expenditure to households are also serious. As Table 8.1 shows, little more than half of income and less than half of expenditure could be allocated.

Why is this? CSO statisticians are faced with the problem that there is no clear way of allocating income from corporation tax, commercial and industrial rates or loans raised in the money market. Equally, spending on services such as defence and the maintenance of law and order are for the general benefit of society, while capital expenditure is for the benefit of future citizens rather than today's households. These may all be termed indivisible benefits.

Benefits received from educational provision and health care facilities are allocated to households on the basis of what is known about the take-up of the service. Here, too, there are criticisms. The system used is both crude and based on costs of provision, rather than benefits received. The crudeness is that households are allocated a share of total expenditure based on household size without any consideration being

TABLE 8.1. *Allocated and unallocated items of government revenue and expenditure, 1980*

	Percentage of total revenue			Percentage of total expenditure	
	Allocated	Unallocated		Allocated	Unallocated
Income tax	23	–	Goods and services (e.g. education, health)	20	25
National Insurance contributions	9	5	Grants to UK citizens	23	1
Local rates	6	2	Subsidies	3	2
Other expenditure taxes	20	8	Capital expenditure	–	11
Other receipts (net)	–	15	Debt interest	–	11
Borrowing requirements	–	12	Other	–	4
Total	58	42	Total	46	54

Source: Central Statistical Office (1982), No. 339, January, p. 97. Reproduced with permission from the controller of HMSO.

given to the actual level of spending on members of that household. This may vary from region to region (as in the case of health care), local authority to local authority (education) or family to family, depending on the age of children (primary schools are cheaper to provide than secondary but the survey lumps the two together). The argument about costs is that they are not necessarily an accurate proxy for the benefit received. The amount spent per patient in a coronary care unit, for example does not necessarily provide a measure of the quality of health care given to any patient (M. O'Higgins in Sandford *et al*, 1980, p. 35).

The CSO's attempt to assess distribution across all policy areas is undoubtedly ambitious. Our discussion of some of the major methodological weaknesses should not be taken as an argument that it is worthless Our concern is simply to point out that there are problems which need to be borne in mind when interpreting results, particularly because the formula gives an impression of precision and accuracy.

In broad terms the results for 1980 (CSO, 1982, p. 97) give cold comfort to those who allege that British taxation and social policies favour the poor. A senior CSO official accepts that the evidence shows the tax and benefit system as a whole to have had little impact on the level of economic inequality (G. Stephenson in Sandford *et al*, 1980, Ch. 2). Another, pithy, conclusion is that 'income redistribution in Britain represents much effort for little output' (M. O'Higgins in Sandford *et al*, 1980, p. 43). The latest survey, covering the year 1980, contained three main findings. First, taxes and benefits did reduce, quite substantially, inequality between households. The original income (*OI*) of the poorest fifth of households — largely pensioners — amounted to only 0.5 per cent of all original incomes, whereas their final income (FI) had gone up to 7 per cent. The wealthiest fifth suffered a reduction from 45 per cent to 39 per cent. Second, however, in the 1976–80 period the spread of incomes actually widened (despite there being in office for most of that time a Labour government committed to the reduction of economic inequality). And, third, the rise in unemployment had added to the level of inequality (and since 1980 there has been a further doubling of unemployment, which suggests that future CSO surveys will reveal additional cause for concern about the impact on society of job losses).

The detailed results indicate the importance of old-age pensions and social security benefits in reducing the range of incomes by adding substantially to the income of the poorest households. But the overall impact of the total package of allegedly redistributive policies is much less marked than many people imagine. A pointer to this was our evidence in Chapter 4 that there is a sharp difference between notional rates of income tax and rates actually paid. These CSO findings are in line with the work of the (Diamond) Royal Commission on the Distribution of Income and Wealth in the mid-1970s. This, too, concluded that redistribution was marginal. It also found little change in the distribution of final income between 1961–3 and 1971–3 (results and discussion in Field *et al*, 1977, pp. 183–5).

The empirical findings of the CSO and Diamond Commission can be interpreted in several conflicting ways. Some argue that the tremendous bureaucratic effort of the welfare state is simply not worthwhile: that public services should be abolished and replaced by larger cash benefits. Others that in a liberal democracy there are severe limitations on what can be achieved in the way of redistribution, because economic and social forces act as a constraint on government. Another view is that government is inefficient and needs structural and managerial reform in order to improve the design and implementation of policy. There are, no doubt, other views too.

CONCLUSION

Our review of the study of policy impact has made four broad points about practical politics and about the methodology and findings of research into the consequences of government policy.

First, impact studies are essential. Pragmatically, they offer a test of effectiveness, helping to ensure that governments obtain value for money, that policy outcomes match intentions, and that governments are accountable for their actions. Morally, they measure the extent to which redistribution of resources takes place and allow us to judge the fairness of public policy.

Second, practical politics has been characterized by a lack of concern with the measurement of policy impact. Politicians and senior advisers are not always anxious to undertake more than a partial or anecdotal analysis, probably because they are aware that outcomes often do not match expectations or political claims and that they are better placed to control structures, systems, processes and cash flows than they are to influence (or even predict) human behaviour and response to new policy products. In short, why look for trouble or produce information which might be used against you? Hence, the attempt to quash the Black Report. Hence, also, the Department of Health's failure to employ any official 'to worry about take-up or to report regularly on the Department's success fulfilling legal obligations to get benefits to the people who were supposed to have them', though hundreds had the task of ensuring that claimants did not get more than their entitlement (Donnison, 1982, p. 42).

In order to judge government, vital questions need to be asked about the consequences of policy. Assessing distribution, fairness, value for money, or effectiveness is difficult but this is not a valid reason for not trying. In Britain only one part of government, the Central Statistical Office, has made a major attempt to study policy impact. Perhaps it is significant that the CSO has no responsibility for public service provision, and, therefore, no vested interest in defending government policy and its consequences. Whether the CSO will be able to continue to improve its methodology is currently in doubt for government is reducing its statistical services and considering curtailing the Family Expenditure Survey in order to save money.

Our third set of conclusions develops this point about methodology. We have, throughout, emphasized many of the problems involved in studying policy impact, including the choice of units, reliability of data, apportionment of costs and benefits, and ambiguity of policy objectives. Our intention has not been to be negative and there is evidence that some, if not all, of these problems are being tackled. The CSO has steadily apportioned a greater percentage of government revenue and expenditure to households; the social indicators movement has developed new and better measures; Le Grand did valuable work in identifying five concepts of equality. However, problems remain and the scholar must be able to question the basis on which studies have been undertaken before accepting their conclusion. A questioning approach is particularly necessary because the results of impact studies are often expressed in statistical form, which gives an impression of precision and accuracy. It is only by understanding the methodological basis of such studies that we can ask questions about the reliability of the data fed into the formula, and about the make-up of that formula.

Finally, the study of methodology has revealed that there are, in practice, no objective analyses of policy impact. Each assessment of impact, whether it be a broad or a narrow study, an analysis of effectiveness or of distribution, must be valuative. Judgments will have been made, but they are not necessarily stated explicitly. Our assessment of the findings of impact studies has involved value judgments. For example, we suggested that the impact of taxes and benefits on households is a cause for concern because studies show that redistribution is limited and that the gap between rich and poor households widened in the period 1976–80. Equally, we implied that Le Grand's findings that the better off benefit most from public spending on social policies were also worrying. Such conclusions represent our values and will not be shared by all, for they are moral judgments.

Our conclusions on methodology and value judgments suggest that the rational and technocratic views of policy making should not be over-emphasized. Similarly, the findings on effectiveness could be interpreted as a critique of bureaucratic government, and of both the conventional and the party government views. The findings on distribution, on the other hand, might be used to support the notion of elite pluralism, or the ruling-class view of policy making. These comments again illustrate the advantages of keeping several views in mind in order to gain a full understanding of the application of policy.

The empirical findings of impact studies suggest that there is some level of policy failure, in the sense that the aspirations of policy makers have not been met. If Aneurin Bevin, creator of the NHS in 1948, were alive today it seems highly likely that he would be dissatisfied with the achievements of the health service. Despite the welfare state, widespread poverty and deprivation remains in many parts of Britain. Every study of policy impact seems either to conclude or imply that there is a gap between aspirations and outcomes. Gradually, we are better able to identify the nature of this gap, a reason in itself for encouraging further research. Impact studies, along with the studies into the carrying out of policy discussed in Chapter 7, complete what is sometimes called the 'feedback loop' in the model of policy making which we outlined in Chapter 1. One idea of such a loop is, in crude terms, that government might learn from its mistakes and steadily improve its performance. Impact studies can lead positively to better and more appropriate policy products.

TOPICS FOR DISCUSSION

1. Take any recent public policy. How might you evaluate it, and what problems would have to be overcome in order to do so?

2. What is policy experimentation? What are its strengths and weaknesses?
3. What should be the key features of a useful Social Report?
4. What factors need to be taken into account in any attempt to assess the distribution of policy benefits?
5. Suggest reasons why government has generally avoided the development of effective techniques for monitoring and evaluating the impact of public policies.

KEY READING

On evaluation see Dye (1978), Ch. 14, and W. I. Jenkins, (1978) *Policy Analysis*, Martin Robertson, pp. 219–40. Some useful general material on both evaluation and experimentation is in Anderson (1975), Ch. 5; while Chs 7 and 8 of Bulmer (ed.) (1978) review two recent British policy experiments—CDPs and EPAs. Carley (1981) considers a range of problems concerned with the handling of information.

Le Grand (1982) offers an excellent examination of distribution within particular policy areas. For a recent case study of the health service see Townsend and Davidson (1982). For studies which look at distribution across the whole range of public policy see Central Statistical Office (1982)—or the most up-to-date version of the annual survey; and Field *et al.* (1977), which offers a useful critique of the CSO methodology as well as itself attempting an overall assessment.

REFERENCES

Allnutt, D. and Gelardi, A. (1980) 'Inner cities in England', *Social Trends*, Vol. 10, HMSO.
Anderson, J. E. (1975) *Public Policy Making*, Nelson.
Boyd, C. W. (1981) 'The Impact of Reduced Service Quality on Demand for Bus Travel', *Journal of Transport Economics and Policy*, May, pp. 167–77.
Brittan, S. (1971) *Steering the Economy*, Penguin.
Brown, G. (1972) *In My Way*, Penguin.
Bulmer, M. (ed.) (1978) *Social Policy Research*, Macmillan.
Carley, M. (1981) *Social Measures and Social Indicators*, Allen & Unwin.

Central Statistical Office (1982) 'The effects of taxes and benefits on household income, 1980', *Economic Trends 339*, HMSO.

Challis, D. J. (1981) 'The measurement of outcome in social care of the elderly', *Journal of Social Policy*, April, 1981, pp. 179–208.

Cooper, M. H. (1975) *Rationing Health Care*, Croom Helm.

DHSS (1982) 'Greater health spending: aimed directly at the patient', *Press Release 82/80*, DHSS.

Donnison, D. V. (1982) *The Politics of Poverty*, Martin Robertson.

Dye, T. R. (1978) *Understanding Public Policy*, Prentice-Hall.

Field, F. *et al.* (1977) *To Him Who Hath*, Penguin.

Hall, P. (1980) *Great Planning Disasters*, Penguin.

Holtermann, S. (1975) 'Areas of urban deprivation in Great Britain: an analysis of 1971 census data', *Social Trends*, Vol. 6, HMSO.

Home, R. K. (1982) *Inner City Regeneration*, Spon.

Horrobin, D. F. (1977) *Medical Hubris*, Edinburgh: Churchill Livingstone.

Illich, I. (1977) *Limited to Medicine*, Penguin.

Le Grand, J. (1982) *The Strategy of Equality*, Allen & Unwin.

McCarthy, M. (1982) *Epidemiology and Policies for Health Care Planning*, Kings Fund.

Maynard, A. (1981) 'The inefficiency and inequalities of health care systems of Western Europe', *Social Policy and Administration*, Summer, pp. 145–63.

Murie, A. *et al.* (1980) 'Symposium on council house sales', *Policy and Politics*, Vol. 8, pp. 287–340.

Rutter, M. and Madge, J. (1977) *Cycles of Disadvantage: A Review of Research*, Heinemann.

Sandford, C. *et al.* (1980) *Taxation and Social Policy*, Heinemann.

Self, P. (1972) *Administrative Theories and Politics*, Allen & Unwin.

Townsend, P. and Davidson, N. (1982) *Inequalities in Health*, Penguin.

Tunley, P. *et al.* (1979) *Depriving and Deprived*, Kogan Page.

PART V

CONCLUSION

9

The Policy Approach Reviewed

'The Policy Approach is concerned with examining what government does (or chooses not to do, or neglects to do), why, and with what consequences for the citizen. It is also concerned with what government should do'. With these words we introduced our Approach on page 12, and we went on to explain in Chapter 1 that we had selected the Policy Approach both because it is comprehensive and flexible, and because it raises important and interesting issues about the effectiveness of government and about the consequences of government policy for society. We can now conclude by using the material contained in Chapters 2–8 to draw out a number of themes about policy making which have arisen during our application of the Approach.

At the very least the Policy Approach has revealed the presence of a number of issues commonly overlooked in books about British politics. In particular we see the extent and division of resources (Chapters 3, 5 and 6), the difficulty of carrying out agreed policy (Chapter 7), and the impact on society of public policies (Chapters 4 and 8) as being issues which deserve to be central to the study of politics. Our review of those issues has revealed just how complex choosing and applying policies is, and the important part that judgment and values play in the making of policy. We shall return to this last point towards the end of the chapter.

Several themes have emerged from our application of the Policy Approach, and have recurred at various points in the book. These can be, and should be, related to the views of policy making outlined in Chapter 2. The exact relationship is a matter for readers' judgments; our suggestions are designed as an aid to discussion and application of the Policy Approach, and are in no sense the single 'right' answer. They reflect our values and assumptions, which are open to challenge.

EFFECTIVENESS AND DISTRIBUTION

Perhaps the most persistent theme running through the book has been the effectiveness, or otherwise, of government. Our concern with effectiveness led us to examine in some detail the tax system in Chapter 4, the ways in which public expenditure is allocated between competing policy programmes in Chapter 6, and the carrying out of policy in Chapter 7. In these examples, and in others elsewhere in the book, there was evidence that governments face severe problems in making public policy effective. Expenditure proved difficult to control, taxes hard to gather in. Government influence on the interpretation and application of laws, rules and guidelines was seen to be diluted by the delegation of wide discretion to those actually carrying out policies such as health care, policing, and education. Take health care policies as an example. Three decades of the National Health Service have not led to the eradication of inequalities in health between social classes. Findings like this suggest that government is a good deal less effective than it sometimes aspires and claims to be.

This leads directly to a second theme, the distributional consequences of government. Public policies are intended to regulate human behaviour, and they modify the resources of each individual citizen. Some reduce his resources (taxation, for example), while others add to them (roads and public transport enhance mobility, state benefits provide an income). Many British public policies have ostensibly sought to alter the distribution of resources in favour of the less well off. The title alone of early housing legislation – 'Housing of the Working-Classes Act' – symbolized this, as does the whole post-war concept of the Welfare State. Yet we have uncovered evidence that a long history of policy initiatives in the housing, health, education and welfare fields (among others) has done a good deal less than is often realized to reduce marked inequalities. In Chapter 4, for example, we found that certain features of the tax system operate proportionally. We showed that the theory that taxation is progressive is open to challenge. In Chapter 8 the distributional impact of all public policies on incomes was also found to be extremely limited, and Le Grand's case studies indicated that some public policies which are commonly thought to aid the less well off (education, for example) may actually benefit the better off.

These findings about effectiveness and about distribution result from the application of the Policy Approach, with its focus on resources and their allocation, but are not explained by it. Explanatory views of policy making can be encompassed within it, and the nine we discussed in Chapter 2 can be applied to our conclusions on effectiveness and distribution. Proponents of the ruling-class view of policy making, for example, might use our empirical material to support their claim that government is not seriously interested in, or capable of, radically redistributing resources in favour of poorer, working-class families.

But this same material can also be interpreted as supporting other views of policy making. Incrementalists might point to the alleged natural desire of policy makers to proceed cautiously as an explanation of the evidence of slow progress achieved by the NHS, or by the Welfare State in general. The administrative dispersion and diffusion view, on the other hand, sees the myriad overlapping and competing public agencies as stultifying. Alternatively the influence of professional and middle-class interests, who would be adversely affected by radical redistribution, could be interpreted as an explanation which accords with the notion of 'elite pluralism'.

POWER, CONSTRAINTS AND CAPACITY

A third theme has been the nature and subtlety of power, a concept which has, of course, been widely explored by political scientists, philosophers, psychologists and sociologists, and tested with empirical studies. In Chapters 5 and 6, on the division of resources, power was treated as the central theme. We saw that power was not simply, or even particularly, a matter of one individual or group of individuals influencing or controlling another. More substantially it depended on the opportunities to gain access to, and involvement in, policy making. Many sections of society do not appear to enjoy those opportunities to any large degree. This applies at all levels of policy making. At the very highest level, for example, it was not at all clear that top policy makers responded to pressure from more junior colleagues (let alone the outside world of organized interests) when determining the level and division of public expenditure.

The Policy Approach has emphasized the importance of access and involvement. These are often affected by factors not immediately apparent to the observer. Two such factors are biases in attitudes and values, and the forms of organization and their operation. They may operate at all levels of policy making, from the overall division of public expenditure to the detailed application of public policy. Access to health care facilities, for example, may be determined not only by the overall level of NHS facilities, but also by the behaviour of doctors' receptionists and by surgery opening hours. Receptionists are an illustration of relatively junior officials exercising some, albeit limited, power; opening hours an illustration of the operation of part of the NHS organization. In both instances it is quite possible that the attitudes and biases of personnel may limit access. The less articulate may have difficulty in getting past receptionists and seeing the doctor; people at work may find the lack of evening surgeries and clinics off-putting. What the public wants, or perhaps, what it will accept, is interpreted by officials at all levels of seniority, and power can thus be seen as not solely the prerogative of 'top' policy makers.

This type of analysis of power is compatible with several views of policy making, particularly those we entitled bureaucratic power, technocratic, and administrative dispersion. Public expenditure policies, the subject of Chapter 6, can also be viewed as rational or as incremental. Indeed power was one of the three main elements discussed for each of the seven structural views of policy making outlined in Chapter 2, and these can now be used by readers as explanations of our subsequent findings.

Our fourth theme concerns the constraints and limitations on government's freedom to act. We uncovered a good deal of evidence about this. Chapter 7, for example, showed how difficult it is to get things done at all, let alone on time and in the way intended. Society cannot, it seems, be controlled and regulated beyond a certain level, partly because this is logistically impossible, partly because it is socially and politically unacceptable. Earlier, in Chapters 5 and 6, we saw how difficult it was for government to alter existing policies and patterns of spending more than marginally. There seems to be an inherent inertia attached to existing programmes, which always generate support from both within government and without. Officials, some of whom may well have been involved in reaching the *status quo*, resist change, and politicians are cautious of policy change because of possible consequences for the key resource of support. This kind of evidence can be related to several views of policy making, including incrementalism, bureaucratic power, and the idea of a ruling elite.

A further limitation on government arises from the complex and often unclear nature of policy objectives, which may be unstated, ambiguous, or even contradictory. As a result governments create, and become limited by, unclear policies. These may be carried out through large-scale delegation of discretion to administrators and professionals, who may receive limited guidance and few targets to meet – a diagnosis compatible with the bureaucratic power and the technocratic views, but not with the conventional view and its central concept of accountability. Contradictory objectives were found in both taxation policy, where the tax system was seen to be both an instrument of social policy and a money raiser for government, and in the example of local government reform where clarity proved unattainable. Unstated objectives include political and personal aspirations such as power, image and a quiet life. These are particularly relevant in the case of symbolic policies. Attempting to hold and attract support causes policies to be dressed up, and packaging and presentation can sometimes obscure policy content. The Policy Approach seeks to unravel this tangle of objectives and purposes, a tangle which constrains and limits government.

Many contemporary analyses of the role of government rightly emphasize constraints and limitations. Often, however, they go no further. The Policy Approach, on the other hand, does also reveal very clearly the ability of government to shape the nature of society. The potential capacity of government is a fifth theme. It can best be considered by examining three issues which have arisen in the book: distribution, access, and the carrying out of public policy.

Government capacity to affect the distribution of resources within society became apparent in Chapter 4 when we found that government does have real choices to make about what resources to gather in, and in what quantities. We discussed this both theoretically (by considering contrasting views about the role of the state and size of the public sector) and empirically through analyses of the tax system and of the size of the kitty potentially available to government. Though there are constraints, there was also potential to alter the nature of taxation. More of the burden could be shifted onto those with large incomes, new taxes could be introduced, tax avoidance and evasion could be reduced through more intensive policing. Similarly, land ownership and its benefits could be altered, and policies on labour and on equipment can also affect the distribution of resources.

In later chapters we went on to discuss the capacity of government to decide on what its resources should be spent, and we considered the overall distribution of costs and benefits between different socio-economic groups. We also found that policy making frequently involves relatively few people, and that government has the capacity to limit or extend access to, and involvement in, the policy process. This could be done, for example, through its approach to issues like open government, public participation, or the methods of selection and recruitment to top posts. In short, government has the capacity and ability to act as an agent of change. Change could bring different demands and needs to the fore, and could produce different policy outcomes. Government is not as unimportant as Dye suggests, or as secondary as some Marxists believe, or as neutral as other scholars have stated.

Government's capacity also extends to the ways in which it seeks to carry out its policies, for these can have a marked effect on society. This was illustrated in Figure 7.1 on page 175. The choices of negative sanctions and of formal controls, for example, were seen to lead, in theory, towards a more repressive regime. Alternatively positive and informal policies make for less repressive government. Finally, in Chapter 3 we became aware of government's considerable potential to create or maintain support, identified as a key prerequisite for policy success.

In short, the Policy Approach indicates that there is a need to balance constraints against capacity before drawing conclusions about government's ability to govern and to make and carry out public policy. In practice government is neither the prisoner of social and economic forces, nor the sole determinant of the extent and shape of those forces. Policy making is more complicated than that. The Policy Approach has thus led us to challenge much of the contemporary pessimism about government and politics, and thus distinguished it from many other analyses. Government is important and relevant.

ACCOUNTABILITY AND ASSESSMENT

A concern with the accountability and responsiveness of government has recurred throughout the book, and constitutes a sixth theme. This concern applies to both elected politicians and to appointed officials. The conventional view of policy making, with its strong emphasis on the concept of accountability, sits uneasily alongside evidence about the massive size and complexity of modern government. Responsibility for a particular policy may be hard to pinpoint, power elusive to locate. Policy making takes place at all levels of government and we have uncovered instances of discretion being exercised by quite junior personnel. In addition, at the highest levels policies may be shaped by political parties or by senior officials, rather than by the representative assembly, and they (like juniors) are only indirectly linked to the official machinery designed to make government accountable for its actions or omissions.

It is, it appears, difficult to have both large-scale government and a high level of accountability. Indeed it may be significant that the concept was scarcely mentioned during much of Chapter 2, notably when we outlined contemporary views of policy making such as party government, bureaucratic power, technocracy, and administrative dispersion and diffusion. The dilemma of modern government is how to accommodate both accountability and discretion and flexibility.

The Policy Approach uncovers this dilemma. In Chapter 3 we identified support as the key resource of government. The suggestion was that one factor in determining the effectiveness of government is the extent to which its actions are acceptable to key sections of society, that government, in effect, is answerable to the citizenry (or parts of it). Later, in Chapter 7, a link between responsiveness and regime-type was made in Figure 7.1. Negative sanctions and formal controls were associated with authoritarian government. In the same chapter the important policy-making role of front-line officials was identified. Their discretion to apply local knowledge of social and economic conditions when carrying out policy could be removed or reduced in an attempt to clarify the accountability of government, but with the possible consequence that policies may be applied in an inappropriate or ineffective manner. The alternative of creating numerous separate public agencies with sharp lines of accountability, each with a stake in a particular policy area, leads to the danger, inherent in the administrative dispersion view, that policy may fail to get carried out at all.

The need to make systematic assessments of the activities of government, but the problems of doing this, is the seventh theme to emerge. Assessments are necessary to ensure that governments (and citizens) are obtaining value for money, that policies relate to intentions, that programmes are effectively carried out, and that informed judgments can be made about the consequences of government actions. Such assessments involve some measurement of public policy, but in Chapters 4 and 8 we identified three main methodological problems. These include inadequate criteria on which to base studies (policy objectives are frequently unclear); problems of defining, locating and measuring intangible factors such as public attitudes; and weaknesses in the data available for analysis. The existence of these problems means that results of studies of public policy need to be interpreted with care, and also gives scope to policy makers to manipulate the findings for political reasons. Hence systematic assessment is difficult, yet it is essential if we are to make sense of government.

JUDGMENT AND POLICY CHOICE

Our main focus in the book has been on the process of policy making, and issues about policy content have been secondary and illustrative. However, now that we have, in the course of the book, developed a checklist of themes to use when studying politics and public policy, we can conclude by asking whether or not there is any objective way of judging between policy options.

At many points we have emphasized that the study of public policy is bound to involve a considerable amount of judgment and opinion. Public policy is too complex to be assessed in a mechanical fashion. Techniques applicable to the laboratory can rarely if ever be utilized, as we saw when considering policy experimentation in Chapter 8. It is not impossible to measure activities such as the provision of public services and cash benefits, though precision may not be attainable. These, however, must be linked to less tangible and less measurable features of policy such as the creation of support. In both cases, services and intangible aspects, assembling data is likely to involve judgments about what to collect and what to neglect, what units of analysis (age, class, and so on) to utilize, and what interpretation to place on the data to be used. As a result, any conclusions are open to debate and challenge. Given that they involve values, this is just as it should be.

These conclusions about the importance of judgment and values already suggest that there is no entirely objective way of choosing the best policy. But we cannot ignore the technocratic view of policy making. In Chapter 2 its main feature was found to be an assumption that there might well be 'best' policies or 'right' answers to policy problems, and that these could be identified by 'experts'. This general idea is also reflected in a widely held view that society would be better off without politics or politicians, and that, somehow, agreed conclusions about courses of action could be reached after an analysis of data and the application of common sense. A broadly similar conclusion, based on different arguments, can be adduced from the work of some management theorists. They base their ideas on the rational view of policy making and emphasize the advantage of using quantitative techniques such as Cost-Benefit Analysis. Such techniques involve measurement and precise evaluation, and can give the impression (though this is not overtly claimed in the literature) that policy choice need not involve political judgment.

Cost–Benefit Analysis (CBA) is one of the best known of these modern management techniques, probably because it has been used to evaluate major policy such as motorways, London underground railways, and the projected third London Airport. The CBA methodology is straightforward. Factors affecting a potential policy option, both its costs and the benefits to be derived from it, are isolated and each is given a value so that the 'cheapest' option may be chosen.

The example of the third London Airport is perhaps the most widely known case, with CBA being used by a Commission of Enquiry to evaluate four possible sites. The 1968 Roskill Commission Report found Cublington to be the cheapest of the four (£4,416 million), and Foulness the most expensive (£4,651 million). Despite this conclusion, the government reacted to a heated political debate by selecting Foulness. Later it abandoned this decision and opted instead not to develop any new site.

Clearly CBA did not, in this case, avoid the need for political judgment. Indeed the process of CBA itself contained numerous judgments. These included the initial choice of which four sites to investigate (a choice aided by a limited application of CBA to rather more sites); estimates of the value to place on costs and benefits like the loss of amenity for local residents or amount of advantage to travellers in being close to London; and the weight to attach to each of the eight items investigated (which included construction costs, meteorology, agriculture, recreation, and residential conditions). Figures for many items were based on a number of (debatable) assumptions (Spiers, 1975, pp. 77–8).

Cost–Benefit Analysis cannot avoid judgments and cannot be considered a wholly neutral way of taking policy decisions. It is best seen as a way of organizing material and identifying assumptions. Like other modern management techniques, it is essentially an *aid to* policy decision, and not a substitute for political judgment. If it gives an unacceptable weight to some factors it will be ignored by politicians – as was the Roskill Commission's CBA.

Advocates of these new techniques accept that they do not enable society to avoid political judgments. But they stress the advantages of having quantitative aids to help policy makers evaluate difficult policy choices about, for example, where or whether to build motorways, power stations, or airports. Opponents see techniques like CBA as positively dangerous, and something to avoid, because they are misleading. The focus on quantity (in money values) causes subjective factors like the quality of life to be underplayed. The false impression of technical expertise given by the analyst has authoritarian and anti-democratic implications because policy makers may be manipulated by 'experts'. Political debate becomes obscured, and the layman is excluded from understanding and participating in policy judgments (Self, 1976, Ch. 5).

Whatever the merits of each, both these sets of arguments accept that choosing between policy options must involve values, and that dispute is inevitable. No technique, however sophisticated, is capable of imposing unanimity and agreement where they do not exist. At the end of the day choosing between policies must be on the basis of moral and political values.

STUDYING PUBLIC POLICY

If policy choice involves judgment and values is it an appropriate subject for academic study? Traditionally there seems to be a widely held view that students of politics should avoid getting involved in issues of policy and simply stick to describing, in an overtly detached way, political institutions and their operations. Most textbooks do this.

The Policy Approach takes a different view. We said in Chapter 1 that it is primarily organizational rather than explanatory. It aims to provide those who study politics with an awareness of a range of possible explanations, and to equip them with a way of understanding different points of view about policy making. The opportunity is now there to select and apply any one or more of the nine views outlined in Chapter 2, and we have pointed to the danger of choosing one and ignoring the rest. That would be narrowing and alien to the strengths of the Approach: its comprehensiveness and flexibility. A rounded understanding is best achieved by applying a range of views, because each draws attention to different features of the political system.

There are, then, some who argue that many of the issues we have raised in this book, such as effectiveness and distribution, should not be tackled by students of politics simply because they involve the application of values. We disagree with that argument, for three main reasons.

First, all studies of politics are valuative, because all studies involve choices about what to study, and how. Mr Gradgrind's discussion of 'facts' illustrated that in Chapter 1. Second, we believe that vital and interesting issues about policy making should not be neglected on the grounds of an inappropriate and misleading ideal of pure neutrality, yet they would be if the content and consequences of public policy are to be ignored. Finally, the study of public policy gives a valuable practical and vocational emphasis to the discipline of political science.

It seems to us, then, that students of public policy can quite legitimately engage in the obviously valuative activity of discussing and evaluating both the machinery of policy making and the content of policy. They must, however, clearly outline the assumptions and values underlying any proposals. This is essential. If it is done, then others can form their own conclusions on the basis of the evidence presented and are not merely subjected to the confident assertions of those putting forward the arguments. The moral choice of what is good or bad is properly left to the individual.

Judging public policy and the actions of government is, therefore, both legitimate and useful. As an academic exercise it provides students with an opportunity to apply their own values and make their own judgments, while leaving the teacher with the task of guiding and ensuring that a range of moral viewpoints are considered. Given the political nature of political study, this seems to us to be the proper way to proceed.

Our hope is that the Policy Approach which we have outlined in this book is found to offer a useful framework for the study of government and public policy. You may, now that you have been able to evaluate it, wish to disagree. By now you will know that the Approach allows, indeed encourages, you to do just that!

REFERENCES

Self, P. (1976) *Econocrats and the Policy Process: The Politics and Philosophy of Cost–Benefit Analysis*, Macmillan.
Spiers, M. (1975) *Techniques and Public Administration*, Fontana.

Author Index

Subject Index